971.603   Armstrong, Bruce.
Arm   Sable Island / Bruce Armstrong ; [fore-
          word, Thomas H. Raddall].   Toronto : Double-
          day Canada, c1981.
             210 p. : ill.
             Bibliography: p. [207]

          1. Sable Island - History.   I. Title.
          0385131135   1285254 NLC

Sable Island

DOUBLEDAY CANADA LIMITED, Toronto, Canada
DOUBLEDAY & COMPANY, INC., Garden City, New York
1981

Sable Island

BRUCE ARMSTRONG

Library of Congress Catalog Card Number: 80-2745

First edition

Design by Robert Burgess Garbutt
Printed and bound in Canada by The Bryant Press

Canadian Cataloguing in Publication Data

Armstrong, Bruce.
      Sable Island
Bibliography: p. 207
Includes index.
ISBN 0-385-13113-5
1. Sable Island — History. I. Title

FC2345.S22A75   971.6 03   C81-094030-2
F1039.S13A75

Photograph Credits

Bouteillier Family Collection: 96
Al Chaddock: 149
Dalhousie University Archives: 112, 162, 163
Collection of Mary Josephine Caldwell Hamilton: 92
Harper's New Monthly Magazine, 1866:   55, 59, 60, 63, 75, 79, 153
Collection of Don Johnson: 114, 129, 134
Library of Congress, Washington, D.C.:   12
Zoe Lucas: 19, 32, 38, 69, 111, 115, 117, 140, 144, 146-7, 150, 155, 157, 168, 172, 181, 183, 185, 186, 187, title page
Ian McLaren: 6-7, 176, 178
National Geographic Society: William Albert Allard, 16, 82, 85, 108-9, 127; Gilbert M. Grosvenor, 137, 139; W. D. Harrington, 1, 42-3, 175; Arthur W. McCurdy, 94-5, 104, 106; John A. Douglas McCurdy, 48-9, 101, 102, 106; map on page 15 adapated from a map by the National Geographic Society
National Portrait Gallery, Smithsonian Institution, Washington, D.C.:   76
Ned Norwood: 8, 24, 45, 56-7, 86-7, 160, 165, 189, 190
Nova Scotia Communication and Information Centre: 3, 10, 14, 124-5
Nova Scotia Museum: Ronald E. Merrick, 40
Public Archives of Canada: 21 (C 9230), 26 (PH 240), 30 (C 92794), 34 (C 40972), 36 (C 40985), 51 (C 93307), 52 (C 14029), 53 (C 14030), 73 (C 42985), 91 (PA 41424), 120 (PA 48047)
Public Archives of Nova Scotia: 64, 68, 72, 99, 167
Collection of Captain Williams: 89, 133

Photograph of Bruce Armstrong by Donna Grosvenor

For Mabel and J. D. Smythe

Foreword

Long ago I lived for twelve months on Sable Island. It was in 1921–22, when that remote life was still untouched by the waves of world change that came in the wake of World War I. In a small shack among the dunes we radio operators talked in dots and dashes to everything from trawlers to trans-Atlantic liners, using an old-fashioned spark transmitter, and taking down their messages with pencil and pad. The lighthouses at each end of the island were lit by oil, and faithful men watched over the lamps and their revolving mirrors during the nights. The lifeboat station was near the west end, and there were three small beach patrol stations several miles apart towards the east.

About three hundred wild horses, whose origin nobody knew, roamed about the dunes and ponds, and fled from all human approach. In the warm days of summer, hundreds of seals basked on the southerly beaches, and migratory birds of many species nested in the scrub bushes or among the tufts of marram grass. Schooners from Nova Scotia and Massachusetts came to fish all around us on the Sable bank, using sails and dories, just as Kipling described them in *Captains Courageous*.

So I knew Sable Island before the twentieth century began to catch up with it, preserved like a fly in amber, which I studied with the curious eyes of youth in every season of the year. In a long life's experiences I never lost my interest or that view.

In this book Bruce Armstrong has gathered the story of "The Graveyard of the Atlantic" in fact and legend. In the course of time and human whimsy a lot of legend has crept into the history. Even so solemn a scribe as the Reverend George Patterson could not resist mingling a bit of fancy with his facts here and there. Nor could Judge Haliburton, or for that matter nearly everyone else who has talked or written about Sable in time past.

You may believe as much as you wish.

Truth unadorned began to emerge when the first lifesaving crew splashed ashore in 1801, the same year in which, far away across the sea, Nelson put the telescope to his blind eye. From that time onward we have the regular reports of the successive "governors" of the Sable Island Establishment, nearly all of them veteran seamen with two good eyes and a matter-of-fact way of writing down what passed before them.

Fact and legend, the story of Sable Island is intensely interesting. Read it and enjoy yourself.

Thomas H. Raddall

I looked about, and lo!
The Moon stood naked in the Heavens, at height
Immense above my head, and on the shore
I found myself of a huge sea of mist,
Which, meek and silent, rested at my feet:
A hundred hills their dusky backs upheaved
All over this still Ocean, and beyond,
Far, far, beyond, the vapours shot themselves,
In headlands, tongues and promontory shapes,
Into the Sea, the real Sea, that seem'd
To dwindle, and give up its majesty,
Usurp'd upon as far as sight could reach.

WORDSWORTH

Contents

Sable Island

PART ONE
Sand, Storms, and Story
1000 to 1800

I *A Dreamer's Return*

IN WINTER, SHE wears white, touched with green; most of the year she favours green, ruby-dotted with berries, or picked out with daisies. Often her serenity is masked by tempest or raging storm; always she is jealous.

These images of Sable Island, written not long ago, continue to haunt me. The attraction of this diminutive island of sand is perpetual. Situated a hundred and eighty miles southeast of Halifax off the coast of Nova Scotia, it lies close to the edge of the continental shelf. Twenty-five miles in its curving length, barely a mile wide with a backbone of dunes reaching up about ninety feet above sea level, Sable has lured many to her shores for good reasons: as a place of escape; a place for anonymity; a location for buried treasure; and a domain where one can stand and shout existence to the heavens.

She clings to and smothers those who draw near. The scent she wears is sweet grass with a hint of the aromatic. Her body is large and surprisingly soft; her curves are generous and comfortable. Her isolation is timeless but she is never lonely.

For some who visit Sable, the experience begins a love affair which lasts for life. I think of the other islands I have experienced in the past. Vancouver Island, off the coast of British Columbia, up near Scott's Point where I felt the desolation and beauty of a true wilderness. The little island we discovered when I was a child, deep in the Québec Laurentian Mountains, reachable then only by our long, red, canvas canoe. I thrilled to the sound of pinewood paddles dipping neatly into the clear lake water as we glided towards our private refuge where a huge turquoise tent was our summer home. But this island on the east coast is different.

She is quite a woman this Giaconda lady. She is at once a refuge and an abyss; a womb and a monster. On her face lies a patina of mystery.

As one who has studied magic in many forms, it is the mystery and illusion of Sable which most fascinates me. Tennyson's verse could have been written for this island.

The hills are like shadows, and they flow
From form to form, and nothing stands;
They melt like mist, the solid lands,
Like clouds, they shape themselves and go.

No man agrees entirely with another in his description of Sable, for the island is in constant change. Its geological age is uncertain. The inward moving of the dunes, the narrowing of the island, are unmistakable on the charts. On Sable, nothing is permanent. The wind is constantly building up new hills of sand and then blowing them away again into the sea. The waves sweep these sand-grains into bars and roll them slowly up to the beach where they do not run back again but sink into the sand and disappear, a continuous and wondrous illusion. But there is a darker side to the island.

Sable wears forever round her throat a necklace of men's bones like the grisly souvenirs of a cannibal.

Chilling; a litany of ship names is chanted forever on the wild winds of Sable, many recorded, many lost to the memory of man. Among those wrecked were, *The Four Sons*, *Stella Maris*, *Hard Times*, *State of Virginia*, *Cora May*, *Gondolier*, *Sylvia Mosher*, *Ruby*, and the *Delight*. One observer, who was shipwrecked on Sable near the end of the eighteenth century, wrote, "Strong winds, blowing sands, exposed forty wrecks in a row and when the sand was blown back it uncovered forty more." Wrecks, their bowed ribs like the skeletons of huge prehistoric mammals, support and hold the very sand that destroyed them.

Ships of all descriptions are buried here: schooners and steamers; yawls and yachts; galleons and men-o'-war. In their holds who knows what treasures there were? Chests of gold, silken garments, perfumes, spices, gems, bullion, books, love letters, diaries—all lost. A captain or a general would travel the high seas with all the possessions he had, his own little universe in a ship's cabin, while he searched for new and larger worlds.

Galleons and men-o'-war have long gone, taking men and treasure with them. This is the twentieth century with fast aircraft. In September 1977 I find myself flying from Halifax to Sable, once again looking for illusions as perhaps others have before me. My first trip, ten years before, was tantalizing to the spirit. This time I am better prepared with archival and contemporary documents. I hope to recapture the excitement of my first trip.

There are seven of us on this adventure. Dr. Ian McLaren, biologist with Dalhousie University, is making one of his many visits to engage in scientific bird-watching, including a census of various species. Slightly built, bearded, blessed with abundant energy, and always cooperative in plans having to do with Sable, Dr. McLaren has been making, since 1967, a special study of the Ipswich sparrow, whose only breeding ground is on Sable. He is the ideal companion; familiar with present-day events on the island, and also steeped in its history, he answers all questions good-naturedly and will succeed in corralling my artist acquaintance, Al Chaddock, and me into exhilarating bird counts. We will be joined in these bird roundups by two biology students, Howard Ross and Estelle Laberge.

Also included on this excursion are two experts from the Department of Mines who will be checking out the pressures on the oil well heads left on the island during the late 1960s drilling operations. Living quarters were constructed by the Mines people during the heyday of wild enthusiasm over possible oil; now the Department of the Environment often uses the house.

We all fit snugly inside a British Norman Islander, a reliable twin-engine aircraft. The pilot, Bob

Lailer, trained during World War II, keeps tight control and bearing of his craft as he makes his one hundred and fiftieth flight to Sable. The sky is filled with brilliant sun and white clouds; below, the shadow of the plane moves across the sea. I am lost in a reverie of names. Santa Cruz, the Holy Cross, Isle de Cruz, Island of the Cross; in the beginning all holy names placating the wrath of heaven. Then, L'Isle de Sablon and Isolla del Arena. I repeat this last one to myself (how melodic it sounds in Italian!); Isolla del Arena, meaning Island of Sand. The very sands of the island are a palimpsest written over by many nations. Fishermen, sailors, explorers, and mapmakers from Portugal, Italy, England, and France, all had a hand in giving Sable a name. When did it begin? As the aircraft drops in altitude, the ocean whitecaps leap into focus.

Perhaps it began down there when Sable was an extensive strip of land, exposed during the Ice Age. Geologists believe it is a remnant of a series of sand shoals or banks that may have extended from the Grand Banks to what is now America. The rising ocean waters slowly closed over this extension until all that remained was Sable. In the sixteenth century, fishermen and traders of western Europe became acquainted with its waters. Joam Alvarez Fagundez, a Portuguese explorer, was granted many territorial rights to the New World in 1520, which included what is now Nova Scotia and several islands; one of the islands was Sable. In Hakluyt's *Voyages* there is mention of a rumour that the Portuguese had put pigs and goats on the island during the 1550s.

Portuguese fishermen were aware of the steepsided sandbars that surround Sable Island. They knew that if a ship sailed into the main shore, chances of survival were good with the use of small boats or ship-to-shore lines. But if it struck an outer bar, a vessel was stranded and rescue was just about impossible. At each delicate extremity of Sable are shoals, deceptively innocent but like the inner and outer bars they are more dangerous than the island itself. Counting the length of the shoals, the island presents a fifty-mile sandtrap for vessels. These dangers are heightened by veils of thick mist which often surround Sable.

The Portuguese were, perhaps, among the first to lose men and vessels to Sable's waters, consequently they probably knew a shipwrecked body might be carried by currents in a grisly passage round and round the island for weeks until fresh gales would bury it with sand.

Suddenly, there are shouts! The other passengers in the Norman Islander are excited. Below lies Sable and this is how most people first see the island these days, from the air. Shaped like a new moon, it presents a mosaic of pale tans and greens, ringed with white surf. I gaze down in wonder and, as

Laurence Durrell expressed it so well, I feel compelled to "trap that elusive wraith, the spirit of the place."

Now we are closer and one end of Sable comes into view. Surprised by the engine noise, a herd of creatures on the sandspit below begins to scatter in all directions. Ah, the horses, I think to myself! The famous wild, shaggy "ponies" which have galloped in freedom across the sand dunes for over two centuries, the only breed of its kind in the world. It takes a moment to realize I am actually looking at a herd of seals. Now, some horses do appear on top of a grassy dune, then swiftly vanish as we bank in a tight circle for a landing. Our field is a natural one, a large expanse of sand on the south shore. We touch down to the right of a large salt-water lake.

When at last we land, I push open the door of the plane and step over the threshold, on to the island of sand. We pile sleeping bags and gear on to a small trailer towed by a tractor (this being one of the best methods of transportation on Sable), and walk inland a short distance to the weathered A-frame house built by Professor Henry James of the Psychology Department of Dalhousie University. On the door is a sign, "Henry House," which brings a smile, for there is a gourmet restaurant of the same name in Halifax. Upstairs are simple platforms that serve as bunks. Downstairs, the large, comfortable space is part kitchen, part living room.

Landing on the south beach.

There are many windows and the front view takes in the vast stretch of sand upon which we have just landed. Flashes of white, like flags, can be seen as breakers hit the beach.

After we chase out hundreds of cluster flies and set up housekeeping, we all head in different directions. The "birders" vanish over a dune, the painter hikes off in a westerly direction to get an artist's first impression, and I take a stroll along the north beach almost immediately behind the A-frame. Here, the high dunes overlook the ocean waves that roll and unfurl in a continuous line against twenty-five miles of shoreline. I stand on the shore looking out to the horizon, wishing I were on the horizon looking toward shore, for I am wondering what it would be like to approach Sable, not from the air but from the sea. Curious, and not being able to experience it first hand, I recall others who did.

In 1866, *Harper's New Monthly Magazine* contained a nineteenth century historian's description of the approach to Sable: "Gradually the line of low, dark hummocks, that have for some time limned the horizon, loom up and resolve themselves into high hills fringed by breakers. Glistening surf beats in solemn monotone upon the dazzling beach. Bare conical sand-hills, mottled with patches of green, or crested with rank, waving grass, rise up in most fantastic shapes, over and around which myriads of birds are hovering."

A seaman assigned to naval duty on Sable in 1916 recorded his first impression of the island when he

came up on the deck of his ship, anchored a mile offshore: "I peered through a curtain of fog which theatrically parted to reveal the most striking landscape I had ever seen; the island appeared to be made of burnished gold and the hills, which faced me, had the angularity of waves in a storm."

He was right. The world of Sable is made of gold, pale gold, a landscape of sands and dunes melting into infinity. The hills have been blown into lunar shapes, as alien as an Arizona desert. But there are no crags here, no rocks, no soil.

Away from the beach, the dunes are dressed in grass, long waving tresses of marram grass on which the nomad ponies feed. These grasses shelter wild cranberries, strawberries, primroses, and chrysanthemums which abound in miniature forms. There are no glades; only mile after mile of undulating dunes and waving grass.

Over there, a tawny, sloe-eyed, beige-maned mare grazes, unconcerned about my company, the rest of her herd a hundred feet behind. Terns and plovers arc through the skies, sandpipers dart across the beach. The sleek head of a seal emerges from the water to gaze at me with childish curiosity. Playful as a puppy, he swims beside the beach to accompany me as I stroll along the shore. He

gets bored and another cheerful companion takes up where he leaves off. Along the sandbars, older seals bask in the sun; above them, clouds haze into the horizon with muted shades of amber, rose, grey, silver, steel, taupe, and mauve, swirling and melting into illusions. There is, at this moment, nothing I cannot see, nothing I cannot imagine.

Soon I begin to appreciate the unfamiliar air I have been breathing so deeply. From the sea there is the penetrating, salty ozone; Sable itself wears the heady scent of sweetgrass. It mingles with this rich sea air and I seem to be at once in mid-ocean and mid-meadow. There is the never-ending sound of the surf and susurration of the wind in the grasses and I am slowly seduced by the soft gentility of the island.

The scream of a gull pierces the air and suddenly I remember that beneath this lunar beauty, this deceptive serenity, there is only sand. This is the home of a mirage, of sand devils, the dreaded menace of the North Atlantic whose shifting contours have lured ships to destruction, taking to their deaths unrecorded thousands of men and women. And it is now, if never before, that I am swept into the flow of time and events that occurred to shape this unique island.

2 Haughtboyes and Horrors

THE FIRST DOCUMENTED shipwreck of Sable was published in Hakluyt's *Voyages*. The account includes an eyewitness description of the last voyage, in 1583, of the great English explorer, Sir Humphrey Gilbert, painstakingly recorded by Edward Hayes who, as captain of the vessel the *Golden Hind*, accompanied the explorer. Gilbert, after taking possession of Newfoundland in the name of his beloved Queen Elizabeth, decided to sail for Sable Island rather than head directly from Cape Race to Cape Breton across the mouth of the St. Lawrence. He had heard from a Portuguese seaman that there were pigs and goats on the island. If this were true, then perhaps there might even be cattle pasturing in the meadows. By stopping at Sable, Gilbert and his men would have a ready supply of the roast beef of England, and provisions for ship's stores.

For the trip, Gilbert chose to make his quarters on a small overloaded vessel, the *Squirrel*. Captain Maurice Brown took command of the *Delight* which carried Gilbert's books, charts, notes, and precious ore samples carefully collected in Newfoundland. Most of Gilbert's men, unhappy with their stay in Newfoundland, were anxious to see the end of their explorations.

On August 20, 1583, the three ships departed on the voyage south. As they sailed close to Sable Island they soon fell into "such flats and dangers, that hardly any. . . escaped." Differences about which course to take soon developed between Sir

Humphrey and Richard Clark, the buccaneering sailing master of the flagship *Delight*. Clark later claimed that when they were within twenty leagues of Sable, Sir Humphrey came up in his frigate and demanded what course was best to keep. Clark answered that the west southwest was best because the wind was blowing south, night was falling, and "unknown sands lay off a great way from the land." In a blustering rage, Sir Humphrey then gave Clark orders to head west northwest. "The General sayd," wrote Clark, "my reckoning was untrue, and charged me in her Majesties name, and as I would shewe my selfe in her Countrey, to follow him that night. I fearing his threatenings, because he presented her Majesties person, did follow his commaundment."

On Wednesday, August 27, they struck soundings and at thirty-five fathoms discovered white sand. The next day they sighted land and that evening, according to Hayes, "they in the *Delight*, continued, sound of Trumpets, with Drummes, and Fifes: also winding the Cornets, Haughtboyes: and in the end of their jolitie, left with the battel, and ringing of doleful knels."

That evening, under a brewing storm and high winds, the *Golden Hind* crew harpooned a large porpoise and pulled it on deck. Later that night eerie sounds of porpoises were heard by the crew of the *Squirrel* coming from the *Golden Hind*. Hayes wrote of the "frivolous reports by them in the frigate, of straynge voyces, the same night, which scared some from the helm" and compared the evening's revelry on the *Delight* to "the Swanne that singeth before her death."

By Friday morning the violent southeast winds had reached gale force. The storm brought blinding rains and dense fog, and wicked currents played havoc with navigation. Richard Cox, master of the *Golden Hind*, warned that the flagship, which had been "keeping so ill watch," should make immediately for the open sea; they were too close to the treacherous shoals of Sable.

"Land!" cried Richard Clark on the *Delight*. "Land ahead—white cliffs!"

Suddenly, with frozen clarity, he saw the mirage of cliffs dissolve into enormous white breakers smashing on the shore of Sable. Heartsick, he spied sandbars dead ahead. The fleet was in trouble. In desperation, the two following vessels veered sharply away and headed for the open sea to the safety of deeper water. With terrific force the *Delight* struck a sandbar. Driving rain and gale winds lashed her top deck. Huge waves battered the sides of the ship which soon began to roll and lurch as her keel burrowed deep in the sand of Sable.

In despair over these sudden and violent events, Captain Brown nonetheless put up a brave front and shouted encouragement to his men. But the sea was relentless; the swell grew stronger and it struck again and again, sweeping overboard and smashing the bridge into fragments. The main and mizzen masts snapped in two and hurtled to the deck. The screams of the men were carried off by the wind as they were struck by falling timber.

By this time, Clark had worked his way to the stern and nearly lost his life overboard when he made the return trip. His ear was torn and bleeding, his mouth swollen and bruised. He had discovered a small boat, a pinnace, already launched in the water which would hold a dozen men. When Clark informed the captain of his news, Brown ordered him to take the pinnace and with some men attempt to reach the island.

Clark pleaded with the captain to save himself

Sir Humphrey Gilbert.

The *Delight* shuddered convulsively each time it was pummelled by the murderous sea. The huge waves mounted the wrecked decks, taking men over the side to their deaths. The currents began working to firmly trap the vessel; the sand swirled and flowed about the ship to build a wall between her and the ocean. Although she was afloat in this basin, the end was already near. Soon the basin got smaller and smaller until it vanished. The sands began to suck her down. Pressure from the sand and violent seas split open her seams. Finally the *Delight* capitulated, broke apart, collapsed, and sank into the sea. The dark grey ocean waters closed over her until there was nothing.

Some eighty-five men were gone along with brave Captain Brown and Stephen Parmenius the Hungarian poet who had honoured the expedition with his elegant verse. Daniel, a Saxon refiner on the voyage to assay precious minerals, also perished. The fleet's provisions, the special ore samples, and Sir Humphrey's valuable notes and books, all were lost. Grieved and angered at this great loss on Sable Island, the explorer saw all his dreams quickly vanish; the cabin boy became the recipient of his frustration, for "the remembrance touched him so deep, as not to be able to control himself, he beat the boy in great rage."

As the *Delight* was being savagely broken into pieces on Sable, the *Golden Hind* and *Squirrel* took soundings. "Making out from this danger, we sounded one while seven fathoms, then five

by getting into the pinnace. "I cannot forsake my charge!" he replied, and mounting the highest deck he continued to cheer his men as long as he could. Clark and sixteen sailors took their chance in the open but sturdy boat.

fathoms, then four, then but three, the sea going mightily and high. At last we recovered, God be thanked, in some despair to sea roome enough." Captain Hayes, recording these events, wrote that they kept a vigilant eye on the *Delight* through the storm, powerless to help their comrades. For two days they beat up and down as close to Sable Island and the wrecked vessel as possible, searching in vain for survivors, before finally sailing away, unaware survivors existed.

Amazingly, some of the crew of the *Delight* lived to tell their story. Sixteen men crowded into a small boat, distraught and half-senseless, and then laboured back to Newfoundland equipped with only one oar; the other was lost in the ocean. Five men died on the way and at one point they were suffering dreadfully from exposure.

"Thirst, master, thirst!" cried the men. "We die of thirst!"

"Piss, men," Clark called out to them. "Piss and drink it, save yourselves. Land in seven days, pray to God." It got them through. They were picked up by a Basque vessel and returned to England by way of France.

Although he escaped Sable, Sir Humphrey's luck ran out by the time the *Golden Hind* and the *Squirrel* sailed north of the Azores. The ships ran into sudden Atlantic storms and met "with very foule weather, and terrible seas, breaking short and high Pyramid wise." During a brief respite, Sir Humphrey, suffering from a wounded foot, and holding a Bible in his hand, tried to cheer the men of the *Golden Hind*. He shouted across the waves, "We are as neere to heaven by sea as by land!" Not long after midnight, as Hayes recorded it, "The frigate being ahead of us in the *Golden Hind*, suddenly her lights were out, whereof as it were in a moment, we lost the sight, and withall our watch cryed, the Generall was cast away, which was too true." Sir Humphrey and his crew of ten on the *Squirrel* vanished forever.

Alas! Sable, heedless of rank and power, eluded the great Gilbert. Stephen Parmenius in his admiration for Sir Humphrey eulogized him in the lines:

What strange new radiance is this that shines
So suddenly in heaven's changing face?

Thoughts of Sir Humphrey and his death in the icy waters of the Atlantic are active in my mind on this sunny day on Sable. Like a child I shed boots and socks and wade into the sea where large schools of fish move beneath the waves and dart away as I advance. I can feel the pull of the cold sea on my ankles. Here, the icy northern waters meet the warm Gulf Stream to produce swirling currents around the island. Sable is in the centre of a whirlpool of currents as the Gulf Stream passes the island on its easterly course; when the great Arctic current reaches the Grand Banks it is deflected to the west. These conflicting currents are omnipresent and strong enough to carry a ship forward so swiftly that before anyone is aware, it is upon the island. Another contributing factor to the massive number of shipwrecks on Sable was the navigational miscalculations of the exact location of the island; for centuries it had been erroneously charted.

On the south side of Sable, landing by vessel is attempted only after a succession of northerly winds and in fine weather. On the north beach, where I stand, ships anchor in the fine holding sand. They must, however, put to sea if the wind arises from the north. Landing on Sable is not only extremely difficult, but dangerous, as James Millar discovered in the early 1800s. Employed to take charge of some goods from a ship wrecked on Sable, Millar sailed in the late fall on the schooner *Elizabeth*. As he sailed close to the island, three of the crew attempted to land in a smaller craft but it capsized in the heavy seas and they were drowned. This left Millar with only one other sailor to negotiate the schooner. Finding it impossible to safely reach Sable or return to Halifax, they steered for the West Indies. After "many dangers and privations" they arrived at Antigua and were forced to remain until passage could be arranged back to Halifax.

As I wade back to shore I see how the dunes definitely have the "angularity of waves." The tops of their crests are wild and windswept. One of

them, higher than all the others, catches my eye, and carrying my boots and socks I arrive at the top after wading uphill through sand. Over two hundred years ago, before Sable diminished in size, the island could carry eight hundred grazing cattle and some of the tallest dunes were two hundred feet high. Today, less than three hundred horses roam the sand hills and the dune I stand on is less than ninety feet in height. The panoramic view from the summit, however, is stunning. The sea waves, great masses of water lifted by the wind, rush and crash forward; the crested rollers break on the shore with a loud hissing roar. To the east and west, as far as I can see, is a long unbroken line of surf, white 'horses' galloping towards shore. I can actually see the island curve at each end like the curl of a new moon; the dunes roll toward the sea until they dissolve into sand shoals.

The east tip, about four miles long, a thousand feet wide and the favourite gathering place for seal herds, seems to extend itself out to sea a little every year. The west tip, with similar dimensions, has, through the years, slowly eroded. Both tips of the island bear the brunt of terrific ocean currents and are modified, shaped, and changed by the dual forces of continual wind and storm. I can see the veritable stretch of desert sand which forms the beaches of Lake Wallace, named after the first commissioner of Sable Island in 1802. It is the main enclosed body of salt water on Sable and in the 1700s the lake was open to the ocean on both sides to form a lagoon where ships could safely enter. Later, by 1833, the lagoon had filled with sand, and since then the lake has steadily diminished in size. The valley, running between the two parallel ridges of hills, contains small open dunes, ponds, and salt flats.

The island runs nearly east and west and consists of two lines of dunes. The north ridge of dunes is higher and more pronounced, about twenty feet

As the western tip of Sable erodes due to wave and current action, the east end is constantly building and moving eastward. This diagram shows the island's progression over the last two hundred years.

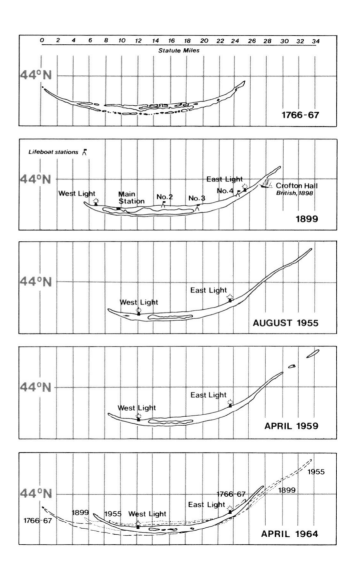

high starting at the west end, rising up in height about ninety feet, and diminishing toward the east tip of the island. From the seaside, the wind keeps eroding the high dunes, while the moving sand from the landward side builds them up again. Thick marram grass, beach pea, and seaside goldenrod anchor the sand hills. One lone, high and narrow sand ridge to the west carries a thin bar of native bluegrass.

The shadow of clouds passes over the sea for a moment and I am reminded of Bernard Shaw's lines of poetry: "The light upon the blue above/ is dark upon the green below." Below me, three seagulls, twenty feet apart, stand erect, sentinels waiting for the sea to serve up food. In the ocean not far from the shore, a large triangular-shaped object juts out of the water. Curious, I stare at it. A whale, a rock? Neither. The blue-green water ripples, then like an illusion the outline of a sunken ship materializes. The triangular shape is part of its boiler. This is a wreck, a real one, the first Sable Island wreck I have seen. Later, I was able to learn this was the *Skidby*, a 343-foot British steamer. She was very old and had just seen repairs when she hit Sable's northwest bar in 1905 and bumped over the shoals. If the captain had kept his engine running he might have worked his way free. Instead, he cut

engines and immediately dropped anchor which left the two-thousand-ton trampship parallel to shore. The crew and passengers simply waded to safety. And there she stuck, "trapped by the shifting sands, forever in eternal sleep." I am, in fact, standing on Mount Skidby, named after that unfortunate vessel.

As evening comes on, the sand dunes creep closer together. Mention of the *Skidby* leads to shipwreck and ghost tales around the fireplace in the A-frame. To cap the moonless night, I brave a lonely stroll on the north beach. I pass the decaying forms of pilot whales, beached to die on shore. Sand cliffs loom out of the dark, the ocean spills its breakers high up on the beach; I feel as if these two elements are pressing in on me. "This dark and sometimes bloody sand," wrote one historian, "could furnish materials for a hundred romances, whose recital could make the blood run cold." Thinking of the wild and strange tales of Sable's past, gives me a *frisson* of delicious terror such as I have never known. The episode of the Marquis de la Roche expedition and brief colonization of the island in 1598 is the heady kind of tale that makes the macabre more real than the commonplace. As I walk along the shore, I look over my shoulder for ghosts.

The wreck of the Skidby.

3 *Early Ghosts and Visitations*

IN 1578 THE Marquis de la Roche, a Catholic nobleman descended from an ancient French family in Bretagne, was appointed by Henry IV as lieutenant general and viceroy of New France. Furthermore, he was given a fur trade monopoly and the power to "bring the knowledge of God" to the Indians. Sable Island was chosen as the first landing point of the voyage in the New World; it was to be used as a military outpost because of its unique strategic location and because it was so familiar to the French navigators. De la Roche took with him fifty of the sturdiest men he could find from groups of seasoned vagabonds and ex-convicts; soldiers were added to keep discipline. A Franciscan monk accompanied the colonists, "charged by his superiors with the spiritual care of the party."

De la Roche, crew, and passengers sailed from France in the vessels *Françoise* and *Catherine*. The navigator of the expedition, a Norman, was Chêtodel de Voteuille, who later turned out to be somewhat of a scoundrel. The voyage passed without mishap and upon landing safely on Sable, de la Roche christened the island, L'île de Bourbon, giving it an entirely new name in honour of the governor of Normandy. With that little ceremony out of the way, the new settlers constructed an outpost with a storehouse and living quarters.

Leaving the main party on Sable with Commander Querbonyer in charge, de la Roche with Chêtodel and a small crew then sailed for Newfoundland to claim fur and fishing rights; de la Roche never reached his destination. As one historian described it, "the gray hummocks of Les Sablons had scarce sunk below the horizon ere a tempest burst upon his ship which rested not until it had blown the Marquis clear back to France again, whereupon he fell ill and languished" unable to do anything for the colonists left behind.

Soon the settlement on the solitary island became divided into two camps. There were those who recognized no law but their own caprices and refused to obey the officers placed in charge of them. The others tried to maintain order under such circumstances and in such society. All this time, the good Franciscan father preached obedience and peace and although he was respected, his prayers, exhortations, and warnings went mostly unheeded.

Violence and bloodshed followed. A convict rogue, more capable and cunning than his fellows, engineered the treacherous murder of Querbonyer and then assumed leadership of the group. They went on to kill Captain Cassez, master of the magazine, and a dozen others. Discipline destroyed, it was *sauve qui peut*.

Thomas Haliburton, in his *Account of Nova Scotia*, published by Joseph Howe in 1829, tells the rest:

These unfortunate people were reduced to the greatest

Sunset on the north beach.

distress. They were compelled to subsist wholly on fish. Their coats wearing out they made clothes of seal skin. The King ordered Chêtodel, who had been pilot to de la Roche, to bring them to France. Only twelve of them were found alive, and when they returned His Majesty had the curiosity to see them in their seal skin dresses, and long beards. Their appearance was so squalid and distressing, that he ordered them a generous pardon for their offences, and gave to each of the survivors a gratuity of 50 crowns.

Captain Chêtodel de Voteuille, having illegally appropriated some of the furs belonging to the survivors, was sued by the twelve men and had to pay the value of the pelts.

Meanwhile, the Marquis de la Roche was relieved of his command and authority and his monopolies were granted to Pierre Chauvin, a Protestant gentleman and merchant shipowner who obtained a commission from the king to trade and fish in the Gulf of St. Lawrence. The Marquis died in 1606, a sad and disillusioned man, but his outpost idea was a sound one. The seven-year settlement, from 1598 to 1605, although short-lived, demonstrated that Sable could be a satisfactory outpost manned by a small army of sturdy, hardy individuals with strong leadership.

The de la Roche expedition provoked several ghost stories and legends; fogs and phosphorescent haze mingled to create the presence of spirits. In those days, legend and fact were apt to become interwoven, and some of the tales were fanciful indeed. For instance, there were at one time, stories of the eerie sounds of clanking chains which began far away on the dunes and swelled to such volume that they struck fear into the heart of the bravest person. They were said to be the chains of the mutinous soldiers of the de la Roche colony, men who had murdered their fellows and were left on Sable to fend for themselves. Restless and guilty, they marched back and forth across the sand dunes. No spirits were seen, no phantoms visible; just the frightening sound of clanking chains in the black of the night.

One of the convicts, so the story goes, was brutally decapitated during the bloody revolt and his spirit was said to have appeared in the most bizarre way. From out of the fog a stallion with a headless rider appeared, galloping across the sands. It travelled at tremendous speed until it reached the spot where the death took place and there it would abruptly stop. Slowly, the diaphanous vision would vanish.

Another tale was about a married woman called Madelaine, who, after spurning the royal advances of Henry IV, was ordered to join the de la Roche colonists on the voyage to Sable. There, she was struck down by one of the men during a fit of jealous rage at the time of the uprising. It was said that her husband, upon hearing of her death, made the voyage to Sable and full of anguish and mourning soon died of a broken heart. His ghost took to roaming the island at night in the mists and his haunting lamentations for his wife and maledictions against King Henry were heard for years afterward.

None of these tales can be substantiated. Through the centuries, writers have confused and altered tales to suit their own style. The "ghost with a broken heart" was without doubt an imaginative elaboration on a report by the Reverend George Patterson which appears to be the only authentic ghost tale of the de la Roche expedition.

Patterson writes that at the time Chêtodel arrived to pick up the survivors from Sable, the Franciscan monk had fallen gravely ill. "I have no long time to live," he is recorded as saying, "perhaps only a few hours. I shall die here in the little hut which I have constructed, in which I prayed for five years as the anchorets of the desert." The men pleaded for him to embark on the ship but he refused. "The winds and the sands will charge themselves with my burial."

Sorrowfully they bade him adieu and sailed away. But the good father's time had not yet arrived. He recovered his health and lived many years as a hermit on Sable. Prayer and meditation filled his hours and he tended his little garden faithfully. He gathered shellfish and berries, and with his vegetables, this made up his daily provision. Numerous shipwrecks on the island gave him the opportunity to exercise his charity, and fishermen from Canso, Sambro, La Have, and other Acadian ports, visited him to bring news, to see his "Ways

George Patterson.

of the Cross" he had erected, and to receive the sacraments at his holy mass.

Patterson, in his *Supplementary Notes on Sable Island* written in June 1897, finishes the tale:

When he died and where he is buried is unknown. But his spirit is said still to hover over this desolate region. The fishermen allege they have often seen him marching at a slow pace along borders of the lake or of the shore, or on the bank, as in his lifetime, reciting his rosary; or often standing or on his knees on the cliffs, examining the sea tossed with tempest, watching and praying for the unfortunate mariners in danger of perishing.

Again they have seen him suspended, as in an ecstasy, in space, delineated against the azure sky, or upon the shadow of the dark heaped-up clouds or in the Fog; sometimes his head covered, with his beads in one hand and right stretched out as if to bless, to succour and to absolve.

Again, they have seen him in his dark robe of aerial drugget, girt with the girdle of the seraphic St. Francis, appear upon the bars and around the isle, gliding through the air as the resurrection bodies appear and disappear, or as in an assumption to the infinite presence. By such sights their spirits are revived and their hearts strengthened.

4 *Clash and Disaster*

IT IS A new day and I am plodding slowly through the deep, yielding sand. (I had heard that those who spent a few years on Sable without going off the island during that time, faced great difficulty in negotiating concrete sidewalks and pavement when they arrived back on the mainland.) I am wandering aimlessly along the north shore, enjoying the vagabond feeling of adventure as I look for shells or old coins. The wind is up, the ocean glistens and the sky is crowded with large white clouds, tier upon tier of them. My feet take me into a gully around the base of a high sand-cone and dramatically the picture changes.

I am now in the bottom of a bowl, a miniature valley hollowed out by the terrific winds. Here and there are a few grassy knolls, but there is very little protection for any creature as the wind shrieks through from the sea. The wind gives the sand a life of its own. Sand is everywhere. In high winds the stinging particles of sand get into eyes, hair, between teeth and lodge in ears; sand steals into pockets, it clings to boots, and irritating grains of sand can be found between the bed sheets or in a sleeping bag at night. Once here, as a visitor or settler, one never forgets that Sable is an island of sand.

Climbing out of the sandbowl, I come to a plateau where waving grasses resemble the western plains. The grassy ocean vanishes as I find myself going down through gentle valleys floored with black peat and filled with ripening blackberries, wild roses fading out of season, fragrant lilies, and bayberry. The grounds are strewn with birds' nests and in summer one must tread carefully to avoid breaking eggs. The sweet blueberries and strawberries are gone now, but unripened cranberries crunch and pop underfoot, beds upon beds of them. If I could return with a hundred huge barrels late next month, October, every barrel could be filled with the finest cranberries in the east.

In 1633 a Dutchman, Johannes de Laet, described Sable in his *Novus Orbis*, as having "but one small pond, but no springs of water, many thickets of bushes, very few trees, the soil naked or but slightly covered with grass." There are no trees, but here along the north side of Sable are many limpid and shallow fresh-water ponds where black ducks breed and where creatures now prepare to burrow deep into the bottom of the pond to ready for winter.

With the "rapidity and freshness of a kaleidoscope," as one nineteenth century writer phrased it, the scene changes as I leave the valley and mount the long dividing ridge or spine of the island where the ocean on both sides may be seen at once; a wondrous sight! This lofty point is further east than the first dune where I climbed and saw the wreck of the *Skidby*.

The year after de Laet's book came out, John Rose of Boston found himself shipwrecked on Sable.

Rose and his crew escaped to safety but their ship, *Mary and Jane*, was demolished. Sable was under French rule in 1634, for it had been granted, along with Port Royal and La Have, to Claude de Razilli, brother of Isaac de Razilli, Commander of Acadia, by the Company of the Hundred Associates. Rose and his men were received very kindly by the French on Sable and with their help they constructed a small vessel which took them safely to the mainland. At La Have, Commander de Razilli was most generous and provided Rose and his men with a shallop (a light open boat which they decked with a mast), and they returned to Boston. In his logs, Rose accurately described Sable: "The isle is thirty miles long, two miles broad in most places, mostly sand, yet full of fresh water in ponds. There is no wood on Sable, but much wild pease, and tall grasses. In the middle is a pond of salt water, ten miles long, full of plaice, soles and other fish and there is eight hundred head of cattle, small and great, all red, and the largest I ever saw, and many, many black foxes and sea-horse."

When Rose returned to Boston he approached two merchants and together in 1635 they formed a company to hunt on the island. The journals of John Winthrop, governor of New England at the time, give an account of their visits to Sable:

June 24, 1635:   Mr. Graves in the 'James,' and Mr. Hodges, in the 'Rebecka,' set sail for the Isle of Sable for sea-horse (which are there in great number) and wild cows. The company carried twelve landmen, two mastiffs, a house, and a shallop.

August 26, 1635:   They returned from their voyage. They found there upon the island sixteen Frenchmen, who had wintered there, and built a little fort, and had killed some black foxes. They had killed also many of the cattle, so as they found not above one hundred and forty, and but two or three calves. They could kill but few sea-horse, by reason they were forced to travel so far in the sand as they were too weak to stick them, and they came away at such time as they used to go up highest to eat green peas. The winter there is very cold, and the snow above knee deep.

In August of 1637 twenty company men set out in a pinnace, a ship's small boat rigged with sails, to hunt walrus, but they could not locate the island. In September, they set out again, this time with skilled sailors aboard. They must have spent two years on Sable for the next entry is not until March of 1639, when a vessel despatched to bring back the hunters was wrecked trying to land on the island. Out of the ship's ruins the hunters and rescuers constructed a small seaworthy craft which took them back to Boston.

During the hunters' two year settlement on Sable, there had not been a death or a case of illness among them. They collected a large quantity of seal oil and skins, some "seahorse teeth" (walrus ivory tusks), and black fox pelts. The loss of their vessel, however, destroyed all hopes of profit from the venture. Two years later they tried once more:

June 21, 1641:   This summer the merchants of Boston set out a vessel again to the Isle of Sable, with 12 men, to stay there a year. They sent again in the 8th month, and in three weeks the vessel returned and brought home 400 pair of sea-horse teeth, which were esteemed worth 300 pounds, and left all the men well, and 12 ton of oil and many skins, which they could not bring away, being put from the island in a storm.

Map of Sable Island, 1715.

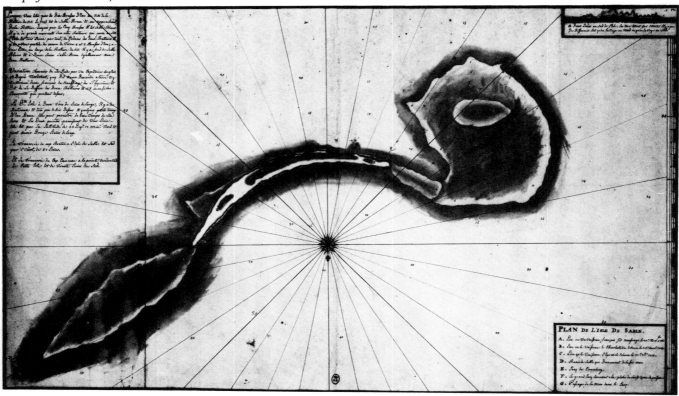

August 8, 1641:   About this time the adventurers to the Isle of Sable fetched off their men and goods all safe. The oil, teeth, seal and horse hides, and some black fox skins, came to near 1500 pounds.

With the death of Commander de Razilli, the French appeared to have abandoned the island in the late 1630s. While they were there, however, the French and English hunted together peacefully. But almost a hundred years later, when Nova Scotia was under British rule and Cape Breton was still in the hands of the French, the two nations were at each other's throats, and Sable Island was to play a minor part in the drama.

In 1745 a hastily recruited militia consisting of raw Yankee patriots captured the "impregnable" Louisbourg fortress on the tip of Cape Breton. Angry ambitious plans were drawn up in France for massive retaliation against the English and a huge armada was put together for this purpose: about sixty-five vessels and a complement of over three thousand men. The flotilla left Brest, France, in the spring of 1746 under the command of the Duc d'Anville. When invasion by the French fleet was rumoured, Boston fell into a panic; the Yankee rag-tag and bobtail army was re-armed, towns were fortified, and the citizenry waited in fear of certain doom.

The dreaded d'Anville armada never once approached the New England shores. Instead, from the moment of setting out, the ill-omened fleet met with such a series of disasters that the melancholy dénouement could almost have been foretold. First they were lashed by storms and suffered great damage and then they ran into a dead calm and for a week rolled about without a breeze for the sails off the Azores. Later, sudden lightning ignited ammunition boxes lashed on deck; these exploded killing many sailors. Ravaged by scurvy and typhus, in early autumn almost one-third of the fleet, unable to continue, returned to France or took refuge in the West Indies.

For the remaining vessels, assaulted by furious winds and storms, the quicksands of Sable were waiting. The gales increased in fury. One battered transport ship rammed into the heavily armed *Amazone*, and it sank quickly with all hands. Four warships vanished one awful night in Sable's shoals. With break of day, flotsam from broken ships littered the ocean. One ship, with rudder sheared off, had jettisoned her guns, her precious armament, to balance the list. The tattered remains of the armada edged slowly away from Sable and with sore hearts and makeshift sails limped into Bedford Basin, near Halifax, where over a thousand men died of pestilence. Too many died at once for burial with bell, book, and candle; too many for a sewn shroud, the pious Latin of a priest, and then over the side to full fathom five in the sea. Many found only hasty, shallow graves. A hundred years later their bones would be turned up by the spade in tranquil backyard gardens.

While these unhappy events were taking place on the mainland, a handful of shipwrecked sailors, part of the d'Anville expedition, made it to the shores of Sable Island. The sixteen survivors were from the corvette *Légère*, a small, fast, naval escort-vessel, which had sailed under the protection of the armada. Her captain, Charles François Guillemin, had just taken some English prisoners of war to France and was returning to his family in Québec when they were driven onto a sandbar on the south side of the island.

During the first wretched days the survivors tried to find some shelter from the harsh elements on the lee side of the dunes. It was their good fortune that they were discovered by a small group of people who had settled on Sable for the purpose of giving aid to shipwrecked sailors. Food and warm huts were shared with the newcomers who were made comfortable until they were picked up a few months later by a New England schooner. Then, after being taken to Boston, they were imprisoned. But Captain Guillemin, with the help of an influential brother, was soon released to return home. This first compassionate attempt at establishing a humane lifesaving service on Sable was the idea of the Reverend Andrew Le Mercier of Boston.

5 *The Enterprising Clergyman*

THE STORY OF Le Mercier's activities concerning Sable is an intriguing one. The Reverend gentleman claimed to own the island for awhile. Perhaps he really did. At any rate he endeavoured to sell it through a very large advertisement inserted in the *Boston Weekly News Letter*, February 5, 1753: "To be sold by me the subscriber, THE ISLAND SABLES, if any Person desires to purchase it, and to know further about it, they may see at my house a Map and Plan of it, or if they Live at a Distance by Letters sent (Postage Free) they may enquire about anything they want to be satisfied in, and I will give them all the Light they desire. I must know their Mind within 2 or 3 Months, that the Crew now upon the island may be disposed of accordingly."

Born of French Huguenot stock, Le Mercier lived in England briefly and arrived in Boston in 1715 where he became pastor of the French Protestant Church. He carried out his duties with great energy, involved himself in community affairs and was highly esteemed by his fellow clergymen.

In 1729 he submitted a proposal to Governor Philipps in Nova Scotia, outlining a plan to establish a colony of French Protestant emigrants. A grant of five thousand acres in Nova Scotia was recommended by the governor but the project was never implemented by the British government. A determined man, Le Mercier next petitioned that a grant be awarded to himself and two partners, Thomas Hancock and John Gorham, both New Englanders. Hancock, a shrewd and wealthy merchant, had his hand in many ventures, which included smuggling and furnishing supplies to new settlements and towns. Captain John Gorham, already a figure of fame, owned military ships and was even a member of the Governor's Council in Nova Scotia. An Indian fighter, he was leader of Gorham's Rangers in America and also would be involved in the Battle of Louisbourg in 1745.

A new Le Mercier petition in 1738 included a plan to stock Sable Island with useful domestic animals. These, he pointed out, would help to keep alive any shipwrecked sailors who safely reached her shores. While awaiting decisions, the trio, with smart dispatch, shipped livestock and a small crew to Sable. The approved petition had to go through the Secretary of State and the Board of Trade in London. Meanwhile, proclamations were issued to protect Sable in Le Mercier's name: one from the governor of Nova Scotia, one from the governor of New Hampshire, and another from Massachusetts; all British colonies at the time. The patient pastor waited two years but Britain gave no indication of interest.

"The land is low with boggy and sandy soil and large ponds or settlings of water occasioned by the overflowing of the tides, he thinks the penny an acre too much for what cannot be improved," wrote Le Mercier in 1740, in yet his third grant application, this time to a new governor of Nova Scotia, Paul Mascarene. In his support of the peti-

Map of Sable Island, 1770.

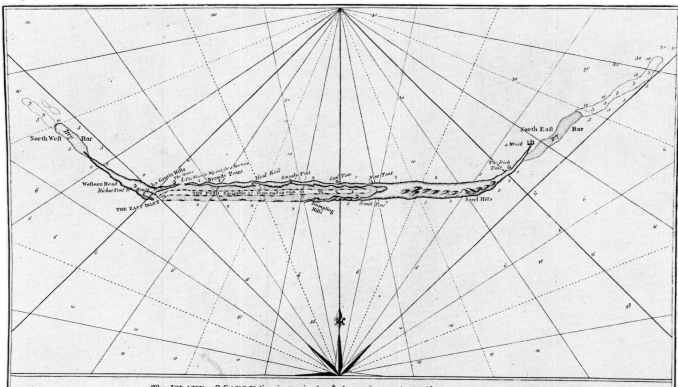

tion, Mascarene suggested to the Board of Trade that the settlement be encouraged. It would, he explained, provide relief to the shipwrecked, and those who owned the settlement could eventually become self-sufficient through profits from hunting. Again, no grant materialized.

A man of lesser will than Le Mercier would surely have given up by then. Perhaps, he reasoned, there was someone he had missed while submitting applications. It was a century when vast land purchases were made by foreign noblemen, and everything was up for grabs.

Grant or no, for the next dozen years Le Mercier attracted settlers to Sable Island. As he hoped, they engaged in raising vegetables and stock, in hunting, and most important, in giving what assistance they could to ships that were wrecked offshore. Le Mercier finally ended his part in this venture by offering Sable for sale to the public. There is no record of a buyer, and since there is no record of possession having been granted to Le Mercier and his partners in the first place, it may be assumed that Sable remained in the hands of the Crown.

The good clergyman seemed to have written the advertisement for sale in 1753, in an honest manner, depicting fairly the positive and negative elements:

There are neither River or Brooks of fresh Water, but every where even upon the Beach, you may come to fresh clear Water by digging about three feet, by which means the Root of the Grass is always kept cool and alive, so that it cannot be much subject to a Drought, as it was experienced three Years ago. The Climate may be called temperate, for in Winter the Snow hardly lies above three Days on the Ground, so it is never extreme hot in Summer, and it is a rare Thing to be frightened by any Thunder.

It produces naturally near 20 sorts of Berries, out of which some People suppose very good Liquors and Wines might be expressed—It looks all green in Winter with the Juniper bushes, and red in Summer with the large Strawberries and other wild Fruits which it bears. —It hath abundance of wild or Beach Pease, which fatten the Cattle very well:—By several Pieces of petrified Wood found there it is supposed that the Sand hath a Property of petrifying Wood.—Within these seven or eight Years of Providence hath opened a Communication between the great Pond (fifteen miles long) and the Sea, which hath made a safe and large Harbour; but the Entrance is barred so that large and sharp Vessels cannot get into it; but as there is about 8 feet of Water, the Bar at High Water there is sufficient Passage (as we know by experience) for vessels of 30 Tons or more, if not built sharp.

The Care of Gardens and Cattle take up of our People's Time in Summer, in Winter they go and kill Seils and boil their Fat into Oyl, as well as that of Whales, which now and then are cast away dead upon the Beach. The island finds them in Turf, and the sea brings them Wood; so they are not deprived of Necessaries of Life, not without Profits of several sorts; besides their having the Pleasure of saving often many Men's Lives, according to the Motto of the Island, *viz. Destruo est Salvo.* When I took Possession of the Island there were no

Pond system.

four-footed Creatures upon it, but a few Foxes, some red and some black (some of which remain to this Day) now there are I suppose about 90 Sheep, between 20 or 30 Horses, including Colts, Stallions, and breeding Mares, about 30 or 40 Cows tame and wild, and 40 Hogs.

The Advantage which do acrue or may acrue from the Improvement of the Place are so great that I would not easily part with it if I was so skillful in Navigation and Shipping as it is necessary: That ignorance of mine induces me (not any Defect in the Island itself) to part with it.

From this document it appears that the first of the stocked horses and cattle had died off before Le Mercier's possession. His description of Sable remains one of the most colourful and complete of the eighteenth century.

6 *Wrecks and Rescue*

It is a tranquil evening. The night sky over Sable is freckled with stars; large and luminescent. Five of us stand outside the A-frame studying the Andromeda galaxy through telescopes and binoculars. There seems to be no end to the universe. The sickle moon (the shape of Sable) dominates the stars, pulls at the sea, pulls at the island; in its grip I feel restless and I begin to walk. Nights like this are exceptionally beautiful on Sable. The bright moon and stars light a pathway through the meadow and between the dunes. The night air is sweet with the exotic fragrance of the island. I pull it deep into my lungs.

Adventurous thoughts, usually associated with a child's fantasy, enter my head and I imagine myself living alone here. Would I be clever enough, I wonder, to know how to construct a shelter, and could I summon up the courage to kill creatures for food in order to survive? The Major Elliott party comes to mind; they were shipwrecked on Sable in 1760 without the Le Mercier settlers to assist them. The Elliott group, which included his wife and two children, were courageous and with Lady Luck riding on their shoulders their story has a happy ending and an unusual sequel.

Major Robert Elliott of the 43rd Regiment of the British army (he had taken part in the Battle of the Plains of Abraham), was returning to New York with his family when his ship was pulled into Sable by the currents and stranded deep in the sands of the northeast bar. For hours the vessel sat there as chilling winds and pummelling waves attacked her. The passengers were helpless, they could see land but it was too far away. The midshipman, shouting over the wind, cried for a boat to be launched, but the seas were too dangerous. The ship was sinking into the sand, something had to be done quickly.

Elliott ordered everyone below deck. They bent their heads to the wind and made their way below where they huddled close together for whatever comfort and warmth they could find. Suddenly, the wind rose higher. With increased horror, the poor travellers felt the ship move under them. Walls of water battered the ship; passengers covered their ears to shut out the thunderous noise. Again, the ship moved. Some people began to sob, others screamed. Elliott and a mate bravely went up on deck to check conditions. They quickly returned with news that the ship was moving; they were released, free of the sandbar! The passengers shouted with joy, but Elliott issued orders for everyone to stay below deck until further word. He went back on deck. The vessel, now free, began to float but soon lodged in the sand again, this time just off the south beach. Disembarkation was still

"A View of the North Shore of the Isle Sable." Aquatint by J. F. W. Desbarres, 1779.

impossible but now their position was much improved and at least they had a fair chance.

Major Elliott ordered everyone back on deck, and announced that an attempt would be made to reach shore. First, however, a line must be carried from the vessel to the island and volunteers were requested. Two sailors, both able swimmers, stepped forward, tied lines around themselves, and without hesitation leapt into the sea. In a few moments the boiling surf took them both under, forever. A third seaman was successful and the lifeline was made fast on the beach.

Elliott and his wife then tied their children securely to their own backs. Shouting encouragement to everyone, they followed the rest of the crew and lowered themselves into the freezing waters. Slowly, painfully, hand over hand, they struggled to safety. Miraculously everyone got ashore, but even though they were utterly exhausted, they had little time to rest. They hastened to build shelters from the sails that were salvaged from their ship to protect themselves from the bitter winds of winter, which had already arrived. Provisions, which were placed in boxes and pulled ashore with lines when the ship was abandoned, were carefully rationed to keep them alive for months.

The Elliott party soon constructed a storehouse and barracks from the remains of their vessel which had rapidly broken up. A month later, another ship was stranded on the island. The name of the vessel is not recorded but the survivors joined the little colony, swelling the number to almost seventy people. More huts were added and the problem of

Vessel appearing over the Land and bearing W.S.W. 2½ Miles distant.

fresh meat was solved when the cattle and wild horses were discovered roaming the island. Major Elliott saw to it that a lookout was maintained and when a sail was sighted, signals were shown in the hope of attracting attention. Their happy rescue was effected by a small fishing schooner. The stay on Sable Island had lasted only two months; the survival program had been successful largely because of the strong, resourceful leadership of Major Elliott.

The most amazing event took place almost a century later, in 1847. By then a lifesaving establishment known as the Humane Establishment had been set up on Sable by the government. One of the crew, doing his rounds on horseback, noticed a strange horizontal black line etched into a sand cliff. He began to dig and soon discovered the site of an old encampment. Many relics were revealed; ammunition, rusty guns with bayonets, old boots, a dog collar with "43rd" stamped on it, knives fashioned from steel hoops, plus some cattle, dog and seal bones. Eighty-one years after their landing on Sable, the remains of the Elliott settlement were discovered, well preserved in the sand.

Sable is so totally a place of sand that any other name for this island would seem unthinkable. The sand dunes have been talked about, written about, or painted by every author with pen in hand or artist with a brush who has marvelled at their colours. Tonight, they stand out in relief against the starlit sky and I think of Desbarres and his water colours.

Colonel Joseph Frederick Wallet Desbarres, who

"A View from the Camp." Aquatint by J. F. W. Desbarres, 1780.

was lieutenant governor of Cape Breton and later of Prince Edward Island, visited Sable many times from 1766 to about 1780. As well as being a notorious lady's man and one of the finest surveyors in Maritime history, Desbarres was also an accomplished artist. His long, horizontal, pale aquatint panels of Sable viewed from the ocean at different locations, now carefully kept in rolls at the Ottawa Archives, are probably the earliest pictorial record of the island.

Desbarres, and Montressor, captain of the vessel that took the painter to the island, arrived at names for the most prominent features of Sable. Along the southern shore from east to west are Mount Knight, Sand Hills, South Tent, Dumplin' Hills, Last Inlet, and finally The Naked Sand Hills, which were "146 feet perpendicular above the high water mark," and always appeared white. Along the northern shore from west to east, there were Mount Luttrel, Gratia Hill, Riches House, The

House, Brandy Point, Smoky Tent, Seal Tent, New Tent, Irish Tent, Entrance to Pond, Vale of Misery, Smith's Flag Staff and the highest hill of them all, the Ram's Head, which has a steep cliff on the northwest and falls gently to the southeast.

Two paintings by Desbarres show activity on Sable during the years he visited. One water-colour, "A view from the Camp at the East End of the Naked Sand Hills on the South East Shore of Sable Island," suggests sealing operations or perhaps horse thieving. Another depicts a supposed "wrecker's den" near the pond on Sable, which could be interpreted as just a romantic whimsy on the part of Desbarres. Yet, according to the *Nova Scotia Gazette* of February 10, 1789, there was a Jesse Lawrence living on Sable who helped the shipwrecked while earning his living at seal fishing. One day he was attacked by people from Massachusetts, "who landed there and wantonly pillaged and destroyed his house and effects, and then compelled him to leave the island." Though he did receive a small compensation from Governor Hancock and the Council of Massachusetts, it was not nearly enough to cover his losses. Lawrence was an unlucky victim of this early wave of pirates and wreckers.

The same newspaper reported that in October 1792, a "fine Spanish vessel, *la Feliz*, bound from Havana with sugar and tobacco was wrecked on Isle Sable." The mixed cargoes riding the sea lanes past Sable Island from England and other ports,

offered special profits to those who could unlawfully get their hands on them. The manifest of the ship *Adamant*, Captain Wyatt, master, which arrived in Halifax in October 1782, included such imports as "an assortment of the best stationery and books; loaf sugar and molasses; wax candles; men's boots and pumps; women's everlasting sarcenet shoes; an assortment of pickles in cases; perfumery; earthenware; optical instruments; guitars, violins and fiddle strings; majick lanthorns and sliders; scented hair powder; Jarr raisons, Valencia almonds; candied citron and orange; troffels, macaroni, morels, vermicelly, pearl barley; comfits, carianter, carraway and other confectionary sorted; cinamon, cloves, nutmeg and mace, etc., etc."

None of these exotic luxuries were produced in the northern New World, and they found a ready sale, legally or otherwise, up and down the coasts and in the towns from Newfoundland to Florida. Criminals murdered for such merchandise and for many years it was believed that Sable was a rendezvous for lawless rogues.

It is another night and I am on the north beach once more. Unseen, primitive forces seem to draw me here after dark. Perhaps it is the security of the long line of sandcliffs so close to the sea; it would be difficult to lose my way here. Or perhaps this is where others from the past still walk.

There are no stars this night, no moon. Mist rises from the ponds and fog moves in from the sea.

Tonight, something invisible is in the atmosphere, "spilling its mysteries" on Sable, as Loren Eiseley would phrase it. Now the fog parts and lets me through. The surface of the sand is wet and the sea strangely muffled as I enter this eerie world. I seem to hear rum-soaked voices from the dunes and the thud of running feet on the sand. Suppose—the thought strikes me suddenly—suppose the voices and the footsteps I hear are those of people long dead? I begin to shiver.

The last shipwreck of the eighteenth century to occur on Sable Island was the sinking of the *Francis* in 1799. Because of the prominence of passengers on board and the valuable cargo, it generated not only interest but a near scandal in both London and Halifax. The two-hundred-and-eight-ton *Francis* was a government transport, sailing from England to Halifax. She was carrying forty people on board as well as the complete equipage belonging to H.R.H. the Duke of Kent, who would become the

father of Queen Victoria. The ship had been detained in England because of an embargo and therefore departed later than planned, arriving in Nova Scotia waters at the peak of the December gales. Caught in a hurricane, driven savagely upon Sable while trying to beat off the northwest bar, the *Francis* was trapped on a sand shoal leagues from land. How she might have become snared on the bar is fictitiously recounted by J. MacDonald Oxley in his book, *The Wreckers of Sable Island*:

A few minutes later the 'Francis' struck the first bar with a shock that sent everybody who had not something to hold on to tumbling upon the deck—a tremendous billow rushed upon the helpless vessel, sweeping her from stem to stern—their wild cries for help that could not be given them pierced the ears of the others, who did not know but that the next billow would treat them in like manner. Again and again was the ill-starred ship thus swept by the billows, each time fresh victims falling to their... fury. Then came a wave of surpassing size, which lifting the 'Francis' as though she had been a mere feather, bore her over the bar into the deeper water beyond. Here, after threatening to go over upon her beam-ends, she righted once more, and drove on toward the next bar.

And there she stayed, to split apart. The end was swift.

Among the passengers of the *Francis* who drowned was Dr. Copeland, the surgeon of the 7th Fusiliers on the personal staff of the Duke of Kent, who, at that time, was in command of all the military forces in British North America. Copeland was also librarian to the Prince and had supervised the removal of most valuable furniture, books, maps, silver plate, horses, and personal effects to the holds of the *Francis* from the Duke's English residence. Responsible for the safe arrival in Halifax of this precious cargo, valued at eleven thousand pounds, Dr. Copeland decided to travel with it; his wife, two children, and a maid servant accompanied him. Of the 7th Regiment on board were Captain Sterling, Lieutenants Sutton and Roebuck, Volunteer Oppinshaw and Sergeant Moore. There was also Captain Holland, 44th Regiment; Lieutenant Mercer, Royal Artillery; Privates Thomas King and Abbott, 16th Light Dragoons; Private Judd, Coachman to the Duke; and stable boys to H.R.H., Nicholson, Johnson, Gardner, and Bloomfield. Every one of them perished at sea.

With the sinking of the *Francis*, rumours of wreckers on Sable Island increased when articles of clothing and personal effects belonging to drowned victims of the vessel began to turn up in private homes on the south shore of Nova Scotia. In a report on conditions prevailing on Sable in 1800 by Governor Wentworth, there is evidence of wrecker activity. It mentions that "no great depredations were made on the cattle and horses until the start of the American War, during the course of which Privateers men and lawless persons of every description frequently landed on the Island." By the time the war ended, most of the animals on Sable had vanished except for a few horses, and many of them were "wantonly shot by persons wintering on the Island for the purpose of wrecking."

An article on Sable Island published in *Harper's Magazine* in 1866, describes the island's reputation: "Then, by-and-by, horrid tales of blood began to be whispered about, and the Isle of Sable became an ill-omened name, at which people shuddered and turned pale, less because the winds and waves were merciless than on account of man's horrid inhumanity to man."

Demands were eventually made to investigate the sinking of the *Francis* to see if treachery was at work. Governor Wentworth authorized Lieutenant Joseph Scambler to make inquiries on Sable about the ship or any other unfortunate vessel that might have been wrecked there during the winter. They were also to land some animals. Scambler proceeded to Sable and landed the small farm animals but discovered no one on the island. However, he spied a schooner at anchor at the northeast spit. Scambler returned to his cutter intending to "beat up where she lay," but the current prevented him. Later in the afternoon he found the schooner under sail. In his report, Scambler tells the rest of the story:

I immediately weighed, made sail and spoke to her; she proved to be the 'Dolphin' of Barrington, laden with

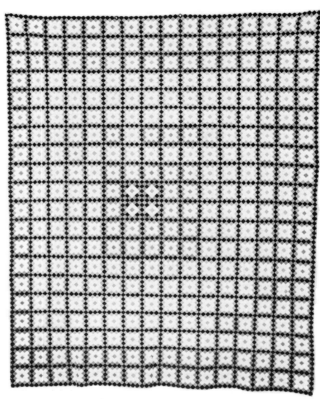

Quilt made from the remains of British Army uniforms carried by the Francis, *1799.*

fish, seal skins and seal oil. She had several trunks very much damaged, on board, and appeared to have been washed on shore. One trunk was directed to His Royal Highness Prince Edward, No. 2, another trunk directed to Captain Stirling of the 7th Regiment Foot, both empty. Also a trunk containing two great coats, the livery worn by the servants of His Royal Highness. The master of the schooner informed me that he had two men on the island this winter, on the sealing concern, who had built a hut on the east end of the island.

Lieutenant Scambler learned that the two sealers had observed a large vessel struggling against the currents off the northeast bar on the second of December. By night time the island was locked into a storm and they were of the opinion the *Francis* must have been driven on the sands and broken up, for there was no sign of her in the morning. Soon after the storm abated, cargo from the vessel was washed ashore: the two trunks, a dozen shod horses, two cows, a bull and two sheep. All the animals were drowned. The body of a woman with a ring on her finger was also found and a number of articles were saved and carried to Barrington, Nova Scotia.

Perhaps it was this report that led to gossip and stories of wreckers and murderers, for there were those who claimed to have seen belongings from the *Francis* in Nova Scotian homes. Indeed, accounts from *Barrington Township* by Edwin Crowell show that in the spring of 1799 a Coleman Crowell and Ziba Hunt were left on Sable Island to hunt seals and "look for wrecks" during the summer. In September, a Captain John Reynolds arrived in his schooner to return the men to Bar-

rington. Foul weather made landing impossible and the hunters were left to fend for themselves during the winter where they survived on "horse-meat and berries." In December, when the *Francis* went down, barrels of biscuits which had been washed ashore supplemented their diet. The sealers also found swollen corpses of animals and humans and several cases of liquor that had been washed up on the beach.

By spring, Reynolds arrived to take the men off the island and load some of the booty from the *Francis* onto his own ship. Unwisely, they failed to notify the government about the articles and "sold and distributed the wreckage stuff all about Barrington." These included soldier's caps, officer's apparel, silk stockings, and red coats. The red coats were the most popular and soon the townspeople were sporting them at meetings and town functions. Some of them were made into warm winter quilts, now cherished in museums.

Captain Reynolds was ordered to Halifax by military authorities for intensive questioning and although he gained a certain notoriety on account of the Sable incident, he escaped punishment. The Duke of Kent, whose equipage went down with the *Francis* later met Reynolds by chance in the street and addressed him in the following manner: "Your conduct, Sir, might do very well for Americans, but it is certainly not suitable for British subjects!" With that, the Duke spun on his heel and marched off.

7 Sable's Pale Lady

MRS. COPELAND, WIFE of the surgeon on the *Francis*, became the subject of Sable's most famous ghost story. Thomas Chandler Haliburton of *Sam Slick* fame spun the tale of "The Pale Lady with the Missing Finger" with a little fact and a lot of imagination.

According to Haliburton, the Duke ordered a Captain Torrens of the 29th Regiment to inquire after the missing *Francis*. Torrens' own vessel was apparently wrecked as he attempted to land on Sable, but all the crew survived. The captain then stationed his men on one end of the island and ordered that the dead washed up on shore from the *Francis* had to be buried, and any of the Duke's effects worth salvaging had to be collected. The burial was "an awful task, and took a long, long time, for the grave was almost as large as a cellar." Once that grisly chore was finished, Torrens set off for the east tip of Sable. There, he spent a few days, along with his dog, Whiskey, scouting the shoreline to check for survivors. His headquarters was a small abandoned hut.

One day he returned at dusk, made a fire, cooked himself a meal, drew some hay from a small loft and made up a bed in one corner. He and Whiskey then went for a walk in the moonlight. As they were returning to the hut, Whiskey stopped and began to growl.

"What's the matter, Whiskey?" said Torrens. "Come on boy, we're nearly home." The dog advanced but continued to growl until they came to the hut.

"Don't stand there, Whiskey, heel boy, heel." A deeper growl this time. "Very well, stay outside if you will. I'm going to bed." Torrens lifted the latch and as the door squeaked open the dog began to bark with fear and excitement. Torrens gasped at what he saw.

There, seated at his fireside, was a woman wearing a torn and soiled white dress that clung to her as if she had just come from the sea. Her long dripping hair framed a pale face, her eyes stared at him.

"Good heavens, Madam, who are you? Why, you're soaked from head to foot. However did you get here?" Outside, the dog howled. "Madam, do you hear me? Who are you? How did you come here? Speak!"

The woman stared at him for the longest time. She opened her mouth and gave the most chilling moan. He felt his scalp tingle. Then out came in a hoarse whisper, "Murdered!"

"Nonsense, woman," said Torrens, recovering himself, "I can see you are soaked to the skin, but you are not murdered, or likely to be. I'm a friend. Do not be afraid." He advanced toward her. Terrified, she flung up her arms.

"Away, away! Do not hurt me. Please, do not hurt me!"

"I do not want to hurt you. Tell me who you are."

She looked around desperately.

"My ring, my wedding ring. I want my ring back. I have come to get my wedding ring. They took it."

"Who took it? Tell me."

"They—they murdered me for my ring. Look!" She held up a hand. The ring finger was missing, nothing was left but a bloody stump.

"My good woman, why, you're bleeding. Let me attend to your hand." Torrens turned to a box he had picked up that morning on shore. It had drifted in from the sunken ship and contained wound dressings. At that moment Torrens felt a rush of cold air behind him and turning, saw the woman slip out the door. He ran after her but she was nowhere to be found. Puzzled, he went back to the hut, not sure of what he had seen. A demented person? A ghost? He must be overtired, he thought to himself. So much danger and death in so short a time.

As he re-entered the hut, there was the pale woman once again, seated as before, staring. Before he could utter a cry she held up her mutilated hand again, her eyes pleading for understanding. Torrens took a step forward and gazed intently at the apparition. The story of the woman washed up on shore from the *Francis* with a ring on her finger, was familiar to him. Perhaps this was Dr. Copeland's wife whom he had met some years before.

"Could—could you be Mrs. Copeland?" asked the captain. "Please, let me help you." He moved closer.

She leaped up and made a pushing motion with her hands.

"Stand back! Don't touch me!" She retreated in this manner, the captain stayed where he was. "I want only my ring. I must go, I must find my ring. They tore off my finger to steal my ring. I can't go back without it."

"Go back, where to?"

"To rest," she moaned, "to rest, for I am murdered. They murdered me to steal my ring, my wedding ring. I cannot rest without it."

"Then I shall find it," said Torrens, realizing he must somehow soothe this tormented spirit. "I'll track the villain down who stole it! I'll have him shot or hanged. You shall have back your ring. I promise you I shall find it."

"Find it," she cried in an unearthly voice as she retreated to the door, "my ring, my ring..." She hesitated and then seemed to melt away.

"Mrs. Copeland, please stay, don't go!" Torrens rushed outside, but there was nothing. "Gone! Like a bubble into thin air." The dog ran up to his master, whining. "Why, hello, Whiskey. I'm beginning to think I've had too much of you tonight."

Sometime later, after he returned to Halifax, Captain Torrens sat in his study reading over a letter he had just written. Lying beside it was a curiously wrought gold ring. His letter described how he first searched the island for any trace of the missing ring, without luck. Then he returned to the mainland to continue his search. Having heard of wreckers in Barrington, he went there and made discreet inquiries about those who were involved in the *Francis* affair. When he questioned Coleman Crowell he was, at first, tight-lipped, denying any-

thing about a lost ring. But Torrens was a patient man.

After a few days, he skillfully drew out the information from Crowell that a sailor in Salmon River had knowledge of the whereabouts of the ring. He made a lengthy trip to what is now the county of Yarmouth, but the man he sought in Salmon River was not at home. Nevertheless, he became intimate with the family by staying with them while pretending to enjoy a fishing and hunting holiday in the area. One evening he turned the conversation towards a jewelled ring he happened to be wearing. The housewife and her daughters were filled with admiration as the ring was handed around for inspection.

"It's been in my family for generations," said Torrens. "This is my coat of arms, you see. It's really meant to imprint a seal. When I close my letters, I seal them up with wax, and just before it sets hard, I take my ring like this," he demonstrated, "and leave on it the impression of my family crest." This delighted one of the daughters.

"What a beautiful design it has!"

"Yes," said Torrens, "it's very delicate. I have never seen one so fine."

"It's very beautiful but not so fine as the ring which father brought home last—"

"Now Susy," her mother broke in, "don't bore the captain with comparisons."

"Not at all," said Torrens, "indeed I'm very interested!"

"Papa said he got it from a rich lady's finger," the girl blurted, "she drowned you see—"

"Susy!" her mother admonished, "what nonsense is this! He got it from a Frenchman in Québec. Never could resist a bargain, your father. Drowned lady, indeed." She turned and smiled at Torrens. "Pay no heed to Susy, sir, she has a head full of cobwebs."

"Oh, no matter for that, madam. Tell me, Susy, shall you show it to me?"

"My husband has it with him, sir," the mother answered for the girl. "He took it to Labrador."

"But Mama," whined the daughter, "he told me he was taking it to Halifax and leaving it to be sold." The mother glared at her daughter.

"Ah, what a pity," said Torrens, "I should have been interested to see it. Well, the light is failing. Time to fish the evening rise. Good place for fishing this, you always catch something."

The captain then hurried to Halifax to seek out the several watchmakers and jewellers. Fortunately, business was slack. In the last shop he visited, the balding jeweller showed him a number of trinkets and charms. To conceal his real intentions, the captain explained he was looking for an anniversary present for his wife. The jeweller brought out a fine pendant. Torrens explained he was thinking more of a ring, something unusual, something curious. The jeweller thought for a moment, opened a drawer, and displayed a ring. "Left by a good client of mine," he said. "He needs the money, poor fisherman you know, from Salmon River."

Torrens held the circle of gold close and tilted it to read the inscription. "*Sublima ab unda*—from the Latin, risen from the waves. Yes, this is very fine. I think I'll take it. Your price if you please?"

"My client asks five guineas, sir."

"A high price you ask for it."

"It is very unusual, sir," said the jeweller.

"Yes, very, for a fisherman especially from Salmon River." Torrens eyes narrowed. "Now, mark me closely, watchmaker. Here are twenty shillings—"

"But, sir—"

"Twenty shillings. You tell your very good client, your fisherman from Salmon River, that when he returns to me the finger that he cut off to get this ring, he shall be paid in full. Tell him that, in full. Here is my card. Good-day to you."

"And so," read the final paragraph of Torrens' letter, "I retrieved the ring . . . I return it to her family herewith in the hope that she who had indeed risen from the waves may now rest in peace. I am, your humble and obedient Servant."

As recently as 1947 one writer was told by an old-timer that four staffmen on Sable Island had seen Mrs. Copeland's ghost, "a number of times" during a three-year span. The hut she appeared in apparently blew down in a great wind storm "and now she appears to the men as they ride patrol along the beach." When seen, the phantom is quite startling, coming at the men with her hand held high so that it can be seen that one finger is missing. The old-timer claimed they did not like the experience of meeting this ghost at all, "but she's here, and we can't help it."

"The Pale Lady with the Missing Finger" is now part of the official folklore of Sable Island. This story and other events surrounding the sinking of the *Francis* gave the governor of Nova Scotia, Sir John Wentworth, much reason to be alarmed about "unfeeling persons who have chosen to winter there." There was reason to fear, he wrote, "that some who have escaped shipwreck had been deprived of their lives by beings more merciless than the Waves."

It was not just the wreckers that concerned Wentworth, but also the crooked schemes carried out to defraud insurance companies. It was suspected that many vessels were deliberately run on shore. Their captains would, of course, choose that part of Sable which presented the least danger. On shore the men would conceal the principal part of their cargoes deep in the sand, and once insurance companies paid out for losses, the owner, or owner's agent, would return to Sable and reclaim his cargo.

Marked by deaths, ghosts, and general lawlessness, the eighteenth century closed, for Sable, on a melancholy note. "That desolate sand," wrote J. Gilpin, "each shifting hillock a dead man's grave—the Pale Lady seeks to fit her bloody finger to the severed ring."

PART TWO
The Sea Samaritans
1800 to 1900

8 *The Admiral*

HERE REPOSING ON sealskin-cushioned chairs before a hearth of glittering copper torn from a shipwrecked keel, and where billets of old English oak, with many a tree-nailed hole, or Spanish mahogany are flickering over carved locker and binnacle, let the visitor listen to the sad stories of the East end look-out man, rare and strange medley of odd assorted things gathered along the bar, or narrow escapes which flow out in so pleasant accents from this self-exiled man; how he found a ship's bell ringing in its own dirge as it was tossed in the landwash; or how he picked a Church Bible from a wreck; or how he pulled the Frenchman with his shattered knee through the ground-swell.

J. GILPIN, on Sable, 1858

I return from the bone-chilling night to the warmth of the A-frame and the last burning log in the fireplace. Everyone has retired, but for me sleep is impossible. A hot toddy of whiskey and lemon will help to dissolve the aura of the past that still clings to me. A walk like that, through mists and vapours, is no ordinary event on Sable. For the first time since arriving here, I feel I have experienced the darker side of the island. How close I was upon the heels of the scattered bones of former actors on this stage. Somehow, my mind had filled the long time-span with wraiths and spirits, with shapes unseen but palpable.

The hot cordial melts my chill depression as I place a new log on the glimmering embers and settle comfortably in the overstuffed chair. Copies of journals and papers are before me, those of superintendents of Sable and reports by Governor Wentworth of Nova Scotia which describe the creation of the permanent Humane Establishment on the island. Now the settlers must outnumber the ghosts.

Because of public pressure that arose from the stories of wreckers on Sable, Governor Wentworth authorized Seth Coleman of Dartmouth, Nova Scotia, to investigate the island in June 1801. Coleman was ordered to "preserve any people or property" he may find there from a recent shipwreck; to observe the possibilities of building a lighthouse; to check on fresh water supplies and edible vegetables and fruit; to report on what animals existed and what kind of fishing could be carried out by residents of Sable. It had been reported, Wentworth told Coleman, that "a Man and Woman of wicked Character" had landed on Sable "for the infamous, inhuman purpose of plundering, robbing and causing shipwrecks." Coleman was to remove them for they were to be considered "trespassers of the worst description."

Coleman found no "wicked" characters on Sable, however he did discover the remains of a wrecked ship, a young cabin boy, and a man named King with his wife and three children. They were living in a small hut and were employed by the master of the wrecked vessel to collect and dry the cargo of cotton which had washed ashore, and wait for the owner who would return with another

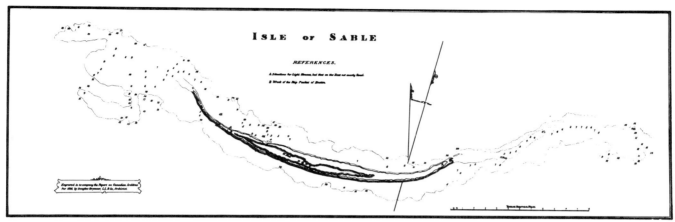

Map of Sable Island, 1801.

schooner to pick them up. Under these circumstances, Coleman felt it was "not prudent to remove King and his family."

He then turned his attention to scouting for a suitable location for erecting a lighthouse. He suggested a wooden building could be made sufficiently secure without a stone foundation, at the east end of the island. He was not on the island long enough to give a reliable recommendation; a wooden lighthouse without a strong foundation might last a week on windswept Sable. But Coleman also felt that Sable could support families and animals.

This was all Wentworth needed; he set the wheels in motion. From this point on, the governor made it clear that everyone would need a government license to remain on Sable, no matter what the reason, or the most rigorous prosecutions would be laid against "such Marauding Offenders." Finally there was a voice of authority for Sable. This was the beginning of a new era for the island. The government had every good reason to establish a permanent, controlled settlement on Sable because the commercial sea lanes were becoming increasingly crowded and vessels laden with rich cargoes and carrying high insurance were taking enormous risks if they ventured too close to the island. Property loss from ships marooned on Sable's sandbars was running into hundreds of thousands of dollars; some of that could be salvaged. Most important, shipwrecked souls were in need of compassionate human beings on Sable.

Wentworth then appointed a three-man commission, with Michael Wallace as treasurer and head commissioner, and asked the Nova Scotia House of Assembly to make provision for expenses to begin the establishment. The funds were to cover construction of buildings, the cost of wagons, clothing, relief supplies, and salaries for a staff of six men under an appointed commandant. Six hundred pounds were allotted for the project and this would cover the two hundred pounds annual salary for the superintendent, and fifty pounds annually to each of the other staffmen.

In 1801 the commissioners advertised a job open for someone who could combine the supreme authority of "a Captain of a Man of War, with the provident, paternal and just attributes of a Supreme Magistrate or Father of a Family." They settled on James Morris, who, having emigrated from England, was looking for a secure future for himself and his dependents in the new colony of Nova Scotia. He acquainted the commissioners with the idea of a "pre-fab" light frame house that could be shipped to the island and assembled right on the sand, "each section to be carried by four men." They were impressed with his vigour and enterprise.

In October 1801, Adam Moore, David Rope, James McLaughlin and Patrick King, were hired by the Sable Island Commission and each took an oath to "remain upon said Island, until the first day of May next, or until a vessel shall arrive from Halifax

Drawings of Sable Island by James Morris, 1802.

with orders from the Commissioners to relieve us." Later, Edward Hodgson and his family would join them, with Hodgson acting as assistant to James Morris.

Backed by fresh southeast winds the government vessel *Earl of Moira* and the schooner *Kitty*, sailed from Halifax on Tuesday, October 6, with the new settlers, provisions, livestock, and building materials. One ship was a veritable Noah's Ark, carrying two young cows with calf, a three-year-old bull, two young sows, a boar, two rams, eight ewes, a male and female goat, as well as a

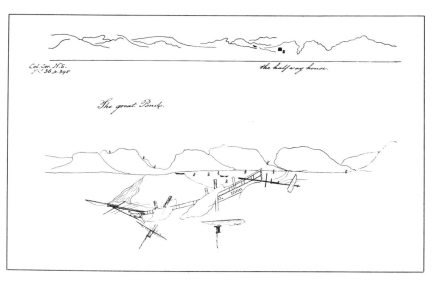

Col. Sor. N.S.
P. 36, p. 398   the halfway house.

The great Pond.

workhorse; a supply of garden seeds, nails, tools, medicine chest, and a whale boat with oars.

Four days later they landed on Sable Island. They could not have chosen a more violent season or harsher introduction to Sable. From October to March of the following year, they experienced continual cruel gales and torrential rains. Morris soon had everything under control, however, and it is to his credit that this first permanent Sable settlement was a success. A man of twenty years experience, with hopes of promotion in the Royal Navy, Morris had perhaps dreamed of being captain in a

frigate of his own. This remained only a dream. Ashore for good, he became determined to make everything ship-shape and Bristol fashion, and he soon envisioned in the prime of life becoming "Admiral" of Sable with a fleet of livesaving stations. Community living finally took root in this desert in the sea, and since that first humble settlement, Sable has never, for a single day, been abandoned by man.

The following spring, in March of 1802, James Morris sent a progress report to the commissioners. Their initial landing, which took several days, was a difficult one and some provisions were damaged. Had Morris not been able to discover flour and meal, probably from a ship that was wrecked before they arrived, they would have suffered from want of bread. As for the stock, the cows gave milk through the winter but the sheep lost their lambs, the goat its kids, while the hardy farm horse was "of infinite service."

The buildings were erected on the north side, a few miles from the west end of Sable. A flagstaff, with a perch for a lookout man, known as a crow's nest, was put up and later a chicken house and stable were built. Within the following year another house, eighteen by fourteen feet, complete with a flagstaff, was built near the east end for the assistant superintendent. With a wry sense of humour Morris commented: "Surely the carpenter that framed the house was either in love or stupid, as many pieces were wrongly numbered, and no braces of any consequence to the building, which gave a great deal of trouble to affix the frame, as a building on this island should be exceedingly well braced on all angles."

In July 1802, a turnover in staff occurred and William Frampton, John Hallet, John Gregory, Guy Morris, and John Myers all agreed to work on Sable. With Edward Hodgson they assisted in rescue work with the first ship to be stranded on Sable since the new establishment began. It was the vessel *Union* of Boston, and Hodgson discovered it from his flagstaff perch at nine o'clock one morning. Sounding the alarm, Hodgson speedily descended to join the alerted crew, which had sprung into action to hitch the horses to the boat wagon. In minutes they were clattering along the hard-packed beach. They headed west to where the ship had struck a sandbar about four miles down from the pond on the south side.

A low ceiling of black clouds rolled along the horizon as the crew made their way over the sand to the unlucky vessel. When they arrived much later, Hodgson and his men found the ship's crew had constructed a raft in an attempt to reach shore. Hodgson shouted to the stranded men to throw a line from their ship, but he could not be heard above the roar of the surf and the high winds. He turned to Gregory and Myers, the burliest of the Humane crew, and instructed them to prepare a line and anchor. Once that was done they were to hold up the line and anchor to ensure that all on board the vessel could see what it was. But the

sailors were too occupied with the dangerous task of launching their hastily made raft. Hodgson knew they would not succeed in the treacherous waters and he was right, for the heavy surf upset the raft, pitching everyone into the sea. They struggled back on board ship as Hodgson kept shouting at them to heave a line. Gregory held up the coil of rope, pointed to the anchor, and mimed a throwing action. Somehow the message got through. The sailors tied a rope to a small anchor, whirled it overhead, and released it. The shot was good. The anchor travelled through the air and splashed short of the beach. The Sable crew made the anchor fast. Now the sailors could come to shore hand-over-hand on the line. From the moment a sailor left the ship, his progress was watched with the greatest anxiety. Could he hold on? Would his legs and arms sustain his weight on that slender lifeline? It was a primitive method for saving lives but if a man was lucky, strong, and fearless, he just might avoid drowning.

The first sailor began his hand-over-hand trip; for a brief spell his head could be seen bobbing in and out of the sea as he struggled to hang on. But the sea was too turbulent. Huge waves engulfed him and he sank from sight to be later washed up lifeless on the beach. A second sailor, more fortunate, made it safely to shore. Spent and weary, half-drowned, the seaman was wrapped in blankets and taken to warmth and shelter by Hallet and Myers.

Hodgson and the others turned their attention

back to the wrecked vessel. The intrepid sailors still aboard the *Union* fashioned yet another raft in a brave attempt to reach safety. By late afternoon, under clearing skies and tranquil ocean, all eleven men were successfully brought to shore. Brief excerpts in Morris' journal say how the captain of the *Union* was most grateful for the rescue and later praised the Humane Establishment in his report to the Sable Island commissioners. It was a difficult and dramatic rescue and the saving of the *Union* crew served as baptism for the new Humane Establishment. This shipwreck and rescue was a scene that would repeat itself in different ways for the next one hundred and forty-eight years.

In a few days the *Union* broke up and went to pieces though not before it had been stripped, for one of the staffmen's duties was to salvage as much as possible from wrecked vessels. What they failed to save was often washed up on shore. From the *Union* they saved the greater part of her two bower cables, anchors, hawser, main and fore-rigging; also a yawl, one longboat with oars and sails, one hundred and forty-one straw carpets, a wooden compass, a copper teakettle and a glass lantern (spelled "lanthorn" in those days). The salvage property was then put on board the next vessel visiting Sable, taken to Halifax, and sold at public auction. Each staffman of the island shared in a small percentage of the sale of shipwrecked property. Saving shipwrecked mariners was not their only work. Experienced boatmen, they also worked as labourers, farmers, handymen, and sometimes even fishermen. Driftwood and timber from broken ships had to be collected for winter fuel. The hay had to be harvested, and the cattle needed daily care.

In one of his reports to the commissioners, Morris complained of head and chest pains. The job of superintendent during those early years must have been a demanding and thankless one, a difficult period of trial and error. The cattle, he wrote, did generally well but at times were afflicted with horn distemper. All the sheep died, except two pet lambs that were brought up in the house. The mysterious cause of their death was traced to a fatal plant on the island; the sheep would thrive, get fat, then suddenly die. Further attempts to maintain sheep on Sable ended in failure. "The hogs," Morris reported, "have no hair from the gristle of the nose to their eyes, in front by rooting through the sand." Some of the hogs, allowed to run free, became wild and aggressive; many perished from lack of ready grain. Poultry was introduced and thrived very well. But rats, escaping from the dank holds of ships, became a serious plague. "We have lately been alarmed in a surprising manner by rats and mice in incredible numbers, but with our dogs, and new invented traps shall, I hope soon exterminate them, the trap takes from 15 to 20 a night."

Morris also reported that bushes and trees failed to take root for very long. He tried a variety of ways to enlarge potatoes and although they were tasty, they continued to grow only to the size of "walnuts." Turnips, cabbages, red beets, and Indian corn, all thrived as long as the tender blades were shielded from the windblasts from the southeast and the drifting sand. For this reason, it was impossible to grow oats, wheat or barley. "I have been much deceived," wrote Morris, "in the nature of the soil on this Island." Experience, he explained, "makes manifest my weak and hasty sentiments at the commencement of the settlement."

It is evident from this sorrowful confession that James Morris was a better sailor than a farmer.

Perhaps when he first saw Sable it was just like England on a summer day. He probably fantisized that with the addition of manure the Sable sands would produce the fruits of the earth in abundance. He envisioned a veritable Eden on this sandy island in the Gulf Stream. This dream, like many Sable fantasies, was rapidly destroyed.

Five years after the colonists landed on Sable the tiny community took on the appearance of order

and permanence. The pine houses no longer looked new and took on the colour of their surroundings: buff, like the sand. Around each dwelling was a white fence enclosing what passed for a miniature garden. One writer of that era described Sable Island and the settlement from a cutter on a calm day in June:

A light breeze scarcely ripples the sea, which now wears its fairest guise. The long belt of surf that fringes the Island glitters dazzlingly in the sunshine, and the gulls and wild-fowls are feeding far out to sea. Seldom has the picture so brilliant a setting. In the hour of this repose a signal-flag is seen to mount the tall flagstaff of the Lookout Station at the West End, and before it has fairly shaken itself to the breeze a responsive signal rises to the mast-head on the high hill at Headquarters, nine miles away. There is a speck in the offing, and with a good glass the long expected cutter is plainly seen standing in, with her red ensign flying at the peak. There is joy on the Island; and if one on board the vessel were near enough to distinguish objects he would observe a commotion in the little hive on shore. Over the sandy hills and along the beach the outpost men are galloping their shaggy ponies in hot haste to Headquarters, recalled by the signal flag. There is bustle and preparation at the barn and boathouse, and the whole community of men and animals seem to have turned out of doors at some unwonted cause of excitement. The dogs bark in chorus, and frisk and tumble in the sand; barefooted urchins halloo and scream; and a patriarch rooster even mounts a post and crows at an unusual hour.

Down gallop the ponies into the very edge of the surf, drawing a lifeboat on a broad-wheeled cart. It is but the work of a few minutes to launch, man, breast the breakers, pull away and board. Then follows many a rough greeting and hearty handshaking in the style of good old fashioned friendship, and such as only those can appreciate who have been shut out from the world for months and seen no faces but their familiar own.

Harper's Magazine, 1866

Governor Wentworth was most impressed with

the Humane Establishment and their efforts to save lives and property and addressed his pleasure to the Assembly: "The happiness derived from reflecting on having stretched forth our hands, and under favour of Divine Providence, to the preservation of so many of our Fellow Creatures, from perishing, renders additional reasons unnecessary to support my recommendations for your providing means, to enable me to continue the Establishment." Fine words indeed and Wentworth was no doubt sincere, but throughout the years of Morris' command on Sable, the commissioners did little to ease his anxieties or the immense workload of that small community. One whale boat for the whole island was the only means of transferring passengers from a stricken vessel to shore. More buildings were needed for survivors and a plentiful stock of provisions should have been on hand at all times to provide for a large number of passengers during unexpectedly long durations on Sable.

The back-breaking work was taking its toll for once again Morris complained of violent stomach and chest pains, especially when he lay down. His request for a long leave of absence and a man to train as his successor resulted in a direct reply from Governor Wentworth. Morris' final decision in November of 1808 was that he was anxious to see his friends for advice and experience a change of climate, but he would continue on Sable until the following spring. In the spring, there was still no replacement and Morris continued through the

summer probably in full knowledge that time for him was running out. He made a third brief trip to Country Harbour to tie up the ends of his new sawmill business. On October 29, 1808, Edward Hodgson informed the commissioners that James Morris died four hours after returning to Sable from the mainland. His son was with him at the time and he and Mrs. Morris and the rest of the family returned to Country Harbour. The first superintendent of the Humane Establishment had given his last breath of life to the support of the island. Mr. Hodgson then took charge of Sable.

Improvements took place on the island under Hodgson's term, due mostly to a report Morris had prepared before he died. His proposals were complete with sketches and diagrams and Robert H. Burton, a captain in the Royal Fusiliers, made use of them when he was sent to Sable to conduct a survey. Burton submitted a report in favour of increased shelters for survivors plus extra quantities of clothing and provisions. The document had the desired effect for more buildings were erected; the most important were two survival huts, one on the south side of the island, the other on the north.

A visitor to the island at this time would have discovered the headquarters in the main establishment on the north side about five miles from the west end. Here were the superintendent's residence, quarters for the crew, and the "sailor's home" for shipwrecked sailors. A short walk further on and the sand hills seemed to part, revealing a large barn and yard filled with stock, large heavy-headed bulls, fat cows, and chickens running about scratching in the sand. Several storehouses, including a hut to keep seal oil, outhouses, and a boathouse made up the "village square."

Standing tall above this snug scene was the hundred-and-twenty-foot-high flagstaff with an observatory platform. (Later in 1829, Haliburton described the flagstaff "made of the spritsail yard of the French frigate, *L'Africaine*.") The visitor

would be urged to climb up to the crow's nest for a panoramic view. As he did so, he would suddenly be struck by the serenity of the village below. Climbing upwards, he would be aware that circling the island of sand was the perpetual fringe of the Atlantic surf; the faint sound of the roaring ocean continually beating upon the shore would be a reminder that Sable was not always an idyllic place. If heavy weather struck while a person was perched on the observation platform at that dizzying height, he would be rocked and blasted by fierce winds. Clouds of drifting, swirling sand would narrow his vision and he would just make out white, angry breakers of the sea. But on a sunny day, to the left and right as far as the eye could see there would be a long, long, ribbon of sandy hills topped with marram grass; the odd fresh water pond would be dotted with wild ducks. Untamed horses, knee deep in tall grass, looked like small Shetland ponies from this height. Aided by a strong spy glass, the visitor might pick out seals on the beach basking in the sun.

A swing of the glass would reveal, about five miles to the east, another station with house, bar, and flagstaff. Over on the south side, as on the north, were the new refuge huts. Here survivors could exist until discovered by one of the outpost crew on horseback. Inside the simple shelter was a fireplace with dry wood, complete with tinder, flint, and steel to strike a warm, cosy fire. Nailed to the wall, out of the reach of rats, was a bag of provisions. Written instructions and a map were posted so that a survivor could dig for fresh water and then find his way to the main establishment.

Morris' soil-cultivation efforts were carried on by Hodgson and for many seasons he was surprisingly successful. Often the settlement could raise two hundred bushels of potatoes and a variety of other root vegetables. In time, with the right soil and technique, the potatoes grew to a fine plump size, no longer the "walnuts" that Morris had raised. But then, there were also years when vegetables were blighted by Sable's destructive winds.

Hodgson complained, one time, of provisions running short, leaving them in a "starving condition." The steamer brought in supplies such as barrels of salt pork and beef; barrels of split peas, rice, navy beans, and brown sugar; a huge cask of molasses; unroasted coffee beans; and wooden cases, lined with lead, of assorted English, Bohea and Souchong teas; barrels of ship bread; a variety of housewares; and usually an iron-bound cask of rum. An isolated community not only needed fresh food, but the supply ship was the sole means of news and gossip from the outside world. It brought a respite from boredom, conveyed happy or unhappy tidings, delivered important despatches, and brought precious letters from loved ones. Its arrival was a great event.

About forty vessels were wrecked on the island during Hodgson's stay. A leaf from his diary describes one day: "June 6. Morning. Wind S.S.W.; cloudy. No reports from the lookouts. Sent the

men and horses to the wrecks to haul wood. Empty barrel came ashore at noon. Wind, evening, S.E." A whole day's existence embraced in a meagre record of two dozen words. As one writer put it: "a waif upon the tide of life as empty and insignificant as the barrel that drifted ashore!" Two other entries are more solemn:

On the 25th October, 1818, the scow, 'Adamant', ran on shore on the north side of the Island, full of water. On the 26th hauled on shore with ropes five out of a crew of thirteen. Four we found dead on deck, who had died from want of food and water. Those saved were very sick and frostbitten.

June 5, 1820:   We have had a tolerable winter, and no wrecks, except the hull of a schooner, the 'Juno' of Plymouth, a fishing vessel, that came on shore of the 20th November, without masts, sails or rigging of any description, and no person on board except one dead man in the hold, whom we got out and buried.

British authorities were finally alerted to the financial strains on the Nova Scotia government to maintain the Humane Establishment, especially at a time when it should be increased in strength due to heavier shipping traffic. In a memorandum from Governor James Kempt written on June 25, 1825, it was pointed out to the authorities that it was rare that a vessel belonging to the province was wrecked on shores of Sable. In addition, Nova Scotia had been bearing the sole maintenance costs for twenty years and it ought to be relieved of part of those costs at least. The merchants of Boston, who frequently benefitted from the Sable humane services formally offered to contribute toward its maintenance. That offer, according to Kempt's report, "was very properly declined, the Province being unwilling to receive contributions from Foreigners." By February of 1827 the Nova Scotia Government House announced that the lieutenant governor had received a letter from the secretary of the treasury in Britain, stating that they agreed to contribute four hundred pounds sterling annually toward the support of the Humane Establishment, "so long as Nova Scotia shall make a provision of an equal sum for the same purpose."

In 1830 Hodgson, like his predecessor, succumbed to the rigours of Sable and once again the island was left without a master. But Sable was never truly mastered; the island simply swallowed up people with their memories and dreams and buried them deeply under her sands.

9 The Rogue

"MAN WOULD NOT be man if his dreams did not exceed his grasp," wrote Lorne Eiseley. The next master of the island, Captain Darby, was a paranoiac who had dreams of absolute control of Sable. I had been told that he was a "colourful and controversial" figure, a bit of a "jolly rogue" with a roving eye for the ladies. These descriptions left me unprepared for the darker side of his character and his questionable activities on Sable.

Darby, captain of the vessel *Eagle*, which carried supplies from the mainland to Sable from 1813 to 1830, had his eye for some time on the position of superintendent. The commissioners agreed to his taking charge because he was familiar with the duties and problems of the island. For the next thirty years the superintendents were to be Darby and later Matthew McKenna. Both able men, they presented an astonishing contrast in personalities.

A storm is brewing outside; gusts of wind shake the little wooden house. Through the windows, the sand hills are but shadows in the night. I can hear row upon row of ocean breakers hitting the south beach like rolls of thunder. Perhaps it was a night like this when superintendent Darby and his men were called upon to save lives on the south side of the island.

They had just spent the previous evening trying to free a schooner, the *Lady Echo*, from a sandbar; the crew was safely landed. By next morning Captain Lowell of the stranded ship had given up all hopes of getting her off the sandbar for the vessel had taken in a great deal of water. Darby's crew began stripping the ship and hauling the cargo to a safe, dry place. No sooner had they finished this exhausting operation, than there was a knock on Darby's door at ten in the evening. A Captain Kimball stood outside, announcing that a sudden gust of wind and heavy northern squalls had thrown his vessel on shore.

The superintendent rounded up his exhausted crew once more. They had to contend with violent seas; the going was rough and dangerous. Slowly, carefully, everyone was brought on shore, taken to the main quarters and bedded down in front of a blazing fire. The following day the staffmen faced more dangers during a violent gale with heavy rains. They crawled on their hands and knees to the north side to check the state of the *Lady Echo*'s cargo and finding it likely to be washed away, rolled some of the barrels up the side of a sandbank. "The sea," wrote Darby in his journal, "was breaking over the schooner and coming down upon us in torrents, it was pouring rain, the wind blowing, and the sand flying."

Fresh provisions were a constant problem, as usual, especially for those at the east outpost, which was at least fifteen miles from the main station. It was up to those men to make the long trip by horse and cart to pick up provisions from Darby, who doled them out in a miserly fashion and even recorded the event: "Adams went home

today. I gave him three and a half pounds of tea as he says that he cannot make three pounds last him three months. I gave him nine pounds of coffee, two gallons molasses, twenty-five pounds sugar, some rice, barley, oatmeal, dry fish, powder, shot, and peas." Some months later, Adams returned with a small bag of stones which he claimed to have picked out of the batch of coffee given to him; it weighed eight pounds. The shrewd Darby wrote in his diary: "I weighed the stones and they were rather above three quarters of a pound. Stevens had them bring up a similar quantity of stones which he says he picked out of about the same quantity of coffee and we have found a larger proportion of stones in what we have used here, they having settled toward the bottom of the cask. This is the coffee that was sent them in the spring of 1844." Speculation from this entry points to someone on the mainland in the coffee distribution business defrauding the government and expanding his profit by adding stones to the casks.

There were those who rebelled against Darby's harsh approach to handling the crews. His diary contains his side of the story for one of the incidents: "William Myers gave in notice to leave the Island in three months in a very insolent manner because I was obliged to speak sharp to him on account of his great neglect of the animals under his care by which neglect we have lost several fine young hogs and indeed I have always had a great deal of trouble with him to make him take care of the cattle. I will have to send him away and get some other person to attend to the stock." Darby's complaint may have been legitimate in this case for the superintendent always had the benefit of the doubt on Sable. Nevertheless, these particular diary entries are an important indication of later problems with provisions, Darby's attitudes, and his treatment of his men, which eventually brought about his undoing.

An amusing extract from the journal of Captain James Farquhar, who wrote about his Sable Island experiences of that time, reveals an intimate glimpse into Darby's many-faceted personality. Farquhar, whose family came from Meagher's Grant, Nova Scotia, spent fourteen years on the island when his father was put in charge of the eastern station in 1849.

Mr. Darby was said to be of a rather religious turn, and, used to hold service at his house on the Sabbath day for the eight or nine men who constituted the crew at head-quarters. He was also known as a great worker, particularly when a wreck occurred. Once a fishing schooner partly loaded with mackerel stranded near his house on a Saturday night. The Island crew could only work at saving the cargo when the tide was low. Bright and early on the Sunday morning, the men were set to work removing the barrels of mackerel from the schooner to the shore. When the tide came in about eleven o'clock, the work stopped and the men went home. About half-past eleven, a large ship's bell, which Darby had erected on a post near his house, was rung for church service. The men who had been hard at work all morning, naturally rebelled. Only one man, the coloured cook, attended the service. On Monday morning, Darby picked up a hammer and said to his wife: "Kitty, Christianity on Sable Island has gone to the Devil." With that he struck the bell with the hammer and broke it to pieces. He did not intend to smash it, but in his temper, he used just a little too much force.

There were times when Darby's temper and aggressive nature were put to good use. In May of 1836 the brig *Lancaster*, sailing from Dublin and bound for New York with sixty-five passengers on board, became stranded on the island. The vessel was carrying a good supply of whiskey and porter. Darby notified the commissioners of the situation, warning them it might turn into a nightmare if the passengers were not immediately removed, for they had become rather riotous from "pulling at the liquor." While waiting for the dispatched ship to arrive from Halifax, the burly superintendent handled the disturbances with a terrible fervour.

Even though there was a watch put on the provision hut, it was broken into and some liquor was stolen on the night of June 17. The next day Darby discovered the culprits, took a bottle away from one of them and "commenced to search for more, found another bottle which I destroyed." In their search for whiskey they found Garrick, the mate of the wrecked vessel, drunk in his hammock. He staggered over to one of Darby's men and struck him a vicious blow. Finally, the others pitched him out of doors, "when he again attempted to strike, cursing and abusing and threatening at a great rate."

Not only were Garrick and another man violently drunk but they had managed, since beginning their drinking spree, to kill every rabbit they could find above ground and even dug up their burrows to brutally destroy all the old and young animals that could be found. Darby, with four men, went after them, placed Garrick in irons and locked him up. "The other drunken lout," wrote Darby, "was shut up in a cellar but he soon broke the door down and began to threaten and abuse everyone." He was put in irons and locked up separate from Garrick, and a staffman was posted to keep watch on the two of them with loaded guns. When the vessel arrived to take off the crew of the *Lancaster*, the two besotted sailors were placed on board and handcuffed.

"Gentlemen," wrote Darby to the commissioners, "if I may presume to give you an opinion as regards the carrying of passengers with wrecked goods from this Island to Halifax, it would simply be this, that if possible, the goods and people should not go in the same vessel, particularly liquor." An understatement to be sure, but he was right. A number of the *Lancaster* crew, upon arriving in Halifax, laid complaints about Darby accusing him of keeping stores from various shipwrecks such as "silks, cottons, cloths, porter and liquor" in his house. They also suspected him of selling the liquor. An investigation of sorts was made, Darby was cleared, and the accusations dropped. But these same charges, and others, would arise eleven years later to reveal Darby in a much darker light.

Darby was considered a God-fearing man, as pointed out earlier, and he had compassionate moments befitting a superintendent of Sable. Once, when a crewman experienced a most painful accident with an axe resulting in the loss of two toes, Darby served as a physician when he and another man stopped the victim's serious bleeding. The man was bandaged, given rum, put to bed, and Darby and others took turns standing watch over the patient for part of the night.

One of the most unusual events during Captain Darby's term of service was the saving of the captain and crew of a vessel in a most "miraculous" way. The subject of this incident later became a lecture that Darby himself delivered before the Athenaeum Society of Halifax during 1858. The event occurred while the superintendent and crew were salvaging the cargo from the stricken schooner, *Lady Echo*, during a terrific gale. Here are the highlights condensed from that lecture, *The Wreck of the Schooner Arno*:

All of a sudden we saw an object to the north side dead to windward which we at first thought was a large bird, but shortly after discovered that it was a sail... we could see that she was a schooner with a close-reefed mainsail set, steering directly for our flagstaff. The sea was breaking everywhere off the north side as far as the eye could see, and it appeared almost incredible that a vessel could live to come so great a distance through such mountains of broken water... we could plainly perceive mountain waves on each side of her that would raise their curled heads as high as the tops of her masts and pitch over and fall with the weight of hundreds of tons, either of which would have been sufficient to have smashed that frail bark to atoms; but miraculous as it may appear, not one of them touched her. At one moment you would see her on the top of a tremendous wave which appeared like certain destruction to her; at another, you would see a mountainous sea rising up before her and breaking all to fragments in her path, but when she arrived at the spot the surface was smooth as glass... the vessel had to pass over what we call the Outer Bar where the sea was breaking with tremendous violence, but that heaven-favoured barque passed through untouched—the sea became smooth before, and she left a shining track behind.

The *Arno* was a fishing schooner that had been caught in a violent gale. With its headsails gone, it was impossible to control the ship in the high winds so the captain dropped anchor in twenty fathoms of water, paid out three hundred fathoms of hemp cable, and brought the vessel to wind. He held like that for several hours but, as the gale continued, he cut cable, put the schooner before the wind, and chose to run it on shore rather than founder. He then sent all but two of his men below, nailed up the cabin doors, and lashed himself to the helm. He directed the two men to roll two large caskets, half filled with blubber and fish oil, up to the fore-shrouds and rope them in position. Next he told them to lash themselves firmly to the barrels and take up wooden ladles. Darby describes what he saw from shore:

Now, here was the miracle. I looked upon this with wonder, awe and admiration, and not without hope. When she approached a little nearer I could see that two men had each a wooden ladle about two feet long, and with these ladles they dipped up the blubber and oil and threw it in the air as high as they could. The great violence of the wind carried far to leeward, and, spreading over the water, made its surface smooth before her and left a shining path behind... the sea was raging, pitching and breaking close to her on each side, but not a barrel of water fell upon her deck the whole distance. The vessel was so old and tender that she went all to pieces in a very short time after the crew, with their clothing and provisions, were saved.

The *Arno*'s bow struck sand close to shore. Darby and his men attached a rope to her bow leading to a sand bank to keep the sea from washing them away as they made their rescue approach waist-deep in water. The *Arno* crew lowered themselves by rope into waiting arms below and were passed safely to the sand bank. They were grateful:

The captain was a praying man, and indeed a clever man; his first act after getting on shore was to go aside with me and return thanks to his Maker for their preservation... thus was preserved in a most miraculous manner this crew of good men; and although the finger of God was seen and felt in this circumstance, yet it was brought about by natural means. I had often heard of oil smoothing the face of turbid waters but I could hardly have believed that it would have been possible to subdue and smoothen so very rough and boisterous a surface.

Darby soon had his own turbulent sea of troubles, for time and events caught up with him. The final years of his tenure were chaotic, as shown by his postscript of his journal entry for December 31, 1846. "To me," he wrote, "it has been a year of misery and unhappiness which I attribute wholly to the misguided policy of the Commissioners." Two men had given their notice to Darby and would not be returning. Two others asked to leave as soon as their time was up. "Some of them will long remember the Perilous and Fatiguing Labour," warned the superintendent, "and will not run the risk of meeting such another job for the same remuneration."

Eight months later, Darby's penchant for bullying came to light. In a bitter and detailed letter to the commissioners, Robert Nichols described the severe conditions one experienced under Darby's command. Nichols, hired by the commissioners in April, 1847, spent a miserable summer on Sable. Poorly cooked and salty provisions were just one of his grievances. He told of working hip-deep in sea water while struggling to save wrecked property, and lying all night on the beach which produced chills, festering sores, and painful boils. When Darby had discovered who had been complaining to the commissioners, he rode in a fury to the East Station, stamped into the house and sent for Nichols. The man crawled downstairs to face the angry superintendent.

"You dammed scoundrel," Darby hissed through his teeth, "why aren't you at work!" According to Nichols, Darby had a three-foot-long, stout stick in his hand which he waved around the man's head threatening his life. After knocking Nichols down with his fist, Darby swore he would tie him to a post and horsewhip him.

"Now that I have got my venom out upon you, you dammed rascal, go to hell out of my sight!" With that, Darby stormed out of the house.

Lest this sound like an old-fashioned "mellerdrammer," it can be seen from Nichol's letter that Darby had acted brutally. Nichols, scarlet from boils and a pain in his side, was forced to walk the fifteen miles back to the East Station. Thirty-six hours later, after lying out in the damp air all night, he arrived at his destination and was ministered to by his fellow workers. Four days afterwards he was

Joseph Howe.

taken to the Main Station where Darby gave him one pound of hard bread and three pounds of oatmeal to last fourteen days. In less than a week and in a "near starving condition," Nichols crawled to the East Station for more provisions. He ends his letter hoping "that your Honour will look into the Diabolical proceedings and dishonesty of the present Superintendent of Sable Island." Darby protested the accusations but many Sable residents quickly closed ranks against him. For some time they had witnessed or heard of illegal practices by their superintendent; others had had a taste of his harsh treatment. It was also the year, 1848, that a reform government came into power in Nova Scotia.

New commissioners for Sable Island included Hugh Bell and James McNab; the new provincial secretary was Joe Howe. A charismatic man, Howe, who later became premier of Nova Scotia, began his reform program by investigating the island and Superintendent Darby. Under Howe's direction, Captain W. I. Townshend carried out this inquiry. Howe himself visited the island for three days, made a personal inspection of its capabilities and conditions and submitted his report to Lieutenant Governor Sir John Harvey in 1848.

The Howe document on Sable Island is an impressive one. It is easy to picture him as a dominant figure during his Sable visit, brimming with energy and curiosity, full of countless questions and laughing uproariously while trading stories with the men. A big man of athletic proportions, he probably led a killing pace in his eagerness to see as much of Sable as possible in three days. As they passed various herds of wild horses on their sightseeing trip, Howe and the men discussed judicious breeding of the Sable horses to improve the herd. Howe's report suggested horses as a main export item to the mainland. He recommended that two stallions, the best available on mainland Nova Scotia, be sent to Sable in early spring and kept in the superintendent's stable. The Sable wild mares, at the proper season, would be driven into the paddocks to receive them. Besides, they were worth a fair price. "Fifty horses, worth from fifteen to twenty pounds each, may be annually shipped from Sable yielding six hundred to seven hundred pounds."

As for fisheries, Sable waters shimmered with schools of mackerel and during his visit, Howe observed five schooners catching mackerel with hook and line. "These fish," he wrote, "crowded the coast in such numbers that they almost pressed each other upon the sands." With a good seine or two, Howe was convinced the Sable staffmen could easily fill a thousand barrels in one day.

Two of Howe's suggestions show his ability to foresee the future, a good attribute for anyone, but

especially for a politician. One concerned the use of power, the other cranberry production. "A small steam engine," he wrote, "which could turn circular saws, a lathe, and other gear, would be invaluable." A substitution for steam would be wind. "A windmill," he said, "would harness the wind to provide power to saw lumber, firewood, and staves." This splendid idea was never implemented. The high and constant winds of Sable could easily harness energy and power, but instead, coal was sent in from the mainland to keep the home fires burning.

In the mid-1800s, only a few barrels of cranberries were picked in the autumn for use by the community. Howe saw the cranberry as a source of income or means of employment on Sable, an idea which never occurred to anyone before. He pointed out that in the United States cranberries formed a branch of New England agriculture where they were successfully cultivated on bogs and waste land subject to flowage. "On Sable Island the cranberry grows spontaneously in many places," Howe noted, "and by a little care, the crop might be largely increased." He suggested the introduction of the American rakes, a tool by which the fruit is gathered, and the seine, by which the bruised or decayed berries are separated from the sound ones. Later, Howe's cranberry scheme was used and the export of these berries in the 1890s reached immense proportions.

In Townshend's report of April 26, 1848, there is quite a catalogue of charges against Darby: general severity, harshness and violence of manner towards the people of Sable; his cruel treatment of Robert Nichols and William Etter; general disrespect towards the commissioners; selling liquor to people in breach of laws and instructions given to him (Darby had already been reprimanded a few years earlier about this practice); entering his eleven-year-old son as cook on the books of the island under a fictitious name, and charging cook's wages and share of wrecks for him; charging wrecked passengers for cooking and other services rendered and taking from them money and clothes in payment; supplying his eldest son's vessel from the stores of the island and selling it to others who occasionally visited it; taking advantage of his position to promote the interests of his family in reference to the wrecked vessels, *Lady Echo* and *Fulton*. These were serious charges and although the committee took into consideration many of Darby's difficulties, they were reluctantly compelled to acknowledge that many of the main charges had been fully proved and that "as respects the last, there is too much reason to believe that undue advantage has been taken by the Superintendent for the profit of his family." These charges were, of course, a reflection of the past corrupt government in Nova Scotia. As far as Sable Island was concerned, Darby was finished by 1848.

10 *The Gentleman*

IT IS LATE in the night and I am still curled up in the chair before a crackling fire. The wind howls and whines outside the A-frame then settles for a while and only the hiss of burning wood in the fireplace can be heard.

The yellowed documents of a past era surround me and I am riveted by the human drama on this miniature world of Sable. It is curious—Darby's journal markings are sparse and inked in the colour of mud-brown. In contrast, the diary of Matthew McKenna, the man who takes over as superintendent, is neatly hand-written on sky-blue paper. Somehow, this seems symbolic of fresh breezes blowing over Sable.

The schooner that took away the Darby family on November 8, 1848, was the same vessel that carried Captain McKenna, his wife and four children to Sable Island. "He was simply the man for the place," was the perfect description by historian Simon MacDonald.

In his brief stay from 1848 to 1855 McKenna brought the Humane Establishment to a high state of order and efficiency. He introduced Captain Marryat's code of signals. (Captain Frederick Marryat, English naval officer and novelist, received the gold medal of the Royal Humane Society in 1818 for saving lives at sea. He adapted to the mercantile marine Sir Home Popham's system of signaling, which was a means of transmitting intelligence at sea, day or night, using naval signaling according to the international code. This was effected by flags, either singly, or in groups, interpreted in accordance with the international code book. Night signals were carried out by means of lights, rockets, or torches.) Before two years had passed, Sable was equipped with more new buildings, for some of them had washed away, including the north and south huts. McKenna also made room for a forge and went through the process of pleading and cajoling for a smith who was very much needed. "I think it strange that I am not allowed a Blacksmith," he wrote the new commissioners, "especially after having asked so often for one. Surely I must be the best judge of what this place requires and I now beg again for a Blacksmith to be sent." The commissioners finally added a smith to take care of the teams of horses which hauled the staff boats across the sands during rescue operations.

The vigorous energy output by the men on Sable called for a hearty diet. The bill of fare for 1853 shows that a stout breakfast included bread, fish or meat, and coffee or chocolate to drink. Oatmeal porridge or bread, meat, and tea made up the rather stodgy, spartan suppers. The dinner menu must have been the highlight of the day, for it featured the most variety—vegetables, meat, pudding, sometimes fish and rice, with soup as an appetizer. At all meals, potatoes were had "according to supply on hand," sugar was allowed for tea but molasses was used with coffee or chocolate.

Fresh meat, fish, and duck in season broke the monotony of the general fare.

One is inclined to look upon Matt McKenna as a romantic figure—tall, strong, lean, and fair-

Matthew McKenna's copy of a receipt for sale of horses, 1853.

skinned with blue eyes—a dependable and compassionate leader. His immaculate daily journals reveal his understanding of his fellow men on Sable:

John Humphrey has given notice of his intention to leave when his year is up, he is a good teamster and a very decent man and I am sorry that he leaves. John Brady is anxious to get away. He has told the rest of the people that he understood there was no work to be done here and that our time was spent either riding on horseback or running from station to station with a gun for companion, but he knows better now. He is no boatman and knows nothing about horses and is a very rough workman yet tolerably smart at what he can do. Morash knows nothing and is nearly blind but he is such a civil, decent creature and so willing to do it if he only knew what for to do, that I think we had better allow him to finish his year on the island.

McKenna's patience and authority, however, were tried and tested many times. During a chilly mid-December of 1852 the vessel *Marie Ann*, sailing with a cargo of codfish from Placentia Bay, Newfoundland, to Halifax, Nova Scotia, struck a sand shoal and sank. The crew of five, plus two younger men working their passage, survived, but one other young man drowned. (His drowning was the only death in rescue work during McKenna's tenure). By the end of March, 1853, the survivors were still on Sable. "The *Marie Ann* crew have been 105 days on the island and during that

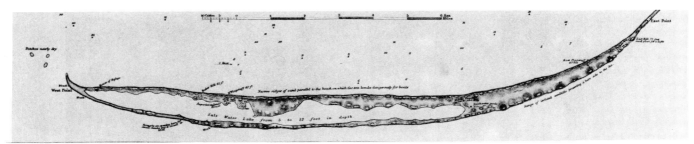

Map of Sable Island, 1853.

time," wrote McKenna, "I have had a great deal of very unpleasant duties to perform." In his letter to the commissioners regarding the two younger men who later filed complaints against McKenna, he explained that "they are a pair of villains and I believe would have given me some trouble while here if they could have raised a party sufficiently strong for their purposes and merely because I ordered all the playing cards on the island to be burned. (Cards were described as the "Devil's Prayer Book" in those days.) A year earlier McKenna found some of the crew of the brig, *Science*, guilty of similar offences. "I firmly believe that if they could have found out who it was that informed on them they would have taken his life. I am willing to allow amusements in moderation, at proper times, but I will not allow cards to be played on the Sabbath day nor will I allow any other games on that day where I am in authority, let the consequence be what it may."

Brady, the carpenter, was one of those unfortunates who stretched McKenna's patience. One bright sunny day, Brady happened to be idling nearby with his hands in his pockets watching McKenna and others load a wagon to which two horses had been hitched. For some reason, the team started moving and headed for marshy ground. Because Brady was closest, McKenna alerted him.

"Brady, catch the team!"

Brady paid no attention. McKenna repeated the request; Brady stood still. Finally, McKenna himself ran after the team and brought them back. Then he turned to Brady.

"Take your hands out of your pockets, Brady, and learn to do as you're told."

"Hell with you," replied Brady.

"What—did—you—say!" McKenna couldn't believe his ears.

"No superintendent is going to tell me to take my hands out of my pockets," Brady answered dangerously, "and there isn't anyone here man enough to force me to work, either."

Faced with that, McKenna instantly "with foot and fist convinced him that he had made a mistake." When McKenna wrote the commissioners of this event, he carefully explained that it had been twelve years since he had had to raise his hand in anger against anyone.

The establishment, or "village," in 1853 comprised thirty-one persons. There was McKenna, who received one hundred and twenty-five pounds per annum, plus commissions on salvage to support his wife and four children. The crew men were paid thirty-six pounds plus commissions on salvaged wreckage. They included people like James Farquhar, who would later write about his experience on Sable, his five children, and his wife, Isabella, who was paid to cook for the men. Their daughter, Alexina, and Isabella Penny were paid as kitchen help. Others were Solomon Knock, whose wife was yet to arrive; William Hodgson, the son of Sable's second superintendent; John Humphrey; John Himmelman; Arch McIsaac; Francis Morash; Martin Clyde; and William Busby. To complete the village, there was Blacksmith Moir, Carpenter George Walker (who was also a boat-builder and wheelwright), and handyman Caspar Graham. These last three were seasonal workers but they often shared the same responsibilities as the staffmen, especially when it concerned shipwrecks.

Work, like the sand, was endless on the island.

Just as the men who toiled under previous superintendents, those under McKenna's charge worked hard. The difference was that work was more evenly distributed than in Darby's days and performed more cheerfully. Horses, cattle, and other stock had to be cared for daily. In warm months, all the necessary attentions were given to the farm; composts were made, fences built, plowing and sowing was carried out, hay was cut and crops gathered. Maintenance of the buildings, which included whitewashing, followed; boats were repaired and painted, supplies were transported to way stations, wood was gathered for fuel, and saddles and harnesses were mended.

One rule that had to be obeyed with absolutely no shirking or deviation was the daily patrolling of Sable to check for wrecked ships, especially after the island had been gripped by fog or a severe storm. Solitary patrols made the circuit on horseback, one rider from the East Station, another from the West Station. It was a lonely trip and often the rider, if he was in a devilish mood, would break the monotony by charging a herd of seals. The herd of bulls, cows, and calves, startled by man and horse bearing down on them, would flip-flop to the shore edge and scatter into the safety of the sea. Feeling cheerful, his mischievous appetite gratified, the rider would keep an eye open for any signs of a shipwreck or salvage; a bobbing barrel, fragment of oar or spar, perhaps even a body. The journey would take them around shallow lakes, through

breeding grounds of countless birds and eventually
the two patrols would meet, compare notes,
retrace their journey, and report their observations
to the superintendent. This way they made a complete circuit of the island. The pattern, probably
conceived during McKenna's stay, was more or less
followed by the Humane Establishment right up to
the contemporary age of radar.

McKenna's recorded observations of a five-
year-old vessel, the *Nisbis*, that was shipwrecked
during a violent storm, demonstrates how important it was to have survival huts on the north and
south side of Sable.

The 'Nisbis' sailed from New York for St. John's, Nfld.,
on the 10th of January with a cargo as per memorandum
enclosed, and struck on the NE bar on the 18th at 10 PM
and almost instantly filled with water. The crew clung
to the wreck till eight o'clock the next morning when
they cut away the foremast, and getting on the floating
spars were miraculously thrown on shore. The gale
raged with such violence throughout the whole of the
19th that it was next to impossible for our men to go the
rounds; and if these poor fellows had not had a fair
wind... and the house of refuge in their road, where
they made a fire and warmed themselves and got Bread
to eat, some of them at least would certainly have perished before they could have got to the Eastern station,
the distance from the Wreck to the station being 7 miles.

Shortly before McKenna was superintendent,

Sable Island became a shelter for a number of luna-
tics. Because no institutions for the insane existed
in Nova Scotia at that time, there were occasions
when "special arrangements" were made to ship
these unfortunate souls, one at a time, to Sable.
During Howe's earlier inquiries into the island, it
was discovered that two insane persons had spent
several years on Sable; they were finally removed.
Another, it was found, had been there for seventeen years, a companion of dunes and wild horses.

The commissioners of Sable received a note from the administrator of the government, authorizing them to permit this man to remain on the island in the capacity of schoolmaster, or to fill any other task as seen fit by the superintendent. The troubled man was often heard addressing the horses.

"Now then, long ears, pay attention, do not eat the grass in school. You are here to learn, and I pose you a problem. If it took a fly a week to walk a fortnight across a barrel of molasses in ten-league boots, how many yards of calico would it take to make a waistcoat for a hippopotamus? What, ten you say? Oh dear me, no! How dull witted you are." This was a man who came originally from a respectable Halifax family of the highest standing in the community. For the first ten years at Sable Island he was extremely violent and troublesome, so that "very harsh measures had to be adopted toward him." But for the last four years of his stay, he was quiet and useful, carrying food and water.

"I have no particular love for my species," said the tireless humanitarian, Dorothea Lynde Dix, "but own to an exhaustless fund of compassion." It was because of compassion that she was fated to be drawn to Sable Island in 1853. Her life work of founding institutions for the insane took her first to St. John's, Newfoundland and then to Halifax. Dangerous storms off Newfoundland resulting in a number of apalling shipwrecks, loss of life, and battered survivors who arrived in St. John's left a

Dorothea Lynde Dix.

deep impression on Miss Dix. Her chief supporter in starting an asylum in Halifax was the Honourable Hugh Bell, whose jurisdiction included Sable Island. Through subscriptions of money, and Bell's position as chairman of the Board of Works, the much needed asylum was eventually established in what is now Dartmouth, Nova Scotia. The cornerstone of the new building, called *Mount Hope*, was laid in June 1856.

It was Bell who acquainted Miss Dix with the Humane Establishment on Sable Island and the tales of the maniacs living out a miserable existence, and eventually she felt compelled to visit the island. In her dedicated pursuit of humane work, Miss Dix travelled by rail, steamboats, and in coaches over rough roads, often subjecting herself to exposure and danger. She journeyed to Sable Island by government vessel in July 1853. Although during her two day visit there were no longer insane persons to visit, she did witness a shipwreck.

Southwest winds, rolling seas, and dense fog drove the schooner, *Guide* of London, bound from New York to Labrador under full sail, into an inner sandbar on the south shore of Sable. After a long, tiring struggle, the crew were brought to safety; only the captain remained on deck and he refused to leave. The actions of Miss Dix, as described in a letter published at the time, undoubtedly saved the captain's life and reason:

The ship was abandoned by all but the captain. He had become a raving maniac and would not leave. Miss Dix rode to the beach on horseback, as the last boat landed from the ill-fated vessel, and learned the sad fate of her commander, who, the sailors said, was a kind-hearted man. She pled with them to return to the wreck and bring him on shore, and to bind him if it was necessary for his safety. They obeyed her summons, and soon were again on the beach, with their captain bound hand and foot. She loosened the cords, took him by the arm and led him to a boathouse built for the shipwrecked, and there by kind words calmed his mind and persuaded him to thank the sailors for saving his life. She trusted that rest and nourishing food would restore him to reason.

Her astute observations of the Humane Establishment and the wreck of the *Guide* led Miss Dix to believe it was imperative that Sable should have modern lifesaving apparatus. In spite of funds from the Nova Scotia and British governments to support Sable, the crews lacked essential mechanical means to assist survivors; all they had were out-of-date surfboats.

Shortly after Miss Dix returned to the United States, this news item appeared in a Philadelphia newspaper: "The Francis lifeboat saved from the ill-fated 'Arctic' and brought here by the steamer, 'Osprey', was tested at noon today, under the charge of Capt. Stotesbury, at the request of Mr. Collins. Fifty-seven full grown men embarked on the boat and were rowed about the river for half an hour, with the bulwarks sixteen inches out of the water. Among the persons on board were a number of sea captains who agreed in the opinion that the boat would have been perfectly safe with sixty persons in it plus provisions and drinking water."

The *Francis* metallic lifeboat was a first class lifesaver and through the efforts of Miss Dix, four of them made their way to Sable. Miss Dix contacted friends in Philadelphia, Boston, and New York and appealed for new lifeboats and other important lifesaving equipment. The response was immediate. Captain R. B. Forbes, chairman of the Humane Society of Boston, made arrangements to have four *Francis* boats constructed. By the end of November, 1853, the lifeboats, *Victoria* of Boston, the *Grace Darling* of Philadelphia, and the *Reliance and Samaritan* of New York, plus a rescue car, mortar, cables, trucks, and harnesses, were all put on public display on Wall Street. The grace, beauty, and strength of these fine craft were a great attraction, but Miss Dix was anxious they should all be taken to Halifax as soon as possible and transferred to Sable Island. There were many delays and it was not until the following November that the first of the lifeboats, *Victoria* and *Reliance* reached Sable. The *Reliance* was housed at the Main Station; the other boat served the south side station. Two weeks had not gone by before the *Reliance* was pressed into service.

At six o'clock in the evening on November 26, 1854, as Sable lay shrouded in a thick fog, the seven-hundred-and-fifteen-ton ship *Arcadia* struck on the southwest side of the northeast bar. Commanded by Captain William Jordan, she was a fine vessel hardly five years old, from Warren, Maine, and bound from Antwerp to New York. One hundred and forty-seven German passengers were on board with a crew of twenty-one, and a cargo of glass, iron, lead, and silks.

"The wreck was sighted at daylight by my father," wrote Captain James Farquhar in his journal, "and he sent a messenger to the Main Station where the lifeboats presented by Miss Dix were kept." As soon as they got the report, the Humane crew hitched the hardy team of horses on the boat wagon. They had twenty miles to cover and they wanted to reach their goal as quickly as possible. When they arrived, they found the *Arcadia* lying on the inner bar, about two hundred yards from the beach "head to southward," with a slight list to seaward. Her lee side under the water, she was mired and trapped deep in the sand. Her main and mizzen mast had gone by the deck and a "tremendous sea was running and sweeping over her bows." The mate and four of the crew had managed to get the ship's boat to shore but found it impossible to return to the vessel. McKenna quickly launched the *Reliance* lifeboat, the crew took their stations, and with the mate they set out for the ailing ship.

"The *Reliance*," wrote Farquhar, "had to be rowed sixteen miles in a heavy sea. It did not reach the wreck until three o'clock in the afternoon. All the passengers and crew were on the forward part and the forecastle." In the first attempt to reach the

which held the oars in the rowlocks. Night fell and work had to be given up until the following day. McKenna's diary records his feelings:

When night came on and we had to haul up our boat, the cries from those left on the wreck were truly heart rending. In the hurry of the work, families had been separated and when those on shore heard the cries of those on the wrecked ship at seeing the boat hauled up —a scene was witnessed that may be imagined but cannot be described. I walked slowly from the place leading my horse, till by the roaring of the sea, the whistling of the winds and the distance I had travelled, their doleful cries could not be heard.

The first wave of survivors were given refreshments and bedded down. Nothing more could be done until dawn the next day. The terrifying thought was that the vessel would begin to break up from the force of the battering sea before the remaining people could be saved. Luckily, the morning brought smoother waters and by ten o'clock the rest of the crew and passengers were brought to shore. According to Farquhar, "some of the rescued were poorly clad. One woman came ashore wrapped only in a table cloth. When she jumped from the boat to the beach, the cloth fell off and she ran up the sand. More fortunate passengers cared for her and gave her some clothing." By two in the afternoon, every survivor was next to a warm fire with hot food and drink in their stomachs.

vessel, the lifeboat was swept to leeward by the strong currents and was forced to land on the beach. Before going off the second time, she was dragged up well to windward. This time, she came alongside and took on board several of the *Arcadia*'s sailors to assist the lifeboat men in handling the passengers. But the passengers began to jump in, and at once the coxswain ordered his men to shove off from the ship to avoid having the boat swamped. When the *Reliance* reached shore with her first load of rescued passengers, one of her crew was so terrified that "he refused to return to the wreck." In six trips, eighty people were brought to safety. Two more attempts were made to search the vessel but violent seas broke oars and thole-pins

The following day the seas ran smooth again and the listing vessel was boarded to remove barrels of bread and flour. By evening, eighty-seven survivors, including women and children, were taken aboard the *Daring* to sail for Halifax. The *Nova Scotian* newspaper reported their arrival: "The passengers have been kindly cared for by the Provincial Authorities, at the Caledonian Hotel, the proprietor of which, Mr. Henry Hesslein, is their countryman. They have been supplied with clothing, and will, we presume, be forwarded to New York at the expense of the province forthwith."

On the night of the twenty-ninth the *Arcadia* finally broke into "a thousand pieces." McKenna's journal records that Captain Jordan was knocked down by a wave and severely cut and bruised while the boat was making the second trip, "which deprived us of Captain Jordan's advice and assistance." The mate, Mr. Cullimore, and the ship's company did "as well as sailors do in such cases." The Sable Island staffmen exerted themselves to the utmost and the boat crew "nobly stuck to their boat and declined accepting the offer of the mate to give a spell with some of the Ship's crew."

The Mariners' Royal Benevolent Society of England, impressed by the gallant conduct and courage of Captain McKenna and his men, rewarded the superintendent with a gold medal; silver ones were given to each crew member. Much of the success of this spectacular rescue was credited to the new metallic boats sent through the efforts of Dorothea Dix.

Miss Dix was also responsible for providing the island with a library. Her appeal to friends and booksellers in Boston netted hundreds of volumes which were shipped to Sable for the use of residents and marooned sailors. The indefatigable Miss Dix never gave up helping others throughout her life. In 1861 she was appointed superintendent of women nurses during the American Civil War and committed herself to war work. When peace came, she continued service on behalf of her hospitals, giving advice and support. She also carried on with her investigations and created new hospitals. In 1887 she turned eighty-five and even though bedridden, exclaimed, "I think even lying in my bed I can still do something."

Matt McKenna was forever grateful to that remarkable woman and would remember her for many years afterwards. "We with many others," he wrote, "have reason to thank God that her good work, has been felt on Sable Island. For my own part I shall think of her with feelings of gratitude while memory lasts."

I I   *Stars in the Ocean*

OUTSIDE THE A-FRAME there is a tempest brewing. The wind has picked up and now a staccato of sand beats on the window panes. I get up and prepare another hot toddy, to ward off the "unknown." Sable can be depressing at times, even terrifying. A knock on the door at this moment would chill my blood. In the days of the Humane Establishment, a knock could mean a wandering spirit or perhaps a survivor stumbling in from another wreck. On Sable, doors were opened at night with nervous caution.

From the beginning of the Humane Establishment, as before, sailors from many countries found sanctuary on Sable. Just as we often do at night, they gathered around warm and comfortable fires, telling yarns. The locale of many stories of the supernatural were transferred from their home-ports to this island with no trouble at all. These tale-tellers had the power to "summon spirits from the vasty deep," and did so for the entertainment and terror of their companions. As the night deepens, I recall some of those tales.

In September of 1856, the year after McKenna left the island, the American brigantine *Alma*, bound from New York to St. John's, Newfoundland, was stranded on the Sable shoals and pitched about on the angry surf a half mile offshore. The lifesaving crew set out in the metal lifeboat *Victoria*, but it capsized before they could reach the *Alma*. A man

in the bow was drowned. There is no record of his name; his body was never recovered. On December 7 of that year the schooner *Eliza Ross*, from Sydney, with Captain Muggah, drifted down the south side of Sable. Again, the *Victoria* was brought into action and the staffmen manned their stations in the lifeboat. They were short one man, for no replacement had been sent for the drowned staffman; the bowseat of the lifeboat was empty. As they rowed out to the schooner, the head of what looked like a man bobbed out of the water near the area where the staffman had drowned. Its eyes were vacant and staring. The spectre grasped the gunnel of the surfboat, pulled itself in, and sat on the empty seat. Then it gripped the missing man's oars and with the others rowed out to the stranded vessel to pick up the sailors from the *Eliza Ross*. The apparition rowed back with the crew without once acknowledging anyone. It just stared straight ahead, expressionless, with eyes like ice. When the lifeboat reached the place close to where the ghost had first appeared, the apparition dropped the oars and, like some creature of the sea, slipped over the side. As the ocean waters closed over its head, the last thing to be seen were those icy eyes, staring. The ghost reappeared many times in this fashion and became most agitated if the bowseat was not free. Those who saw this ghost said "it was as though human, but not alive." Others recalled only feeling the presence of the drowned man.

The murmur rose soft as I silently
  gazed
On the shadowy waves playful
  motion
From the dim distant land, till the
  lighthouse fire blazed
Like a star in the midst of the ocean

THOMAS MOORE

The addition of lighthouses on Sable in 1873 did little to prevent shipwrecks or dispel ghosts of drowned men and women. Ever since 1801, when Governor Wentworth endeavoured to "get two pieces of cannon, one on each end of the Island to answer signals in dark weather, also some rockets to distinguish the Island," the matter of lighthouses on Sable was always current with each new change of government or administration. Nothing came of Seth Coleman's report about a suitable location for a wooden structure. The matter was taken up again in 1802 by Benjamin Lincoln of Boston. Lincoln recommended that "a Wooden Pyramid built with good white pine timber, without sap, covered with seasoned feather-edged boards and these covered with shingles well painted, with three coats of paint, will last for more than fifty years." Little did he know Sable. Following him, Superintendent Morris fully expected lighthouses to be built once the Humane Establishment began. Impatient and surprised at the indecision shown by the commissioners, he submitted his own plans for building two lights. Still, nothing was done; cost probably had something to do with the continual delay. In 1808 a Lieutenant Burton made a report on the matter to Sir George Prevost, then governor of Nova Scotia, suggesting the British government provide funds for lighthouses on Sable. There is no record of any action having been taken.

No further mention is found on behalf of the project until 1833 when a commissioner was sent to the island to make recommendations about the matter. He was in favour of lighthouses and even selected a site. Four years later, a Mr. Millar, on a similar errand, discovered that the selected site of 1833, located at the west end, had been entirely washed away by the sea. Joseph Howe, in his 1850 report, wrote that the lighthouses were a subject that "has been anxiously discussed, opinions were divided as to the propriety of such erection." Both Mr. Cunard, senior commissioner of lights, and Darby's son who commanded a cutter on provision visits to Sable, opposed the measure in the firm belief a lighthouse would lure vessels into sand shoals and bars. "Vessels driven near the Island would find a light invaluable," contradicted Howe. In 1851 a Lieutenant Orlebar, who conducted the admiralty survey of the island, further confused the matter by reporting that he considered a lighthouse at the west end unnecessary for general purposes of navigation, for the west bar "could be safely approached by the lead from any direction." He felt a lighthouse on the east end would be more advantageous, for the northeast bar extended fourteen miles with a very steep drop on the north side. None of these statements did much to encourage the construction of lighthouses. It was not until after Confederation in 1867, when Canada became a dominion and was financially independent of Britain, that a decision was reached.

In 1873 the dominion government constructed two powerful lights, one at the east end, and one at the west tip, at a total cost of eighty thousand dollars. The east end lighthouse, a white and brown octagonal tower almost ninety feet high, was constructed a mile and a half from that tip of the island. With a fixed white dioptric light, it could be seen eighteen miles out at sea. At the west end, a ninety-six foot high white octagonal tower had a revolving white light, giving three flashes at intervals of half a minute, then a cessation of light for one-and-a-half minutes, was visible for seventeen miles.

Eight years later, a series of violent storms shook the island and carved out huge chunks of the west end. The terrified lightkeeper reported that the lighthouse was in grave danger, he could feel it shudder from the combined forces of wind and huge waves. The light was dismantled and the superstructure moved to safety. No sooner was this done when an enormous bank of sand vanished into the ocean, taking the lighthouse foundation with it.

Besides eroding the west end, savage gales can do great damage to the rest of the island. In the late 1860's when McKenna's successor Phillip Dodd was superintendent and before the lighthouses were built, a terrific gale hit Sable that was reported in the newspapers by a staffman's wife. Susan Kelley often performed a man's task at the outpost while her husband, Joseph, coxswain of the lifeboat on the south-side station, was attending to wrecking work.

The gale that struck with such tremendous force blew from the east-south-east and quickly ripped the two flagstaffs from their moorings. The earth cellar, a small building close to the house, was carried off by the winds to disappear somewhere over the Atlantic. Enormous ocean waves then came surging over the south beach to the outpost and smashed into the stable. As the shrieking wind threatened to carry that building off as well, Susan Kelley threw open the doors so that less resistance would be offered to the gale forces. She then loosed five horses, let them out, and made the lifeboat, which was in the same building, ready in case it was needed. She was prepared, if the house were destroyed, to run the boat to Lake Wallace and try to cross over to the Main Station. The wind was so fierce that she was forced to crawl on her hands and knees from the house to the stable and back again.

Meanwhile, Joseph Kelley and other staffmen were at work rescuing sailors from a stranded barque, fifteen miles away. They too, were forced to crawl and at times had to shovel sand into the boats to keep the wind from tearing them away from the beach. The captain and the crew of the vessel were brought safely ashore, along with the captain's sister. But in the confusion of the rescue they discovered, to their horror, that the woman's little child was missing. One of the shipwrecked men, a brave sailor, tied a line about himself, stepped into the raging waters and swam for the barque. The sea was running high and for awhile his efforts seemed

futile. But he persevered, reached the ship, and brought the child safely back to shore.

Back at the outpost, Susan Kelley crawled a short distance out to the dairy hut and propped it up with planks to prevent it from being thrown against the house. By this time the sea had washed in through the doorway of her home to fill it with two feet of water. Susan waded in with an axe and chopped holes in the floor to allow the water to drain. It was a day of heroic action on Sable but also a day when much of the surface of the island was capriciously altered.

Not long after the West Light was first moved, the advancing sea again threatened the new location and it became necessary in 1888 to rebuild a new tower. Made from ferro-concrete, the ninety-seven foot high octagonal tower, with four equally spaced winged buttresses, was built about a half mile or so further east which positioned it half a mile east of the most western area of dry land. It was built on top of a large dune about twenty feet above sea level and its lantern was equipped to revolve every three minutes.

This pattern, repeating itself a number of times, was a clear indication of erosion as Sable slowly shifted eastward. Superintendent Hodgson, as far back as 1814, complained that "the West end is washing away so fast that it is now very near the house..." In the winter of 1916, the foundation of the West Light was once more threatened by battering waves and erosion. A new structure,

one-hundred-and-ten-feet high, was built about a quarter of a mile further east on a broader part of the island. The erosion was too severe, however, and it actually toppled over making it the fourth west-end lighthouse to be destroyed in forty years.

Early lighthouses were fired by coal and wood, oil and candles, but were unsatisfactory for they produced too much smoke and dirt. The Argand smokeless circular-wick lamp, developed in 1782, became the standard light source for a century. These originally used porpoise and sperm oil and probably the fumes lay heavy in the air up in the light tower. By the time Sable lighthouses were constructed, cheaper vegetable oils had replaced

sperm oil. Fitted with catoptric (mirror) apparatus at first, the more expensive and effective dioptric (refractive) equipment was introduced later.

Living quarters were provided close to each lighthouse on Sable, where a keeper could be joined by his wife and family. The keeper was responsible for keeping the tower neat and tidy, floors and stairs were scrubbed, with attention given to any repairs needed.

Each lantern weighed almost three tons and had to be kept in perfect working order. Made of brass and glass, these huge lights floated in a vat of mercury. As the atmosphere changed, mercury had to be added or drained off to keep the light balanced.

Every four hours the lightkeeper wound up heavy weights situated at the bottom of the lighthouse. They were geared so that a man could wind them without too much trouble and the gear system kept the light revolving. The light would turn on ball bearings at the top but floated delicately on a well of mercury.

During the latter part of the nineteenth century, it was a rather lonely vigil for lightkeepers, especially if a man were single. Not all keepers were suited to this lonely work. One lightkeeper's log tells of deep frustration and bitterness:

February 9:   Handed in my resignation, also assistant keeper withdrew his on a promise of being shifted from West light. Accepted a bag of good Potatoes this time, I thought, but only on top of the bag were 74 good ones —the rest frozen and about the size of your thumb.

March 7:   Showing new man routine. Mending pots and pans so I can use them. Slipped on stairs, bruised and wrenched my back so bad I could hardly stand up.

March 9:   Back terrible sore. Hobble around but doing my relief. I shall have to forget any aches and pains I have here.

April 5:   Boat arriving tomorrow. Everything ship-shape, light in good running order. Station thoroughly cleaned up.

April 6:   So long everyone and good luck to all. Not one minute relief in six months and sixteen days. I could not give in to anyone—but just try to CRUSH ME, ANYTIME, ANYMORE.

A very angry man who never came to terms with his isolation. A wife and family might have given the lightkeeper the sense of security he needed during his term of duty on Sable.

To make matters even worse, Sable historian, the Reverend George Patterson, points out that in a fourteen-year stretch, from 1874 to 1887, the number of shipwrecks on Sable were the same as in the fourteen previous years, 1859 to 1872! One might have expected an increase in shipwrecks because of the heavy commercial traffic, which grew year by year, but there had been vast improvements in navigational equipment and better trained navigators. Perhaps, one could reason, the number of shipwrecks should have diminished, but since the number is the *same* in both fourteen-year periods, one must finally conclude that the early lighthouses actually had little effect in preventing shipwrecks on Sable.

The early Sable lighthouses were, however, magnificent structures. According to Patterson "They serve as a house of refuge, a flagstaff, a lookout, and, glistening in the sun, they are useful as a day beacon, as well as a light by night."

Connected with the lighthouses is a chilling tale which is told to this very day. Not long after the construction of the lights and on a bitter winter night when the savage northwest wind brought blinding sleet and snow, a French schooner was driven into a sandbar. A small boat was lowered into the raging waters and three men, the captain

and two sailors, began their dangerous trip to shore. Huge waves overcame them and before they could land, the boat capsized in the surf. The men struggled ashore, drenched and frozen with the cold. It was pitch black, they could see nothing. They bent their backs to the storm and stumbled, crawled, and were sometimes blown until they reached Lake Wallace. Here, one man collapsed from exposure. The others tried carrying him but it was no use; they were near exhaustion themselves. They left him and went on. Another man dropped to the snow. The last man hurried on for help. Then a faint glow appeared through the storm; it was the West Light. As the man went on, the silver beam from the lighthouse got stronger, but utterly beaten and weary, he had to crawl. He crawled a long way; the next day the Humane crew could see where he had crawled for a distance of a quarter of a mile.

At the lighthouse, the keeper's wife awoke to noises outside. It sounded like, "Mmmmmm-aaaannnnn-mmmmmmaaaaannnnn!" Lost seals, she thought, calling for their mothers. They often flipped over the bank to the lighthouse at night. Then a faint knocking brought her and her husband out of bed. When they opened the door, there was a sailor collapsed in the snow, one foot bare and nearly frozen. They carried him inside and wrapped him in blankets and made a fire. He was so chilled he resembled a corpse, and when revived

West Light, 1940.

with rum, he kept moaning over and over,
"*Capitaine, Capitaine!*" He held up two fingers and
gestured with them. Two, he meant, there were
two, the captain and one more. He spoke no
English.

The only communication from post-to-post on
Sable at that time was by horse. The lighthouse
keeper saddled up and rode the five miles to the
superintendent's house. The superintendent
rousted up a crew of three men and they began an
island patrol to search for the sailors as they made
their way to the West Light in the violent storm.
Shortly after leaving, the superintendent heard a
furious barking and looked behind to see a black
dog running along the bank, not a quarter of a mile

from the Main Station. Thinking it was his own dog following, he commanded her to return home, and continued with the patrol.

The patrol returned to the Main Station but at daybreak resumed the search. The wrecked ship was found broken to pieces on the north side of Sable. One sailor was discovered by Lake Wallace; he had been the first to drop. So severe was the storm that his body had to be chopped out of the ice. A short while later, the superintendent came across the black dog lying in the shelter of two small dunes. Its head was resting on the body of a man, its master. The captain had crawled there for protection against the storm and perished during the night. The dog, seen by the superintendent only a few hours before, was in fact not his own, but the dead captain's, a Newfoundland dog. It had been trying to attract the attention of the patrol. The superintendent was devastated over the affair; a deep feeling of regret followed him for a long time.

Among the captain's personal effects, the superintendent discovered a bill of lading with the name of Captain Lamarchand, who was sailing from St. Pierre Miquelon with a cargo of fish destined for Boston, Massachusetts. A third body, that of a sailor from Brittany, Noblance by name, was washed up on the north shore. All three men were buried in a little plot north of the Main Station.

The captain's black dog mourned its master by howling at the grave for months. It would not leave the grave even to eat and would have starved had it not been for food left by the Humane crew. But in time the dog shunned all food and strangers. Eventually the unhappy animal died from cold and grief.

For years afterwards, at the West Light, the howling of a dog was often heard. Real or imagined, on winter nights it mingled with the winds. The keeper of the light would shiver; he remembered the story of the dead captain and his black dog on the dunes.

I 2   *The Governor*

SABLE TAKES ON a deepening autumnal colour. The coming winter can be seen in the bright space of sky, in the heavy coursing of ocean waves, and in the changing shapes of clouds.

The secret and remote abysses of the sands of Sable hold more than just men and their dreams. Today, I am in the vicinity of the East Light where I discover a slag heap, or refuse pile, at the bottom of a deep, blown-out sand hollow. Down here, I find various artifacts of a past civilization, from the turn of the century: a half jaw bone of a sheep or possibly someone's pet dog, with three teeth almost intact, turning a very interesting shade of green; a small piece of an animal trap, probably for fox; aged marlin spikes; and a small handle coated with rust, which belonged to a door or a pressing iron of the day.

Climbing out of the pit, I tuck my archaeological finds in my knapsack and head towards the old East Light house. This two-storey building is sturdily constructed and has been here probably since the early 1900s. It is situated near a very high dune, almost as high as Mount Skidby near the west end but not with nearly as spectacular a view. However, from the top I can see what remains as traces of a hollowed-out canyon. It is difficult to believe, but what I am looking at according to the journals I have been reading late into the night, is actually a man-made road running for miles through the dunes. This amazing feat did nothing whatsoever to help the fragile environment, but back in Super-intendent Bouteillier's days, commerce was an important matter. A road like this subtracted many miles from a long, roundabout wagon journey along the shoreline.

Now, as I look around Sable, I can almost see, advancing through the haze from another era long vanished, the figure of a man seated in a two-wheeled flat wagon pulled by a pair of horses. The driver, whip and reins in hand, is dressed in a tweed cap, jacket and vest, with white shirt and black trousers; he has a round face, full red-brown beard, and intelligent eyes.

At the age of twenty-five, six-foot Robert Jarvis Bouteillier had his first experience with Sable. Highly skilled in constructing houses and contracting, he went to the island in 1879 to carry out repairs on the buildings. During this introductory visit, he was swept up in the events of saving lives from the S.S. *Virginia*, forced on the sand shoals by a violent storm. The young, burly Bouteillier found himself joining forces with the lifesaving crew and rowing out in the turbulent sea to reach the stricken vessel. They were successful in landing one load of passengers safely on shore, but during the second transfer the surfboat overturned and nine people lost their lives. The only body to be recovered was that of a small boy, which was buried in a little valley not far from the Main Station. For many years afterwards the boy's mother sent flowers and flower seeds to Sable Island to be planted on his grave. This annual ritual, a mother's devoted love to her lost son, continued for many years. Bouteillier was very affected by these events on Sable; he returned to take charge of the island in December of 1884. Thoughts of his family coming in the spring sustained him through the long winter.

It was a cloudless, sunny day when Bouteillier's family arrived on a supply ship and anchored off shore. Sarah Beatrice, the youngest, fondly nicknamed "Trixie," saw her father approaching in a surfboat. Excited, she shrieked for her father over the waves, and when they met, Bouteillier wel-

Robert Jarvis Bouteillier with his nieces Mary Josephine Caldwell Hamilton (top left), Dorothea Bartlette Caldwell-Bannerman (bottom left), and his nephew William Arthur Caldwell.

comed his wife and family into the surfboat. Besides Trixie there were Bertha May, Clarke Jarvis, Clarence Edwin, and Richard Stanley. Mrs. Bouteillier gave birth to James Woodbury McLellan shortly after arriving on Sable, the only Bouteillier baby to be born on the island. The family would later be faced with hardships, illnesses, and deaths, but on this day Sable was a fresh new adventure in their lives.

During the spring they settled into their new home. When summer came, they joined in with the rest of the community in strawberry picking, a big event on the island. There were six stations by this time, all named in sequence by number, and each station keeper's wife would prepare chicken, potato salad, cakes and pies, and lemonade. All the families from the different stations then travelled by horse and wagon to No. 4 Station where the sweet wild berries were most abundant. Here in the great Victorian tradition, they would picnic, sing songs, and gather berries for eating and preserving. Sometimes they were harassed by a huge Jersey bull that would send the picnickers scampering to safety on top of the flat wagons. The men would then spend the remainder of the day trying to lure the huge animal away from the berry patches. One morning, after an event like this, Trixie woke up to discover the bull bellowing under her window. With his forefeet, he had dug a hole so deep, that "he was up to his rump in dirt."

Cranberries were picked in October to make stew and jam. Cranberry sauce was always on the kitchen table and visiting officials were often so taken with the Bouteillier recipe that they would invariably ask for a jar to take back to the mainland. Trixie later recalled that the demand for these tokens was so pressing she put up forty-eight jars of cranberries one year just for visitors alone. But, she complained, after asking each visitor to send back the borrowed preserve jar, "none were ever returned." Visitors badgered her for the recipe, including Colonel Gourdeau, one of the Ottawa officials. "Nothing to it," claimed Trixie, "just sugar, water, and berries!" But no one could make cranberry jam quite as tasty as Trixie.

Attempting to find a teacher, there was "a strong desire on the part of the parents of children on the Island," wrote Bouteillier, "to secure Miss Ancient's services"; she was the daughter of the Reverend W. J. Ancient of Halifax. At that time the dwelling at the old No. 2 Station was abandoned and it was decided, that with repairs, it would serve as a schoolhouse. Miss Ancient arrived to take charge of fifteen children for five days each week, and here they chanted arithmetic tables, practised penmanship, and took turns reading aloud. The arrangement was a practical one and was successful for a number of years.

There were other visitations from outsiders, like those of the Reverend J. Ruggles, who, at the request of the bishop in Halifax, often journeyed on board the government steamer *Newfield* "to attend to the spiritual needs of members of the Church of England, of whom there are about sixty on the Island." If the Reverend Ruggles was unavailable for this trip, then the Reverend Almon would carry out services, sometimes to baptize new infants or to hold communion. Father Moriarty would visit Sable from time to time to celebrate mass. Sometimes on the same vessel that carried the ministers there would be a doctor, called to Sable to treat various ailments. "Mr. Smallcombe was examined for fractured ribs," wrote Bouteillier, "and the doctor pulled a very badly decayed and ulcerated tooth for Mrs. Horne and extracted a large fly which had been in the ear of one of A. Tobin's children for 4 months."

Arthur Tobin was the "senior" resident, having moved to Sable in 1872, the year of his marriage to Annie Knox, and remained there for some thirty years as keeper of the East Light. Tobin's father and grandfather became members of the legislative council of Nova Scotia, were well known in business and social life in Halifax, and had a street in that city named in their honour. Annie Knox Tobin was a fearless and loyal partner for Arthur, as seen by this entry in Bouteillier's journal: "Find by complaints that Mrs. Tobin and George Sellon are quarelling. Sellon says the wicks of the Light were tampered with and that she hit him over the head with a chair. They were about evenly matched with the odds on the woman." In all of Bouteillier's journals and letters there is very little mention of

Old Main Station, 1899.

insubordination or trouble; he ran a well-organized, tight little ship.

August of 1894 was a black month on Sable for everyone. The summer had been scorching and dry. Feeling faint and oppressed with the heat, Mrs. Bouteillier took to her bed where her daughters did their best to make her comfortable. The next day a plague of locusts landed and proceeded to ravage Sable. The community must have been thunderstruck; where on earth did the locusts come from and why did they choose Sable Island which was isolated miles off the coast? There was little

time to ponder. The hordes destroyed all the vegetable gardens and stripped a vast portion of wild grass making it impossible to secure enough fodder for the stock during winter. The cows, because of damaged pastures, began to "fail in their milk." The high buzzing of the locusts, these sudden and unwelcome invaders, was unnerving. Bouteillier was so alarmed at conditions that he even suggested the wholesale slaughter of the wild horses. "In another month," he wrote, "the whole Island will look as though fire had run over it." The only respite from the pests were high winds

that blew them out to sea, though as soon as the wind died, the locusts would swarm back and continue to strip acres of wild peas and grass. When the pests finally left, the relief from their departure was immense; the damage horrendous.

Bouteillier was then dealt another blow almost immediately, when his wife suddenly died. He wrote to his superiors to inform them of the death of Mrs. Bouteillier of paralysis, "which occurred here after an illness of nine days. The body was interred today at 10 A.M., enclosed in a coffin coated inside and out with pitch." It had happened so quickly that Mrs. Bouteillier never had the chance for a doctor's visit on Sable.

By this time Trixie had grown into an energetic tomboy and was quite capable of keeping up with her brothers. Often after school, mounted on tamed Sable horses, they raced each other to Lake Wallace where they enjoyed sailing or boating. The boys, among other activities, became amateur ornithologists; Sable was a paradise for a large variety of birds. Sometimes Trixie and the boys rode with their father on beach patrols.

The patrolling system had become a carefully controlled and sophisticated operation since the days of McKenna's tenure. Ever since that cold, tempestuous night when two shipwrecked French sailors froze to death on Sable, the Humane Establishment had adopted the idea of patrol already in use on Cape Cod. Similar to Sable Island in structure and its shipwrecks, Cape Cod began to do

Bouteillier boys fox hunting.

something about shipwrecked mariners on the Cape as far back as the eighteenth century. They placed huts, or way stations, at equal intervals apart, each containing fuel and food. Sable had been using a way station idea for some years, but after the death of the sailors more huts were constructed. The specially devised patrolling system

used on Cape Cod also proved useful on Sable; it was a clever ticketing scheme that ensured complete patrol coverage of the island starting from the west end.

In Bouteillier's time the six residential stations were from two to five miles apart, extending some twenty miles, and at all were lookout posts; these were the check points for the patrollers. The rider would go along the north beach where he would stop at his first check point, then on to the next and at each point someone initialed his ticket. The patroller would continue on down to the East Light and return on the other side of the island. When the rider and ticket arrived back at the Main Station at the west end with the signatures of all the check point men, the superintendent knew that every foot of Sable had been covered.

On foggy or stormy days, riders covered all the beaches twice including the extreme ends of the northwest and northeast bars. In case they found a shipwreck or castaways, patrollers always carried bottles of stimulating liquid to give to the survivors. From there, the patroller galloped to the nearest telephone to alert Bouteillier; in 1884 all the stations were connected by telephone making communication continuous and immediate. When any casualty was reported, Bouteillier quickly obtained all the facts and gave orders to his men at all stations.

In a newspaper article J. Parsons, the agent of the marine department in Dartmouth, Nova Scotia, described the contents of the "stimulating" liquid given to survivors:

The patrol proceeds to the stable, gives his pony a few oats and then milks one of the cows, filling a wooden bottle similar to what soldiers use... Strapping this bottle over his shoulder he saddles his pony and away. In his pocket he carries a sealed two ounce bottle filled with a mixture of liquid ammonia, capsicum, essence of ginger, etc., and when castaways are found the contents of the vial are poured into the milk and this nourishing stimulant is passed around among them. If there is no call for the stimulant, the vial is not opened, and the plain milk is drunk by the patrol himself when nearing home and he is sure there are no shipwrecked people.

Nothing was wasted in those days! Parsons even tried the mixed drink himself and found it "palatable and nourishing." The effects of a tablespoonful were "noticeable and beneficial and a much larger draught is not dangerous or injurious."

To prepare for saving lives from shipwrecks Bouteillier and his staffmen devoted fifteen hours a month, once a week, from March to November, to lifesaving drill. These drills, which included boat and rocket drill, had been routine for the staffmen who were boat crew probably since the beginning of the Humane Establishment. The children especially found the rocket drill quite thrilling, for it promised the visual excitement that only a rare storm with lightning could provide on Sable. The rockets were cylinders of metal carrying a small projectile in front and an explosive charge in the rear for propulsion. After Bouteillier's time a Lyle gun was used to propel the "shot line" from shore to ship. Made of brass, it resembled a miniature cannon. The line was attached to the eyelet in the projectile and when the charge was lit, there was a noisy "crack!" and the line would sing through the air to land on the deck of the trapped vessel.

But in the 1890s the rockets were still in use and once the line landed across the deck of the vessel, then a breeches buoy could be sent out to the ship. A survivor wore the buoyant canvas breeches buoy like a pair of shorts and could be conveyed by lines and pulleys over the waves to safety on shore. It was slow work, but many lives were saved by this fine reliable method.

The rescue of survivors from the wreck of the *Raffaele D.*, the only ship lost on Sable in 1896, showed the effectiveness of well-drilled staffmen. On the afternoon of July 8, during heavy southwest winds and dense fog, Mrs. Smallcombe of No. 2 Station went outside to investigate why their dog was barking. Hearing shouts above the roar of surf from the south side, she alerted the staffman on patrol duty, who instantly mounted his horse and rode hard to the beach. There he met several Italian sailors who, in broken English, explained that they had come ashore through the breakers from a barque that was stranded to the west. The ship was already breaking up; their captain and four men were still on board.

The patrol spurred his horse to a gallop back to the station and phoned Mr. Bouteillier. The alarm was given to the outposts ordering staffmen to the scene of the wreck as quickly as possible. In less than fifteen minutes horses were hitched to the rocket wagon and the lifesaving apparatus, consisting of rocketgun, whip line, and breeches buoy, started out at breakneck speed with a run of eleven miles before them across the deep yielding sands.

As soon as they arrived, the rocket apparatus was placed in position. The outline of the vessel's hull could barely be seen through the fog. The dim forms of five men could be made out as they clung to the mizzen chain plates on the upturned side of the ship. As historian Dr. S. MacDonald described the events, the seas were "bursting over her constantly, drenching in a smother of foam the unfortunate men in their perilous position." He was visiting Sable at the time of the shipwreck and accompanied the staffmen on their rescue mission.

The *Raffaele D.* was fifty-four days out of Genoa, bound for Bathurst, New Brunswick. Captain J. Batta Caprile, in his report, stated that for six days prior to stranding on Sable, he experienced heavy southwest winds and dense fogs. When they struck they were carrying "upper main and fore topsails, forward main topsails and jib topsail, and staysail, and steering a course N.E. by E." From dead-reckoning he supposed the ship to be thirteen miles east of the east end of the Sable bar, but could not be sure, for they had not seen sun for two days.

Captain Caprile had just ordered the lead to be thrown when broken water was seen to windward and the next thing he saw was shore breakers dead ahead. Before he had time to heave to, "the barque's keel grated on the bottom and a minute later she struck heavily on the inner bar, about two hundred yards from the beach, where she swung on broadside. After taking the bottom, the seas came leaping aboard fore and aft and she thumped heavily and was on her beam ends. At the same time, the main and mizzen masts went by the board lifting her outward."

As the spars split and fell, the captain became entangled in the rigging and was thrown into the lee scuppers, injuring his left arm and face. His men rescued him from this dangerous position by placing a rope under his arms and hauling him to safety with the others on the bottom of the upturned vessel.

Just after striking Sable, seven of the sailors managed to get a small boat launched in order to reach shore. Waves hurled the boat shoreward with such force that it overturned and the men were thrown into the sea. The boat rolled over and over dangerously close to the men as they were repeatedly washed towards shore, then pulled back by the undertow. Finally, an immense wave tossed them clear of the breakers and miraculously they swam to safety, where they had attracted the attention of Mrs. Smallcombe and her dog.

The lifesaving crew was now ready to fire the

Land drill for boatmen on lifesaving crew, c. 1895.

rocket. The surf was breaking heavily on the bars with a confused current sweeping the beach. Dr. MacDonald recorded the drama in this fashion:

Every moment was now precious. Quickly, yet with extreme care, the gun line was paid out of the faking box along the beach, made fast to the rocket, aim taken and the port fire applied. Next instant the rocket shrieked through the air, carrying with it the life line. Every heart seemed to pause while the result was being watched. Fortunately the line fell among the men, who seized it and began to haul out... on the arrival of the lifesaving apparatus they all prepared themselves for the struggle among the turmoil of waters between the ship and the shore by divesting themselves of their clothing... to the gun line, the whip line was made fast... slowly the line crept out under the hard conditions of the hauling, the men having to hold on for their lives by one hand while the waves made a complete breech over them. The whip line block was now made fast to the chain plates, there being no other elevation, the masts having gone out of her shortly after striking, and the signal for hauling given to the surf men. Here a hitch took place owing to one of the men on the wreck having a lifebuoy and insisting on going ashore on the whip line. After some minutes, which seemed hours, the breeches buoy was made fast and the whip line manned by the Island people and sent to the vessel, who eagerly seized it and the work of landing the men began.

Night was fast closing in. The first man landed ashore was the steward in an exhausted condition and almost naked. The third trip brought the injured captain, who from some trouble in placing him in the breeches buoy correctly, overturned in the surf twice before landing, rendering him almost unconscious. As each one came to shore within reach the surf men rushed in and dragged the almost helpless men clear of the breakers and handed them to the care of another who administered restoratives. The last man was landed as dark came on and a short time after the ship collapsed.

Superintendent Bouteillier, in his letter to the marine agent, wrote that it was a matter of "congratulations that we were able to get the five men off the wreck before night, otherwise there is no doubt of their being washed off during the darkness and lost."

There was no lack of statistics on produce and exports in Bouteillier's time. In 1897 the island produced, for its own consumption, two hundred and twenty bushels of potatoes, thirty bushels of turnips, twenty of beets, and a hundred and forty tons of hay. Stock, killed for meat, included ten beef, three pigs, and seven calves. Export items for sale on the mainland were varied: three bushels of salted seal hides, two and a half casks of seal oil, forty-five Sable horses, and four hundred barrels of cranberries.

Cranberries followed blueberries in the cycle of growing things on Sable. The island's meadows and shallow boggy basins were perfect for growing carpets of the largest, most delicious cranberries to be had anywhere in the Maritimes. Government authorities wisely embraced Joseph Howe's suggestion that cranberries could be an island industry worth cultivating for export. The big red berries, which grew without any assistance from the islanders, became the chief item to be sold on the mainland.

Picking, cleaning, and packing the cranberry crop required considerable skill and was an extra workload for the staffmen on Sable. The berries grew chiefly at the east end of Sable, between Stations No. 3 and 4, and were picked by the staffmen with members of their families using wooden scoops with tines. These tools looked like large claws thrusting through the cranberry vines which were bedded close to the earth. Next, the berries were placed in large barrels, teamed to No. 3 Station, and from there to No. 1, where they were dried on huge tarpaulins. After the winnowing process, done in a large shed, the berries were poured onto a table which had six-inch-high boards around the edges to act as walls. Holes, or pockets, were cut into the table at strategic points. A clean, empty cranberry barrel was placed under the table at the pocket. A worker sat and separated out the perfect berries, directed them into the barrel; the residue of dirt, old berries, leaves, seeds, and vines was discarded into a bucket on the floor.

Picking and cleaning began in the second week of October, and both these operations continued daily until the end of October when the full crop was picked. Then the coopering of barrels was completed, the berries were packed, and finally they were shipped to reach Halifax by the middle of November for marketing.

For the Bouteilliers and the rest of the community, the 1897 October cranberry season was more than abundant. The following July one of the most famous persons of the nineteenth and twentieth centuries, would have the chance to taste Trixie's cranberry jam.

13 *Century's End*

THEY STOOD ON the deck of the S.S. *Harlaw*, which was anchored off Sable, watching the morning break across the sky. He was tall, bearded, dressed in jacket and britches. She appeared almost as tall as he with her long, full skirt, tight-waisted sacque coat with peplum and a hat with two feathers. They were deep in animated conversation, hands clasped like lovers, wide awake to the wonders of the world in that early dawn of July 29, 1898. Superintendent Bouteillier saw them before they were aware the surfboat had pulled alongside the *Harlaw*. He shouted a greeting. Dr. Alexander Graham Bell turned and waved. He nudged his wife. She, too, turned, waved, and smiled.

Once Bouteillier was on deck, Dr. Bell explained his mission. He had a government permit to land and search for evidence of close friends, a married couple, who had drowned during the *La Bourgogne* ship disaster, a sinking which had occurred sixty miles off Sable Island in June, 1898. The rest of the party came up on deck and Dr. Bell made the introductions before they boarded the large surfboat to take them to the island. They were Marian, Dr. Bell's daughter, Mr. Arthur McCurdy and his daughter, Susan. A servant travelled with the party. Once the surfboat reached the Sable beach, the ladies were carefully lifted from the boat and carried to dry sand, thus revealing their high-button fashionable boots of the day under long, trailing skirts.

In honour of the great inventor's visit, the superintendent hoisted the American flag at the Main
Station. It was a red-letter day to have a man of
such genius, the inventor of the telephone, on the
tiny island. Dr. Bell had already made tremendous
contributions to medicine in the field of eugenics.
He had carried out extensive research in electricity
and marine engineering. As a humanitarian he was
"the greatest single influence in the English-
speaking world in successfully integrating the deaf
child with society." Helen Keller was Bell's out-
standing success. He also helped his wife, Mabel,
overcome the handicap of deafness, the result of a
childhood attack of scarlet fever.

The Sable visit was to be a short one. Bell and
Bouteillier set out in a buckboard drawn by a team
of horses, to tour the island. A saddle horse
tethered to the wagon followed them; forays could
be made on horseback close to the sea to look for
washed up wreckage or corpses. *La Bourgogne* had
sunk south of Sable without survivors from her
listed five hundred and forty-five passengers. No
bodies or debris were recovered while the Bells
were on Sable.

During their stay, the Bell party was treated to a
full tour. They went to see the East and West
Lights and met the crew members and their
families. They had their picture taken as they posed

The Crofton Hall, *1898.*

in the entrance to the boathouse, flanked by its broad doors. Inside the building was one of the metal lifeboats donated by Dorothea Dix in 1853. Dr. Bell and Mabel, holding hands as they often did, and unaware they were camera subjects, were snapped by Arthur McCurdy, official photographer and secretary. Then they all went down to the south beach to see the *Crofton Hall*, a ship stranded there in April of that year. She was beached on a spit of sand, parallel to the shore and at first glance appeared to be in excellent condition. "A splendid vessel," Dr. Bell noted, but sadly added that her hull was broken in two amidships and she would never sail again. Buildings, sand dunes and even horses were often named after shipwrecks. Just before the Bells arrived on Sable, the guest house they were to occupy had been christened Crofton Hall, from the recent wreck.

The Bouteilliers (the superintendent had remarried by this time) gave a dinner party with Dr. Bell as guest of honour. Mr. and Mrs. Smallcombe, keepers of the Island's No. 4 Station, were invited to attend. The subject of two-way communication with the mainland arose; Bell was amused and fascinated with the superintendent's descriptions of a "pigeon patrol" experiment tried in 1893. It was decided that Sable Island would make an excellent testing ground for carrier pigeons. For the first experiment, Bouteillier told his guest, the pigeons were taken from the mainland out to sea and released. None of them arrived on Sable; seventeen

died, seven escaped, and fifty-five were lost. During another trial two dozen birds were released. They became confused with high cross-winds; some ended up in a flock of seagulls, and many were lost to hawks.

The lost "pigeon patrol" discussion turned to the science of flight and kites. (At Baddeck in Cape Breton, Nova Scotia, Bell would later embark on a series of kite experiments with his assistant, "Casey" Baldwin, which would lead to new theories of flight.) Bouteillier became most interested in Bell's theories; the inventor's enthusiasm was contagious. The discussions were resumed the following day, for the superintendent's journal records that he was in conversation with Bell and McCurdy on "the feasibility of transmitting messages by water by means of a kite or balloon attached to a float on which the message is placed." Next day they constructed and flew "a Blue Hile Kite, at 1:30 P.M., wind south at 12 miles an hour, which flew very well...had a few floats made to test kite on the Lake...discussing new construction of frame of Hargrave Kite, small round pipe to make a hinge to collapse."

Dr. Bell's party departed the next day, August 3, and at ten in the morning two buckboards and a saddle horse were sent on to Crofton Hall to pick up the visitors and take them to the surf boat for their return to the S.S. *Harlaw*. From there they steamed up to No. 4 Station to pick up two Sable ponies Dr. Bell had arranged to purchase. Govern-

ment authorities charged him the going price of sixteen dollars for each pony. One of the ponies was given to his grandson, Melville Bell Grosvenor, who would one day become editor of the *National Geographic Magazine.* The pony found a home with young Melville in Cape Breton and he would later recall that "Grampy brought back several ponies to our summer place."

The Sable Island guest book of that year, now in the possession of Superintendent Bouteillier's grandson Robert, who lives in British Columbia, was signed by the visiting party along with their impressions of Sable. Dr. Bell's wife wrote, "It is one of the most fascinating places and the water, sky and sand of the most beautiful shades of colour I have ever seen." Their daughter, Marian, agreed entirely with her mother, adding that it was the most fascinating place she had ever known. "I would like to have a cottage on this lovely Island," wrote Susan Winnifred McCurdy, "near the south shore and come here every summer to spend a month. I never wanted to stay any place so much. We might call it—'The Crofton Hall'!" Her father, Arthur, penned a rhyme for the occasion; "Comrades, leave me here a little, while its yet still early morn, leave me here and when you want me, I'll be off to Crofton Horn!"

Dr. Bell, according to the custom and courtesy

Alexander Graham Bell with Robert Jarvis Bouteillier.

of the day, left a letter for Superintendent Bouteillier to read after he left Sable. In it he thanked the Bouteilliers for their kindness and hospitality and said that he would cherish pleasant memories of Sable Island. Dr. Bell promised that when he corresponded with government authorities he would take the occasion to tell them of

...the high state of efficiency in which everything seems to be maintained. The appearance of order and neatness prevading all the Stations is most striking...I have been much interested in your plan for communicating with the mainland by means of a kite towing a float carrying a bottle or sealed case with despatches. The plan is certainly practicable and I wish you every success...a few hours would suffice to bring the apparatus to the shore with the wind in the right direction and even if it failed to land it would certainly be picked up at sea, for a kite in the air would be a most conspicuous object attracting attention even at a distance of many miles.

A few weeks after they had left, Bouteillier wrote in his journal on August 18 that he had "made a new kite and tried it towing a float on the Lake at 7PM, wind 10 miles an hour. It towed a piece of plank 3x9x7 feet long, 2½ inches thick, at about 4 to 5 miles an hour and by making fast on the side of towing end, can make about 2 points to windward or with a SW wind can make a NNE course." Bell would have been happy in the knowledge that he now had a disciple on Sable.

The Bells and Bouteilliers kept up a friendly cor-respondence. Mrs. Bouteillier described their let-ters "as visits of our friends on Sable." The winter of 1899 was a stormy, cold one with continuous gales from early January until February 12th, when the *Moravia*, a German liner carrying coconuts and wine, was lost to Sable. "I stand at the window to watch the foaming white mountains of surf," she wrote to the Bells, "I have only one daughter at home with me this winter, Sarah. Bertha has gone to the mainland. She has always wished to take up the study of nursing. I feel it is better for her as she needs more social life." Her husband's note, sent in the same envelope, tells in a short sentence a great deal about islanders at that time anywhere in the world: "Of course, we are like those marooned, constantly watching for a steamer smoke and within the last fortnight all are out of tobacco,

which to many of them is more serious than if out of beef." In isolation, the Bouteilliers had no idea of the tragedy to come. Soon they would learn that their daughter Bertha, the student nurse, had died very suddenly from typhoid fever on the mainland. Later, in another letter to the Bells, Mrs. Bouteillier wrote that the hardest part for them was the fact that the same steamer which brought the news of Bertha's death "also brought her Christmas remembrances to the household and she had been laid to rest nearly two months."

The superintendent resigned his Sable duties in 1912 when his wife had to go to the mainland for surgical treatment. He applied for and secured a position in the naval services as a surveyor of stores, in order to be close to his wife. Her illness was a serious one for she soon died of cancer. During the following years, Bouteillier frequently lobbied for salary increases for staff members on Sable.

Bouteillier's tenure had its melancholy periods. His first wife had died; the eldest daughter passed away at twenty-five; young Clark Jarvis went off to sea to become the youngest captain on the Pacific coast only to die of tuberculosis at thirty-seven; now the superintendent's second wife was dead.

The rest of the family went their separate ways

The Bells.

to live interesting and for some, long lives. Trixie, the tomboy, married to become Mrs. Merton Embree of Naksup, British Columbia. Her adventures did not end when she left Sable; right up to her death, at one hundred years old, she experienced a full and adventurous life. At Sable she learned the basics of operating the Marconi wireless and sent code messages to the mainland. This experience served her well later, when from 1911 to 1913, while visiting her brother at Grindstone on the Magdalen Islands, she acted as third operator of the Marconi station and became one of the first women Marconi operators in North America. In 1967, in her late eighties, she returned to Sable. "I would dearly like to...stay for a whole summer," she told a journalist who described her as a "vivacious widow." "It wouldn't bother me, all that change on the island," Trixie said, "because it's happened all my life. I would like to ride and take notes on Sable, I would really like to do that. I wouldn't mind if I died and was buried there."

As for her father, Robert J. Bouteillier, his governorship of Sable was an astonishing achievement. His tenure was and remains the longest of any superintendent on the island; twenty-eight long and arduous years, plus the few years on the mainland, almost thirty years. He had arrived during the fading Victorian era and stayed to govern through the early Edwardian age which saw the beginning of the twentieth century and two-way communication between Sable and the mainland.

PART THREE
Soundings
1900 to the Present

14 *The Brass Pounder*

"ON TUESDAY AFTERNOON," said the *Nova Scotian Journal* on June 30, 1905, "Sable Island picked up the Camperdown wireless station in New Brunswick and the first telegraph message ever received from the Island came in." On June 27th, messages were also sent to the Marconi headquarters, and to Dr. Jonathan Dwight in the United States who had visited Sable to study birds. Now, with two-way communication, Sable Island finally had a lifeline to the outside world. The effect was tremendous: emergencies could be handled more speedily than before, important messages could be sent to relatives, and medical advice could be relayed by wireless telegraphy. Sable's total isolation was finally broken.

The wireless operator was a new breed in a new century, and to some, it seemed an adventurous and romantic occupation. With a small staff of operators Sable began to relay weather information to Toronto. This valuable service continues; reading the weather by measuring upper air winds with special balloons and tracking them with sophisticated radar has turned out to be the main function of the island today.

David Rosebrugh joined the Canadian Navy as a wireless operator and was assigned to duty on Sable Island in 1916. In an article, "The Graveyard of the Atlantic," written for the *Canadian Geographic Journal* in 1932, Rosebrugh gave a general description of Sable and wrote about some of his impressions. Though they seldom had

newspapers when he was on the island, the operators copied the wireless press bulletins from Arlington, Virginia, and Cape Cod each night. The next day Captain Blakeney, superintendent at the time, would read the bulletins to the people at the other stations over the telephone. "What those bulletins meant during the war years," wrote Rosebrugh, "can be readily imagined."

The addition of wireless operators on Sable meant more Sunday dinner preparations for Captain Blakeney's wife. The operators always looked forward to each Sunday, the day they were invited to the Blakeneys for Sunday service and afterwards, a hot dinner. Blakeney was an old salt who had navigated steamers for many years for the Department of Marine and Fisheries. He remained a fascination to the wireless boys. After dinner, as pipes were filled and hoarded tobacco rolled into cigarettes, the superintendent would light a fire in the fireplace, sit in his favourite chair and spin yarns. The living room was filled with curiosities he had collected on his sea travels. In one corner of the room stood a huge, gleaming tusk of a narwhal, or sea-unicorn, personally given to Blakeney by the famous Arctic explorer of the day, Captain Bartlett.

Rosebrugh and his fellow operators spent much of their spare time "walking along the beaches, swimming in the surf, hunting amongst the ponds, and horseback riding on Sable ponies." The sandhills and cliffs were of "graceful contour, steeper

and more abrupt than ordinary hills on the mainland." On their beach walks they looked for rare
finds such as "sea-beans from the Mississippi, the
eggs of the deep sea ray, sea–horses, or even
swordfish swords." Often they saw the "bleached
skeletons of wooden ships imbedded in the sand."

Many young men were sent to Sable as "brass
pounders," a nickname given to wireless operators
who tapped out messages in Morse code on a key
which was made of brass. Thomas Raddall, the
Nova Scotian author known round the world
today, spent a year on myth–ridden Sable as a
youthful "brass pounder" and immortalized the
island in his novel, *The Nymph and the Lamp*. A
lively and agreeable man whom I liked at once,
Tom Raddall welcomed me at the door of his home
in Liverpool, Nova Scotia. He had promised me an
interview. Handsome, giving little sign of his seventy years except for a touch of arthritis, Tom kept
me on the varnish of my chair for two hours with
talk of Sable: impressions, information, and anec-
dotes, all presented in the engaging style of an easy
raconteur.

   Among the many books he has written, Tom's
favourites, *Halifax, Warden of the North* and *The
Nymph and the Lamp*, happen also to be mine. *The
Nymph and the Lamp* is a haunting and eloquent

Thomas Raddall, age 20, with his dog, Sparks.

love story about a chief wireless operator on Sable Island who visits the mainland after ten years isolation and brings back a bride. There follows a triangle of love, a conflict of emotions. The novel presents a fictitious place called Marina, a miniature world where the island "imposes its own reality in terms of its own nature." It is a story that one is not likely to forget, and the leading character, Matthew Carney, might very well have been Raddall himself, except that the writer spent only a year on Sable. Tom once admitted that when he had finished his year in isolation in 1921 at the age of eighteen, and boarded the *Lady Laurier* for the trip back to Halifax, he was so happy to be going home that he kneeled down and kissed the deck. He may have been happy to leave, but time has proven that Sable made a deep impression on this extremely intelligent young man.

In 1921 the Sable wireless station crackled with communications between Halifax, North Sydney, Cape Sable, and Cape Race. Trawlers and liners from all over the world flooded Sable Island with messages to be relayed to Halifax or Montreal through Cape Race, Newfoundland. The wireless building on Sable was quite new, for the original one had burned down in 1919. When Raddall was there, it was a one-storey wooden construction containing a small apartment at one end for the chief operator. There was an engine room, watch room, bathroom, and three bedrooms for the unmarried wireless operators. Oddly enough, the designer failed to realize that it was necessary to heat the operator's quarters. The engine room was kept warm by the constantly running gas engine and the watch room was made cosy by lighting a coal stove. But during the winter months the occupants froze in their bedrooms and were kept busy using a blowtorch to thaw the bathroom pipes. Tom recalled for me that old station of 1921.

"Somewhere under all that sand, if the old station is buried and no doubt it is, there's a cement slab around the base of the old mast in which, while the cement was wet, I took a stick and wrote the names of the three operators and the date. I presume it's still there, I don't know what they did when they pulled the mast down. The mast was a piece of Oregon pine. The chief operator had discovered that rot had set in at the level of the sand all the way around. He sent a message ashore. There was still a lot of perfectly good wood in it. On the next boat they sent down a lot of cement and told us to cut out the rotten wood and then build a cement slab around the base of the mast to prevent any further rot, which we did, of course. We had a hard job to make cement aggregate there because there were no stones to mix with it, so we went to the ruins of the old station which was burned. Some old rusty machinery was still in there, and we took sledge hammers and broke that up and used the chunks of iron to mix up our aggregate."

The three operators referred to were Bill Williams, George Cope, and Mike Walsh. Walsh was

Boiler tubes from the wreck of the Skidby.

history, like "walking over a big tomb." He recalled the old Scotch boiler tubes on the wrecked *Skidby* that was carried over the shoals and up to the main beach on Sable. Over the years the ocean destroyed the whole superstructure except for the Scotch boilers which Raddall often thought would make a "great advertisement for the makers because the boilers were still firmly fastened to the bedplates and that was all that was visible. When the wind got into a certain quarter," he said, "it wasn't quite east, it would set up a moaning in those tubes. The first time I heard it was in the middle of a graveyard watch and it certainly made my hair stand on end!"

A house, buried deep in the sand and described in *The Nymph and the Lamp*, was no imaginative creation. When Raddall was on Sable, a sand dune had started to bury the building. The staffmen tried different methods of halting its progress, but the high winds kept building up the dune. They built a storm fence to protect the house. When that got no results they tried shovelling back the sand. Finally, they had to give up and the dune buried everything but the attic window in one gable end.

"If you went down inside the house," Tom said, "it was like going into a mine and it was a very weird sensation. And when you got down in the kitchen you had the feeling that if you opened the kitchen door, Davey Jones or somebody would be on the other side. Well, you couldn't open the door because it had been nailed shut when they aban-

the chief operator, and, as Raddall arrived to begin his duties, Walsh was leaving to get married. Three months later he returned on the next supply ship, bringing with him not only a bride but a piano. Somehow, with the help of the operators, they got the piano over the dunes and into the wireless shack without so much as a scratch on the fine finish. That made two pianos on Sable; the other was located at the Main Station. Cope, an Irish chap who was the son of a Dublin music teacher, was an accomplished pianist and violinist; the dunes of Sable often echoed to the strains of Beethoven.

Often Raddall had strange feelings of Sable's past

doned the house, but it was the weirdest sensation being down inside that house. You felt it was in the grip of some sea monster and your voice and everything else was dead because the house was gripped in this solid mass of sand."

Ten years ago I experienced this same sensation, but in a different house which no longer stands. I remember the sand spilling in through the spaces left by the windows, and the rooms mysteriously dark and cave-like in the sombre light that seeped through cracks.

"I wasn't superstitious, of course," continued Tom, "and I used to poke fun at a lot of the yarns. However, there was one unusual incident. I was to have the graveyard watch one night and I was getting some sleep. Bill Williams was on watch and George Cope was there engaging him in conversation. In the watchroom there was a window that looked out toward the base of the mast, and then on the right hand side there was another window around the corner. It was a thick foggy night and Bill was sending a message; Cope was sitting down smoking and all of a sudden Williams stopped and cried out. Cope asked what the matter was and Williams turned, and Cope then saw something white outside the window. Of course, my room was along there so they came piling into my room, hauled me out of bed, and accused me of playing around with a sheet on the boardwalk that went around the building. I told them I didn't know what the hell they were talking about and finally convinced them I'd been fast asleep. Then Williams explained that he saw something, like somebody dressed in a sheet, and they assumed it was me pulling their legs.

"Well, I wasn't, so when midnight came and I went on watch Williams said, 'Well, Brud, I wouldn't want to be on your watch tonight.' It just occurred to me that maybe they were setting me up for a little game of their own, you see. So I had a Smith and Wesson 32 revolver that I kept in the receipt chest and I went out and brought it in, loaded it and put it on the table. Cope said, 'What are you doing that for?' and I said, 'Well, if I see something white go past this window, I'm going to fire at the damn thing right through the glass window, just in case they had any ideas.'" Raddall broke into a hearty laugh, and then continued.

"Well, anyway, they went off to sleep and I suddenly remembered that I had read somewhere about the spectre of the Brocken, in which the shadowy image of the observer is projected on the mists about the mountain-top; this was first observed on the Brocken in Germany. When you look at the mist you see what appears to be the apparition of the human figure and it turns out to be your own. So I thought of this in this thick misty night with just enough air stirring that swirls of fog would be going around. At one stage during the night the graveyard watch was a very dull one; very little went on then, since you'd take an hour off to pump the station water tank. So, in the middle of the night I took my trusty 32 and I went up and sat on this concrete slab, the base of the mast,

and I looked down towards the instrument room. Well, I had the solution. The lights from the room made a shaft right into the fog and that's when I could see these swirls of fog which looked just like white, diaphanous ghosts floating by!"

One evening before going on watch, Tom went for a walk. As he was returning at dusk, he noticed a square black hole in the side of one of the dunes. He ventured closer and discovered a hut, probably built by castaways. There he could see that it had been built from ship timber and was now uncovered because of the high winds. Raddall had no time, nor a light, to investigate. Hurrying back to the station he reported his finding to his fellow operators. There was immediate excitement and talk of treasure and plans to find the hut again as soon as possible. A sudden storm, lasting two days, delayed their search. When it was clear again, the little party set out to find the hut, but with one dune looking much like another, it was nowhere to be found. The winds and sand had buried it again completely. That may be the real secret of Sable; like a fan-dancer, she teases with a glimpse and a quick cover-up.

About fifteen years ago, Tom had a visit from a chap who was stationed with the meteorological station on Sable. While taking a walk after a severe storm he came upon the exposed remains of a hut that had been burned. Inside he found human bones, a pistol, claspknife, sword, musket and balls. The bones were collected and sent ashore to Dalhousie Medical School. They reported that the bones belonged to a young man who had probably died of starvation. Oddly, the hut contained a fireplace built with good-sized rocks, which certainly were not found on Sable Island. They could have been part of a ship's ballast. The pistol appeared to be an eighteenth century weapon. How the hut came to be burned with the young man inside remains a tragic mystery.

Practically all the dunes are sitting on top of human remains and huts. The most prominent ones, well-anchored with marram grass, were given names, Tom explained, "And I remember one that was called Smoky Hut and it was still called Smoky Hut when I was there in 1921. They have been given different names by different cartographers, but you could still identify them. There was one called Frenchman's Hill. The staff men told us that some years before I arrived there, someone became curious about this name and they supposed, correctly, that it was so named because some bodies from a French vessel wrecked on the island had been buried there long ago. So some of

them went and dug and found a part of a skeleton that still had a wooden sabot on the foot." The sabot was brought to the Main Station and added to the odd little collection of skulls, bones, and objects, all kept in the rocket house. Many of the relics disappeared when visitors and others took them for souvenirs. When Tom was there, the walls of the lifeboat shed were literally covered with name boards of ships from all over the world. The preferred keepsake, however, was the name of a ship on a transom. This unique collection was quite large at one time but most of the items have since vanished.

The idea of making a movie of the *Nymph and the Lamp* has been around for a long time and eventually it probably will be made. "I would like to see the film done in its proper habitat," said Tom, "and I would like to see it filmed in the time of the novel, 1920. It's a chance to recapture a time that's gone forever. Sable Island and Cape Race at that time were the most important stations on the Atlantic coast because everybody travelled by sea in those days: business men, military people, famous actors and actresses, and financiers and so on. All their messages came back and forth to our station and Cape Race, Newfoundland, so Sable was a very important radio station. To operators at sea in the North Atlantic, VCE was Cape Race and VCT was Sable Island. These letters were the outposts, the speaking trumpets of the continent."

IT WAS A wild night, everyone slept in fits and starts. We arise to continuing blasts of wind and rain shaking the A-frame. It seems as if we might be hurled into the ocean. Everyone feels weary this morning, but we don oilskins and face the weather to the West Light to pick up supplies.

Outside, the whole world is one of flying sand, as though devils are at work. The stinging sand particles tear at the face and make breathing difficult. As always, Dr. McLaren strides ahead, seemingly undaunted by this phenomenon. My head is twisted down and sideways for this is much like being caught in freezing rain and vision is impossible. My hands cover most of my face; a shield, or better still, goggles would be helpful right now. As we stumble blindly over the dunes, tufts of torn-out marram grass and other debris fly past and it is only too evident that the description of a storm on Sable by the historian, Simon McDonald, is no exaggeration:

The sun often rises clear, giving indications of continued good weather, and with the exception of the sea breaking high on the bars, and the fretful moan of the surf as it breaks along the shore, there is no premonition of the coming storm. Suddenly a dull, leaden haze obscures the sun, clouds gather from all directions. The sky assumes a wild, unusual appearance. The wind begins to rise in fitful gusts, carrying swirls of sand before it. The darkness increases as the low, driving scud shuts in all distant objects. Now the gale bursts in awful fury, whipping off the summits of the hummocks, carrying before it a cloud of blinding sand-drift. Darkness adds to the horror of the scene, while the rain descends in a perfect deluge. No human voice can be heard above the tempest. The crinkled lightning for an instant lights up the mad waves, as they rear and leap along the beach. Then a sudden calm ensues—a strange calm. A few short gusts at first break this period of tranquility, and in a few minutes the hurricane bursts again from the opposite quarter. The darkness still intense, is relieved only by the crashing of the thunder, as it strives to be heard above the howling of the blast. Gradually the storm ceases, the clouds break and pack away in dense black masses to leeward, and the sea alone retains its wild tumult.

The more violent of these storms "strike the boldest with awe, if not terror," wrote Reverend George Patterson, and the full force of the Atlantic beating upon Sable's shore of fifty miles seems to cause the island to quiver to its foundations.

"The winds are mad," wrote Robert Burton, "they know not whence they come, nor whither they would go: and these men are maddest of all that go to sea!"

In the March 1928 issue of the *Canadian Magazine*, C. H. J. Snider gave a skillful account of numerous aspects of Sable and expressed his outrage on behalf of the fishermen who were drowned near the island. "Last year," wrote Snider, "fifty-six men were lost in two vessels out of Lunenburg. The Nova Scotia Workman's Compensation Fund has been drained to the extent of $350,000 for these

disasters. A toll of lives, taken not by ones and twos, as in highway homicides, but by tens and centuries, challenges attention and clamours for cure. Until an earthquake sinks Sable Island a thousand fathoms deep, the price of Atlantic fish will be the lives of men."

Snider urged improved broadcasts of storm warnings. He was convinced that schooners would be better equipped to survive if they were built wider. Outside ballasts might help, for as he pointed out the schooners were proportionately narrow vessels, "five beams to a length, and as their ballast is inside, not necessarily very low." Snider described the saltbanker as:

. . . the highest form of sailing development since the era of the vanished clippership. She is so swift, so staunch, so able, that yachts are built on her lines. She treads the trackless wastes of the Atlantic in spring gale and winter blizzard, in summer zephyr and autumn storm. She goes from Nova Scotia and Newfoundland to South America with her fish, after they are caught, cured and cargoed, and she comes home with salt from Lisbon or Turk's Island, for the curing of next season's catch. She rides our Caribbean cyclones and the westerlies of the roaring forties. One combination of weather and one only appears to be her master—the August backlash of a West Indian hurricane on the shoals of Sable Island.

The Bluenose.

One of the most famous of these saltbankers was the *Bluenose*. Its captain, Angus Walters, had his greatest fight with the sea when he sailed the famous schooner clear of Sable's deadly sandbars in April, 1926.

The *Bluenose* came into existence on March 26, 1921 and was designed to race and win against the finest Yankee schooners in competitive sailing. She was a big vessel, 143 feet from bow to stern, with an astonishingly short keel for her size and perfectly stepped masts. With Captain Walters at the helm, the *Bluenose* won many races to bring international acclaim to her captain, and glory to Nova Scotia as a shipbuilding province.

They were anchored sixteen miles off the West Light of Sable and already spent two splendid days of fishing under fair April skies when a sudden breeze turned into high winds and snow. Walters called in the dorymen and took soundings: only twenty-eight fathoms, not much maneuvering room so close to Sable. The *Bluenose* was under terrific strain as she was tossed about while anchored with a hundred and fifty fathoms of cable. "I kept sounding," Walters told writer Snider, "until I got only eleven fathoms. When I got that I sounded no more. We had no chance really, after it had shoaled to fifteen. The seas break from the bottom then. An enormous wall of water struck the *Bluenose* broadside, snapped the anchor cable, tore away part of her rail and bulwarks. Another blow like that would have shattered her."

Angus Walters lashed himself to the wheel and faced the attacker. With the ocean spilling over her decks, Walters attempted to beat the storm and work the vessel around the treacherous Sable sandbars. She kept heading up, biting her way into the gale. It was the most vicious storm Walters had ever faced on the banks and all they could do was hang on and keep her going; it was a miracle they survived. They had come so close to Sable that sand had "choked the spinner on the taffrail log, and it lay thick on the deck of the *Bluenose* when daylight appeared." Feenie Ziner's book, *Bluenose, Queen of the Grand Banks*, describes the incredible courage it took during a sea storm just to cross the deck of a tossing ship. Some men would climb the rigging to avoid the seas pouring over the deck below them. Some simply froze with fear. Others would crawl below deck to await death. Against overwhelming odds, there were times when the captain and crew would capitulate to allow their vessels to be swamped by the raging seas and carry everyone to a deep green grave. But with Captain Walters, "the *Bluenose* was an extension of himself. His courage, judgement, and skill were at stake. He loved his vessel; this brought the *Bluenose* to safety."

During one of the wild hurricanes described by Snider, the fishing schooners, *Sylvia Mosher* and *Sadie Knickle*, sank off Sable in August of 1926, with all sixty hands aboard. Once a hurricane struck any ship, cables would snap and sails would rip. The shattered schooner would float aimlessly and "if her drift and drag take her islandward, God pity all." Using the prizefighter as an analogy, Snider tells about a schooner caught in an August hurricane:

Even if the stout double-ought storm-canvas holds, and the schooner gallantly hurls back the hurricane's gauntlet, she fights against fearful odds. The invisible geography of the Banks is an open book to the fishermen. It is read by the sounding line. He sees, smells, tastes, the samples of sand, shells and mud the tallow arming of the lead brings up, knows where he is, and shapes his course away from danger. But if the fight forces him on Sable Island, he is like a dazed boxer driven to the ropes. Under the scourge of the hurricane, for twenty, thirty, even fifty miles out from Sable Island the Atlantic becomes not a range of charging mountain peaks, but a chaos of spouting maelstroms, with no rhythm to their range. One after another the splendid schooner can climb the charging mountain ranges and ford their fearsome valleys. But in a hurricane, as though it were some writhing dervish of sand, Sable shoots out bars like feelers and suckers, there one hour, gone ere the next tide. No man can chart these. They make the maddened ocean harder to stem than the Niagara whirlpool. There is no regularity in the violence of the wind and wave then, nothing but wild uproar. When the seas "break from the bottom" the schooner is tossed up, thrown down, hurled on one side, spun around, like butter in a churn.

A year after the loss of the *Sylvia Mosher* and the

Sadie Knickle, August hurricanes screamed across the banks at a hundred miles an hour and, without warning, demolished an entire North Atlantic fishing fleet near Sable. Two schooners were out of Lunenburg and between them fifty-six men lost their lives, as reported by Snider, with the result of the huge financial compensation delivered to widows and bereft families. The vessels were named the *Joyce Smith*, *Clayton Walters*, *Ida A. Corkum*, *Mahala*, and *Columbia*; American and Canadian, all names commemorating a newborn child, a favourite daughter, or the owner of a ship. At least eighty-five men perished, twenty-two alone from the famous *Columbia*, out of Gloucester, Massachusetts. The Americans took the loss of this ship heavily, not only because of the dead, but also because they claimed she was the only vessel ever built that might have out-sailed the *Bluenose*. Now these lovely ships were no more, except for the *Andrava* which luckily escaped the maelstrom.

The *Andrava*, with no radio or engine, was caught in the raging storm which burst the foresail, broke the main gaff in three pieces, swept dories off the deck, smashed chain tackles, and brought down the boom onto the ship's wheel. Battered and leaking, the *Andrava* had come perilously close to the shore of Sable. There were two alternatives for her skipper, Captain Knickle: to continue on a suicide mission on the present tack, or to sail across the submerged northwest sandbar. Taking the gamble that might cost eighteen lives, and not knowing how deep the sandbar was submerged beneath the churning ocean, Captain Knickle chose to try sailing the vessel over the bar in order to reach the north side of Sable and the safety of deeper waters.

Mate Isnor volunteered to steer the craft and he was lashed to the wheel. Others tied themselves down to pumps as best they could. Isnor steered the *Andrava* toward the bar where she struck again and again and each time she was lifted onward by another wave and then slammed into the sea. Some of the crew prayed, others cursed as they became almost senseless and half-drowned. Finally, after what seemed like an eternity, the *Andrava* moved forward smoothly, free at last of the sandbar to sail in deep, calmer waters. The storm subsided by 3 A.M. and the crew toiled until daybreak repairing what damage they could. When dawn came, they could see the deck of the *Andrava* covered with a massive amount of Sable Island sand.

The *Andrava* and her crew were safe but the port of Gloucester never recovered from the great disaster of the lost schooners. Mass funerals were held for the dead, and wreaths of flowers were taken out to sea by a schooner and scattered over the ocean in memory of the brave, lost men. Sadly, it brought an end to salt fishing and saltbankers in that area. Today, sealed flasks of yellow sand from Sable Island sit in curio cabinets of many parlours in Lunenburg; mementos of an entire fishing fleet demolished near Sable.

Sable was a place where spirits haunted the living and even ships returned as apparitions. Not long after the 1926–27 disasters, the keeper of the East Light complained of seeing visions of the *Sylvia Mosher*. The apparition would appear through a glowing phosphorescent haze; the ship would seem suspended in space, hanging above the ocean. Ghostly figures of the crew could be seen in motion on the decks. They were in panic as winds gripped and shook the phantom vessel. The keeper watched the terrible spectacle as a steady trickle of men leaped over the sides, one after the other, to vanish into the raging sea below. Their bodies made no splash as they struck water and like a silent film of that era, the action was soundless, adding to the horror of the vision. The lighthouse keeper begged to be taken off Sable Island.

During the same year the cook took it into his head one day to "escape" from Sable in a dory fitted with a sail. He sailed a good distance before being picked up by a passing schooner and taken to the mainland. Perhaps, like the lighthouse keeper, he had his fill of visions and ghosts. Neither the keeper nor the cook ever returned to Sable; they were soon replaced and there were no further reports of a ghost ship.

The storm has abated as we return from the West Light with our backpacks bulging with frozen supplies. The sun tries to break through the dense clouds and the sea remains tumultuous. We come

across an immature herring gull lying crumpled in the sand, obviously exhausted by the high winds and probably blown over the dunes from the ocean. It is best to leave it, the sun will warm its shivering body and dry its matted feathers.

At the Main Station we stop for a spot of tea. Our reception appears rather lukewarm. On my initial visit ten years ago, the staff greeted me with open arms, for visitors were a rarity at that time.

Now, with an increased traffic of scientists coming and going, and oil people, our presence is taken for hum-drum, neighbourly, dropping-in.

As I drink my tea, I look through the window to the west. The superintendent's old house, a weather-wracked shell eroded by years of rain, wind and sand and vacated in 1950, is no longer standing. Built at the turn of the century by R. J. Bouteillier it served, for awhile, as a home during World War II for Don Johnson, whom I like to call "the last of the grand, old-time governors of Sable Island."

16 *The Atlantic Cowboy*

THE INTERVIEW WITH Don Johnson took place in his comfortable Halifax apartment. The short, powerfully built ex-superintendent made me feel as though I had actually been on the island during the 1940s. Donald Stuart Johnson has an unmistakable air of authority and on Sable he exercised the prerogative of power to the full. As he said, "If the governor of Sable Island wanted to call Christmas day in the middle of July, he could do it."

Don Johnson's affection for the island began when he was a very small boy in the early 1900s. His father, who was captain of the *Lady Laurier*, the supply ship to Sable, used to bring him to the island to play on the sands. When he was sixteen, Don spent a year at King's College in Windsor, Nova Scotia. Restless and feeling the pull of the island, he asked for an appointment and was taken on Sable as a member of the Humane Establishment. Two years later he returned to the mainland to join the RCMP as a constable. After receiving an honourable discharge he was a quartermaster on a vessel running from Boston to South America; a drill sergeant for the Nova Scotia Provincial Police; corporal-in-charge of the RCMP detachment in Sydney, Nova Scotia; an observer in seaplanes for the flying squad; a commercial artist and cartoonist. Completing the circle, he returned to his beloved island as a staffman and largely due to his extensive experience handling men, he was appointed superintendent of Sable in 1939, just prior to World War II. There is no doubt that life on Sable suited him. I asked him why he was so fond of Sable.

"They called me the Atlantic Cowboy because I broke in horses and rode all over the place," he said. "I liked that island so much because of the variety. For instance, when I first went to Sable a fella could ride horseback and go down all over sod right to the lake beach, then on good hard beach to No. 3 Station and the horses would hardly make a print in the sand. Then when you got to No. 3 you could drive on sand and go right to the East Light. And there were lilies down there and freshwater ponds and all kinds of flowers like daisies and buttercups. I loved it.

"Now, in Bouteillier's time," continued Johnson, "a couple of crates of roses were shipped to Sable. They were planted and when they bloomed in the summertime you could smell them for hundreds of yards around. They were wonderful. You couldn't walk among them because of the thorns. But they thrived in the sand. Had to put a picket fence around them which was always painted white, and beautiful roses, oh, just a profusion of roses!

"I had a good bunch of men there, too," he added. He also had a new bride and when she arrived she found the main buildings ship-shape with a coat of fresh paint and the kitchen floor shining like a mirror. Each day for a week she would add some womanly touch to what was once Johnson's bachelor quarters and each day the superintendent would return from his duties, stand in

the doorway and remark, "Well, it's looking a little different again!"

Mrs. Johnson arrived during the interview from a shopping trip downtown. A warm and friendly person, her eyes danced as she greeted me. She put on the kettle for tea at once and talked about Sable. Her first week there had been a lonely one, she explained, and she cried for awhile out of home-sickness for her parents and friends on the main-land.

"The days weren't long enough to do the chores I had to do, which included housework, gardening, and cooking." Mrs. Johnson brought in tea and cakes. "I tried everything in the cookbooks. We couldn't eat it all, of course. We used to have after-noon teas. There were two other women on the island, Esther Eccles, wife of the weatherman and Eileen Morner, whose husband was a lighthouse keeper. It was quite sociable."

Johnson's duties, like those of all superintendents before him, included being a part-time physician. When he first arrived on Sable the only first-aid supplies were two bottles of horse liniment, some bandages, and one bottle of iodine. He wrote to the National Research Council in Ottawa requesting a medical kit for the island. The next supply ship brought in eight large packing cases of supplies like sulfa drugs and penicillin with instructions on how to deal with different viruses. At that time, in the forties, patients could be flown to the mainland during any emergency. With the new supplies, Johnson took care of most ailments.

Mrs. Johnson asked, "What about your own leg being broke, Dad, you set it yourself and nearly drove me crazy and kept me awake!" She turned to me, "He broke his leg when he was coming back on the boat."

"We were trying to get back on the small boat," Johnson continued the story, "and I was on the beach and tried to scramble up the beach when the sea lifted the boat up and it came right down on my leg."

"I had some job to get his rubber boot off."

"I was probably in shock and I wanted one of the men to cut the rubber boot off but I couldn't make them understand, so instead some of them pulled the boot off and took me back to the house."

"It was terrible!" exclaimed Mrs. Johnson.

"But then I got the leg set after awhile, with a bit of help—Mom here kind of dozed off to sleep—and I worked and worked on my leg until I got some feeling back into it and had splints made up and ready, all wrapped with cotton wool and everything."

"The whole story was," said Mrs. Johnson, "he wasn't going back on the supply ship to the main-land where a doctor could look after his leg. He was going to do this job himself, but I didn't know that. I went to sleep and he woke me crying about his leg. His toe was braced at the foot of the bed. He'd clicked his leg back into place."

"She would towel the sweat off my forehead and I'd let a yell out of me 'cause I'd feel myself lapsing into unconciousness. The bone was broken right

Don Johnson on Sable patrol.

below the knee and you could put your two fingers right down between them and there was no feeling at all down there."

"Dad and I finally got it set expecting we were going back on the ship to get it looked after. When the time came for the ship to leave he wasn't going. Well, then I didn't know what to do 'cause it was the Christmas ship and here was winter coming on and the lighthouse wasn't working properly."

"And this is what he had in mind, see, he wasn't going to tell me but anyhow, the ship left and we were still there and we went through the winter—"

"Yeah, but two weeks after, the light really went on the blink."

"When the boat returned in the spring, the doctor examined his leg and said he couldn't have done any better himself. And that's the story. That was the first winter we were there."

It was also the winter that Canada was fast becoming deeply committed to World War II and its effect was felt even on Sable Island. On June 2, 1941, while Johnson was in Halifax having x-rays for his leg, a low flying RCAF twin-engine Lockheed Hudson bomber on a patrol sweep out to sea during foggy weather struck one of Sable's radio beacon poles shearing off a wing. The bomber tilted and dove into the rough sea about one hundred and fifty yards off shore. The staffmen managed to recover five dead airmen; they had been decapitated from the terrific impact of the crash. The bodies were flown to Halifax. At the request of the officer commanding Eastern Air Command, Johnson flew back to Sable to recover secret codes and equipment.

In 1944 a Liberator bomber, a four-engined aircraft, experienced heavy icing on its fuselage and wings, and was forced to land on Lake Wallace, striking the water nose first. Although the aircraft could not be salvaged, the whole crew escaped unharmed.

In January 1942 Don Johnson requested leave to go to the mainland to join the armed services. Ottawa's answer was that he was too important a man to leave the island during wartime. "Well, I figured I could do more in the service so I resigned from the civil service. Of course I was asked if I was interested in staying there for more money—I said no." Johnson, always in control of his own destiny, joined the Royal Canadian Air Force; they were happy to have him and gave him the rank of squadron leader. Ottawa refused his resignation and insisted he remain as superintendent of Sable. "I had two jobs. I was in the air force and superintendent of Sable at the same time. So I was put into a queer situation of acting as a navigator every time a navy corvette would go around Sable. And any-

thing that would go wrong on the island, I used to have to fly out. I built the Fleet Air Arm on Sable. No one knew anything about it." I asked what its function was.

"The Fleet Air Arm on Sable from 1942-44, was the Navy's air arm and it was logical for them to be stationed on a spot of land out in the ocean. We had a Canso, a Grumman Goose, two Walrus aircraft. The land-sea craft took off from the lakes on the island. Landing was pretty bad there because you couldn't tell how the wind was when you were coming down. The pilots got used to it and after awhile they could make a good landing but at first takeoff they'd be skipping and banging and all that kind of stuff. One time, when the wife and I were returning to Sable, the pilot asked me to come up to the cockpit. He asked me how the wind was on the lake. I explained how the wind swirled all around the island and he said, 'God, I thought it was altogether different!' So he set her down a little wrong and we bounced when we hit the water and went way up in the air and came down just like an old truck going over a bridge.

"The wife thought that was just great! Everyone else was speechless. They were catching their breath and thanking God they were alive. And I'm sure we went thirty, forty feet in the air and then came down with three big bombs on each wing!"

I asked about the German submarines for it was well known that during World War II, U-boats sometimes escaped detection and came very close to Halifax harbour. "Oh yes, the subs were out there. We could hear them over the waters, refuelling their engines at night time."

D-Day saw activities in Europe stepped up to fever pitch for what was hoped would be the final Allied offensive. Sable, with the Fleet Air Arm established there, was more important than ever. Johnson was asked to take up full-time duties on the island. He was mustered out of the air force in one day rather than having to wait the customary month, and a week later he was back on Sable. Not long after his arrival he and his staffmen were facing the serious danger of explosions on the beaches.

It all began when the S.S. *Independence Hall* grounded on Sable in the afternoon of March 7, 1942. Within hours the massive ocean waves broke her in two and she sank. Nine men were lost overboard and three of the bodies were recovered by the staffmen eighteen miles away from the Main Station on the south side of the northwest bar. They were buried in a little graveyard plot across from the West Light. Part of the vessel's cargo contained tins of sodium.

Two years later, in 1944, the sand and water uncovered enough of the wrecked hull of the *Independence Hall* so that somehow, the tins of sodium were released to rise to the surface to be washed ashore. No one knew what they were. A labourer with a construction crew on Sable was taking a casual beachcombing stroll along the shore when he discovered one of the tins. Curious, he took some of the sodium out of the container and poured water on it, causing a chemical reaction which triggered an explosion and set the man on fire. In severe pain he attempted to make his way back to camp. Attracted by his screams, his co-workers rushed him to the Main Station where Don Johnson treated the patient for face, leg, and arm burns as well as for general shock. The following day the patient suffered intense pain in his eyes; his lips and mouth were badly swollen and burned, and it was necessary to fly the man off the island to a mainland hospital.

During another exploding incident, two staffmen were cut about the face and hands from what seemed like shrapnel. A third staffman had his thumb and two fingers blown off by one of these surprise detonations. Superintendent Johnson applied a tourniquet and gave morphine shots, but like the first victim, the wounded man had to be flown to a hospital. Johnson warned those on the island not to tamper with the containers, but it was a situation difficult to control; for weeks there would be no trace of explosives, then a gale would change the formation of the beaches to uncover more sodium tins. Sometimes the tins would rust under the sand and, activated by the salt water and air, they would detonate without warning and explode with tremendous force to cover a wide area. It was like a World War II minefield. Eventually the tins were buried deep in the sand and the danger passed, but for awhile Sable was a "front line" island.

While Johnson was on Sable there were five shipwrecks, and he talked about some of them, describing rescues, the violent storms, and high seas. It must have been hard to leave the snug comforts and security of the superintendent's residence at such times. Don Johnson reminisced: "We had oil lamps then. There could be a storm a thousand miles off, South America maybe, and when the seas hit Sable, well, you could see the oil in the lamps just quivering from the vibrations of a thousand tons of water hitting the south beach. I've seen forty feet of the banks go in one storm. But inside we never gave it a thought, for our house was made so well by Superintendent Bouteillier that once we went into our bedroom it could blow a hundred miles an hour and you'd never know."

Among the five shipwrecks during Mr. Johnson's tenure, there was the *Alfios*, a five-thousand-ton Greek freighter. According to Farley Mowat's book, *Grey Seas Under*, she was travelling at nine knots when she shuddered into Sable's offshore bars during the fog-thick night of April 23, 1947. Lacking any radar equipment, she had no warning when she went aground on the sands; her bows almost lodged into the shore dunes of Sable. The captain sent an urgent SOS which was intercepted by the *Foundation Franklin*, a deep-sea salvage tug. When the tug arrived, she tried every which way to tow the *Alfios* loose, but the freighter would not respond. The tug had to release her tow line when high winds and enormous waves began to slam both vessels.

By dawn it was all over for the *Alfios* for she was listing twenty degrees and sinking. To the last moment, the stubborn captain and his crew refused to leave the ship. The Sable staffmen finally made the rescue attempt in the surfboat, reached the *Alfios* and took all the crew ashore. If they had waited another hour, Don Johnson told me, the captain and his men would have drowned.

The *Alfios* vanished under the Atlantic. But she rose from her grave after a wild storm in the summer of 1955 and showed herself almost clear of the sands. The startled Sable staffmen, who were riding patrol on the lonely beach, carried the news back to the Main Station. The *Alfios* was on view for six months and then vanished as mysteriously as she had reappeared, faithful to the tradition of ghost ships and illusions of Sable Island.

The last recorded sinking off Sable occurred when another Greek freighter, the *Manhasset*, ran aground and sank in much the same fashion as the *Alfios*. The *Manhasset* was steaming from Newport-News, Virginia, to St. John's, Newfoundland with a heavy cargo of coal when she became trapped on a sandbar at 9 P.M. on Friday, July 4, 1947, only three months after the other vessel sank. There were some interesting highlights to this last sinking. It was during this historical event that Superintendent Johnson had to face a small crew of sullen sailors bent on anarchy. It could have turned into the same kind of nasty nightmare experienced by Captain Darby in 1836 when drunken survivors had to be quelled with violence.

It all began when the *Manhasset*, caught on a sandbar, took a savage beating from the sea all night long, just like the *Alfios* and hundreds of vessels before her. In addition, an unexplained engine room explosion rendered the boilers useless and severely burned the hands of the chief engineer. The skipper, Captain Luis Marangos, sent out a distress message which brought the Canadian freighter *Argofax* to her aid. But the larger ship found it impossible to navigate through the sandbars close enough to get a line aboard the stranded ship.

The following morning, twelve of the crew went ashore in a lifeboat after the vessel began to

Don Johnson (middle) with members of the Manhassat *crew.*

list. The heavy surf, rising sometimes to a height of twenty feet, made it impossible for the men to launch the lifeboat back into the sea for the return trip. A breeches buoy was then rigged from ship to ship to Sable, but by the time it was completed the *Foundation Franklin* tug arrived. Efforts to free the *Manhasset* over the weekend were fruitless and the remainder of the crew, nine of them, were taken off in one of the *Franklin* lifeboats. Four trips were made over the turbulent waters before the rescue was completed. A few days later the men were taken to Halifax and the injured engineer, Victor Luliac, was flown from Sable by air ambulance and admitted to the Royal Canadian Navy hospital.

As for the twelve crewmen who landed safely on Sable, they were to spend a number of days there until the fog cleared enough to allow an aircraft to land on Wallace Lake to take them to Halifax. The first few hours of their arrival were tense ones. The crew was a rather undisciplined lot who paid little attention to their captain at any time. Now, without his presence, they decided to take matters into their own hands. When asked to take quarters at the East Light, they refused. Perhaps the effect of being on an island coloured their attitudes. At any rate, anarchy was on their minds and the glint of knives appeared from under shirts and jackets. No one was going to tell *them* what to do.

Superintendent Johnson would simply have none of this behaviour. Approaching the hostile group on horseback, he calmly patted his holstered pistol and told them he was governor of Sable Island and that everyone followed his orders. The men glowered. To emphasize his point, Johnson pulled out the gun, displayed it, then slid it back in its case. He was prepared to use it if necessary, he explained. He made an imposing figure in the saddle as he ordered all knives and other weapons handed over to him. Something in the tone of his voice, probably from those years of police experience, convinced the shipwrecked men to do as they were told.

Johnson dismounted, went over to the group, squatted, and as he casually rolled a cigarette, chatted amiably with the defused crew. The hostilities soon faded, some faces began to crack with grins and the atmosphere changed from dangerous to the lightness of an afternoon tea party. Soon the sailors were in good spirits as vehicles took them over the sandhills to bunk in tents near the East Light.

Meanwhile, the listing vessel sank deeper and deeper into the sand. Built in 1923 at Sparrow's Point in Maryland, the freighter was christened the *Wilton* and renamed the *Manhasset* in 1942. Beyond salvage, she came to rest not far from the *Alfios*. The last vessel to succumb to Sable all but vanished except for her main mast which was exposed for the next twenty years.

In 1948 the Johnsons had to leave Sable because of family illness on the mainland. For them, the island was a paradise. "I loved it," said Mrs. Johnson. "I cried when we had to leave but that was on account of my mother who became sick. I would have loved to stay down there five or six years more." The Johnsons felt as many did after living on the island for some time; Sable was the only real home they ever had.

17 *The White Mist*

AS I FINISH my tea at the Main Station, I can remember when I first became interested in Sable. It was 1967 and CBC Radio producer Peter Donkin put forward the suggestion that together we assemble a radio documentary on the island for national network release. The idea hung in the air for awhile until one day I chanced upon the September 1965 issue of the *National Geographic Magazine*. Inside was an article on Sable Island by Melville Bell Grosvenor, now Dr. Grosvenor, known and honoured the world over as president emeritus of the National Geographic Society and editor emeritus of the society's magazine. Dr. Grosvenor told how, accompanied by members of his family and friends, they reached the island aboard their yawl, the *White Mist*, aided by radio detection equipment. The result was a superb account of the landing with a rich, informative text, colour plates, maps and charts, and black and white photos from 1899 showing men "with elegant mustaches posed with ladies in flowing skirts and bonnets." The article, the first and most thorough contemporary coverage, brought Sable Island to the attention of the world. The crew of the *White Mist* knew of the dangers surrounding Sable and yet dared to attempt their landing in the summer of 1965.

"One foal, a wild kicking thing," wrote Dr. Grosvenor, "I tamed before I was ten. Sometimes she threw me, but I found her worth the bruises for she came from a place where the only industry was danger." Dolley, the pony he tamed as a boy, became the famous editor's symbol for Sable Island. When his grandfather, Alexander Graham Bell, brought Dolley to Melville, he told him it was no ordinary horse, but "one of the rare Sable Island breed, like no other horse in the world!" Dr. Bell's tales of Sable piqued Melville's imagination. Later, on transatlantic voyages he often saw the steady flashes of Sable lighthouses. "Once my ship passed at daybreak," he wrote, "and Sable lay so close... we could see its pale dunes lying low and ominous. On other ships, we passed cautiously in fog. Every time, the captain had sighed in relief, 'Sable astern!'"

It was not until that summer, however, that Dr. Grosvenor experienced the magic of Sable for himself and decided to try a landing on the island. Canadian officials had made it clear that "No small craft should approach or attempt landing on Sable, there is no harbour. The weather is calm for a three-week period, only in mid-July. The surf at that time is low enough to allow small boats to beach on its shores. Even so, it is a fifty-fifty chance and there is almost continual fog." The Grosvenors, neither dismayed nor deterred, headed for Sable, cautiously determined to make the attempt.

The *White Mist* had already earned an excellent

The White Mist *landing on Sable.*

reputation. The forty-six-foot craft, equipped with auxiliary motor, had been designed by Sparkman and Stephens, built in 1950 by Nevins in New York, and had given a good account of herself in numerous international sailing races. Capable of a steady seven and a half knots under mizzen and jib, at this time she was carrying the Grosvenors from the warm winds of Bermuda to their summer home in Cape Breton. They hoped to visit Sable on the way.

"We had left the tropic weather and run into fog," wrote Dr. Grosvenor who was on night watch. "Fog thick as milk had settled around our yawl...and a faint breath of wind moved us north by east at a silent three knots. I am still not sure how the sound began—a rippling or faint chuckle on the sea. Was this the jumping of tiny fish or squid? I studied the water and saw dimples like the splash of raindrops, or were they small whirlpools? For half an hour the rippling continued, then ceased mysteriously as it had begun. Checking tidal charts, I found the cause of the ripples." They had reached, of course, the rendezvous of the two great ocean rivers, the Labrador current and the Gulf Stream. The *White Mist* was now in the chilling fogs and treacherous currents that surrounded Sable and carried so many other skilled mariners to their demise on the sandbars. Would the currents carry them off course, too? They had to be on guard.

Now in the dark of a foggy night, with Sable off their starboard bow, they knew the worries of the old skippers. Dr. Grosvenor was anxious to land on the island but determined that their yacht would not "leave her lovely hull in this boneyard." In the early dawn, as the fog grew thicker, Dr. Grosvenor ordered the yawl slowed to five knots. Later, when a break in the fog allowed it, the navigator, Gil Grosvenor, made a quick sun shot with his sextant. Their course had been plotted to keep well clear of the west tip but like many ships in the past, the contrary currents put their instruments awry. Because of the mist, the horizon had proven false. It was easy to understand how early navigators stranded their vessels on Sable. A new course was fixed and Alex Grosvenor, as helmsman, turned the *White Mist* thirty-five degrees westward. All was well. By noon, they were receiving accurate bearings from Sable Island's radio beacon, indicating they had sailed thirty miles farther west than planned.

As night arrived they chose a long course around the west tip of Sable, staying clear of any shoals and sandtraps. The *White Mist* changed course at 1:15 A.M. "to run down on Sable radio beacon, bearing 197 degrees." They took no chances. Even though the fathometer registered "no bottom," they took soundings with a hand line. Soon they touched 150 feet, then 120, then ninety-five.

"As pale daylight brightened the fog," described Dr. Grosvenor, "we began to hear breakers on the starboard bow. This was the notorious surf-pounding West Bar. Chill water and fog carried the sound for miles. Surf with this calm sea—what would it be like in a storm, I mused." The yawl drifted slowly towards Sable until the sounding was ten feet. They could see nothing; down went the anchor; the fog was a blanket. Soon, just as naval officer Rosebrugh had observed fifty years earlier, as if on a silent cue, the fog curtains parted to reveal the island. The sailing directions had said, "Blow your horn." They blew. Nothing happened. Again the horn; louder this time. Again, no answer. With sails down and motor chugging slowly, they followed the shoreline taking soundings all the time. When the lighthouse tower and rooftops came into view, they anchored, left a watch on board, and rowed ashore in their little cockleshell of a "pram," a flat-bottomed row boat about eight feet long.

The first living thing to greet them at the west bar was a wild, black stallion. Immobile, high on the rim of a dune, he stood scenting strangers. Suddenly, he snorted and flashed away with streaming mane and tail to warn his mares. Sable horses—symbols of free spirits—a boyhood dream fulfilled. The tribe of Dolley had survived.

The landing party clambered up the sand dune and discovered lying below them a tiny Shangri-la of houses and green meadows. A man and a woman were picking berries. As no word had been received on the island of their coming, although a message had been sent, Norman and Christel Bell,

busy filling their cans with strawberries, were badly startled by the sudden appearance of these husky sailor men! Their berries were spilled, but when Dr. Grosvenor introduced himself, and when the Bells learned that his grandfather had been Alexander Graham Bell, the welcome was warm. The Bells maintained the diesel station which provided the electricity for the island, and lived nearby.

At the Bell home the Grosvenor party was made

Dr. Grosvenor meeting Norman and Christel Bell.

comfortable and given tea. Doug Harrington, a bushy-bearded man in charge of the weather station, arrived shortly after to take the visitors around the island. This tour was not unlike that given for Dr. Bell sixty-five years before when Superintendent Bouteillier had conveyed the inventor to all points of interest on Sable. The twentieth century visitors were taken across the south beach in a trailer drawn by a tractor, and then out to the east tip of Sable where they photographed seals.

On their way back, the *Manhasset* wreck provoked comments for only the mast was visible; shaped like a cross, it was a grim marker. Further down the beach in shallow water stood a headless woman hitching up her skirts. This apparition proved to be a wonderfully carved wooden figurehead from some forgotten ship. Uncovered by the shifting sand, like the ghost of Mrs. Copeland, she seemed to have "risen from the deep." The headless lady now stands on display in a Halifax museum.

The visitors saw two riders galloping along the hard-packed shore. They were meteorological technicians who were picking up bottles washed ashore and collecting them in saddle bags. This was part of a special experiment in which bottles were released from the mainland in order to study ocean currents. In one of these experiments, acccording to Dr. Grosvenor's article, 827 bottles were released off the coast of Nova Scotia; of fifty-six

that returned, twenty-four were from Sable, indicating the possibility of a huge eddy ringing the island.

The final stop was the Main Station where they sent radiograms to the mainland announcing their safe landing on Sable and shared a hearty meal with the staff. The early evening sun touched the dunes with its soft light as the tractor rolled across the sand taking everyone back to the beached pram of the *White Mist*. Back under sail, steering clear of the dangerous sandbars and breakers off the west bar, they headed out to sea. Doug Harrington stood on the beach waving farewell for a long time. Watching that solitary figure, Dr. Grosvenor defined an aspect of Sable in a single sentence:

Preparation of a radiosonde balloon for flight.

"The only permanent thing about Sable Island is its loneliness."

"A boy's will is the wind's will," wrote Longfellow, "and the thoughts of youth are long, long thoughts." For Melville Bell Grosvenor, the vision of Sable which had been but a dream, was now a cherished memory.

Here at the Main Station there is little change from that day the *White Mist* paid its visit or even from ten years ago on my first visit to Sable. I wash my tea mug in the same kitchen area where the cook, Bill Desroches, used to prepare meals. Fred Androschuck was officer in charge of the weather station, which used to be under the jurisdiction of the Department of Transport. Now it is referred to as the Atmospheric Environment Service under the Department of Environment. The electronic equipment in the operations room is slightly more sophisticated these days, but the function of sending up a weather balloon to explore upper air winds remains the same.

The lives of these technicians may sound less romantic than those of the men who once rode patrol on horseback to save lives, but all men on Sable are affected by the same powerful loneliness. One young man actually took his own life by hanging in the late forties. Today meteorological observers spend less than one year at a time on the island.

In a modern building near the Main Station I watch as these "Explorers of the Empyrean" prepare a radiosonde balloon for flight. Chemicals and water are mixed and the resulting gas flows into the inverted tear-shaped balloons measuring about five feet in diameter. When ready and on schedule, the huge doors to the building are opened and the balloon, shining red in the mid-day light and bearing its precious radio transmitter, is sent aloft. Easy enough on a fairly decent morning but most treacherous at night in a forty-knot gale.

The technicians have a half hour to prepare and send up a second balloon if the first take-off is a failure. The helium-filled plastic envelope soars up and over the Atlantic Ocean to a height of sometimes a hundred thousand feet. Twice a day the floating ball goes up and its transmitter relays readings back to a receiver at the Main Station, including windspeed and direction, humidity, temperature, and barometric pressure. Because of the diminishing air pressure these balloons get bigger and bigger the higher they go. Eventually they burst and disintegrate; the remains flutter to the earth. Usually this happens over unpopulated areas, but occasionally part of the equipment is found by someone and returned to the Atmospheric Environment Service. The weather observations are sent hourly from Sable and all this data is internationally co-ordinated with global weather stations to provide information for aircraft and vessels to and from North America and the European Continent.

In the reading room at the Main Station I discover a 1960 journal containing some light-hearted entries by one young meteorological observer who proved to be most resourceful:

November 23rd: It's been a hard, hard day. Pickled 70 eggs yesterday and the house has taken on an air of a buried tomb. Made some Nectar of the Gods, today. I used two dozen oranges, one and a half dozen lemons and three pounds of raisins plus three grapefruits for flavour. I put them all through the meat chopper and along with five pounds of sugar and a package of yeast, plus three gallons of warm water, I set it beside the furnace in the basement.

November 27th: Stinky was away for three days, but the prodigal cat returned this evening, only to eat a can of salmon and take off again. Stinky must be in love or something. The Nectar of the Gods is starting to come to life now. It has begun to lose its horrible orange and lemon taste and is now taking on a wonderful new flavour!

December 2nd: We had a big explosion this morning —scratch one gallon of brew.

Liquor, as a rule, was not allowed on Sable during the Humane Establishment years. There are records from the turn of the century of men who often took employment on the island for the purpose of reform from drinking. One letter to the superintendent mentions that "Thomas Graham lost his grip on himself through liquor and requests to be sent to Sable." Others had no choice in the matter. James Joseph O'Rourke, who stole some of his own father's clothes, was ordered to serve two years suspended sentence on Sable, "so as to endeavour to overcome the ravages which liquor had made upon the young man's system." The fresh air, industrious life, and Sunday services in that time were a help to those addicted to intemperate use of alcohol.

Long before the young technician made those entries in the 1960 log book, everyone on the island enjoyed the benefits of electricity, just like people on the mainland. This electricity was produced by a diesel station generator. Diesel is oil and practically the whole world runs on oil, even remote Sable. In 1959 oilmen had arrived on the island to explore the possibilities of finding oil, and in 1967, the year of my initial visit, drilling operations began.

I arrived in a Canso, a land and sea aircraft belonging to Mobil Oil Company. It is a somewhat heavy craft, so a special bed of wooden planks under the sand surface acted as a landing field. I remember that, because of the oil operations, quite a community existed on the island at that time. Prefabricated buildings were erected: a cookhouse and a bunkhouse to accommodate thirty-six men.

A million dollar oil rig, lying idle in England, was brought across the Atlantic to Sable and stood, as writer Barbara Hinds described it in the *Atlantic Advocate* magazine, "like a towering 20th century monument to man's ingenuity pointing its lofty trellised head into the fog banks of Sable, its shaft rooted in the earth for more than a mile." Although the presence of oil-seekers may have worried some, I recall that a number of younger members on the weather staff welcomed the regular contact the Mobil people had with the mainland by aircraft; they would receive their mail more often and be able to enjoy the latest reading material. Mobil sank three million dollars into the project and at that time it was costing the company six thousand dollars a day to drill a hole in the sand, using Sable as a convenient platform to suck up the "gold" trapped in sediments on the ocean floor. In later years floating oil rigs would be placed around the island to drill for oil and it was hoped that gas wells would materialize.

Norman Bell's job, as pointed out before, was to tend the diesel station that generated all the electric power on Sable; by the early seventies even that job became automatic and now the Bells live in retirement in Newfoundland. I remember the wonderful little greenhouse that Norman built for Christel and here she spent many hours with her plants and flowers. A poetic storyteller, Norman talked about storms and ghosts.

"The wind we mind the most here on Sable, is the northwest wind. It's a bitter wind. Well, now I've been around the world and have gone through hurricanes on a ship in the North Atlantic, and it's a fearful thing. But a storm on Sable Island is altogether something diffferent. The wind starts to blow, and it blows and blows and blows as though it's going to blow forever. And very strong. This house will dance on its foundation, literally, pound on the foundation. You hear the wind shrieking in the tower, in the guy wires of the tower. When the wind is high the sea gets very rough. Along the north shore, it booms, the waves boom, they come up against the sides and it sounds like cannonading. On the south shore it's like a troop of very large trains going by, a steady roar. We can look out our window and see the spume over the top of the dunes, like sailing ships, one after the other, like a great white sail going by."

Mr. Bell was not much of a believer of ghosts on Sable. "If anything cannot be written down," he said, "it's not so." Mrs. Bell said that their house is supposed to be haunted still, "but we haven't yet met whoever is in the house. There have been reports before of knocking, walking around upstairs, feeling the weight of someone else's body on the bed when you sit on it. We haven't yet experienced that. It is really easy to explain too. If you would be out here in a storm and you heard the wind howling through the tower wire, well, anyone with imagination can see or hear anything they want. It's all in your mind, more or less. And if you walk in the fog, well anything in the fog looks much bigger. A horse would look like a giant."

"You see," Norman said, "we have a heavy fence around the house now to keep the horses out. We have nothing against the animals. In the winter on a stormy night, with a horse plastered with snow, his face covered with snow, and the horse looks through the window at you—it could be anything!"

Horses, little horses, roam the Sable dunes in herds. In the bitter months of winter they huddle together, rumps to the wind. In summer they can be seen grazing belly-deep in waves of rippling grass. They wander about the meadows and ponds and race along great stretches of lonely beach, free to split the wind.

The Spirit of Sable

18 *Ponies*

"The wild horses dot the landscape of Sable," wrote Arthur Silver in 1905, "and seem to give colour to the Grecian myth that whenever Neptune struck the earth with his trident, a horse appeared." A little family of six horses can be seen grazing not far from the Main Station. Partly hidden behind a tall dune, I skirt its base and keep low while a small black horse looks up to catch my movements. Almost prostrate in the grass to remain out of sight, the tall spires rise on either side of me like a wall, a vivid green against the blue sky. There can be heard the gentle susurration of the wind in the grasses. The rustle grows louder and suddenly the small black horse, a young mare, appears in front of me.

She moves closer, sniffing the air. The rest of the herd materializes. A little shy, they keep their distance. But the dusky black mare is daring and curious. She advances, nostrils quivering. I keep very still and talk to her in low tones. Brazenly she walks right up and begins to nuzzle me. Her soft nose travels up my legs, along my chest, and over my face. I can feel her warm breath whiffling my neck. Carefully, I raise myself to a full sitting position. The mare now nuzzles my hair and gives me an affectionate butt with her head. She continues to graze, pausing now and then to use my back as a scratching post for her forehead. By this time, the small herd has moved closer around me until I am surrounded. Ten years ago it was impossible to come any closer than fifty feet to the animals. Later, I learn this particular family always grazes close to the Main Station and is therefore more friendly than other herds. The group before me is one of forty to fifty family herds scattered over the island and consists of some young horses, one or two mares, and a lead stallion past his prime who seems content with this modest family.

I am more aware of the island sounds by now. The music and rhythms of Sable surround me: the faint thunder of the ocean on the far beaches, the whisper of dune grasses, and the sound of the animals cropping the more tender shoots. Autumn clouds sail over the dunes. The salt air is on my lips, the wild herbs give off their fragrance and the aroma of the horses is pungent and penetrating. Suddenly, I have the most extraordinary sensation as a strong bond of sensuality begins to grow between the animals and myself. My head begins to spin, time is no more, and it seems as though nothing else exists but the horses and myself on this lonely island—I am marooned! The sensation is brief, but delicious.

Turning to study the mare, I note that the shape of her head matches the description of the Sable Island horses by Daniel A. Welsh, who wrote his

Ph.D. thesis on the animals after observing them
on the island for a number of years. He noted that
some of the horses "most closely resemble the
Barb of North Africa with small, rounded, wide-
set ears that are slightly tipped inward, and have
fine muzzles and thin, curved nostrils. Roman
noses are common, although a few have finely
dished faces. Their hooves are small and round, but
often become overgrown in the soft sand."

The small family of horses that I am looking at
are coloured in different shades. There are some
bays, a palamino, and the black mare. A dark stripe
runs down the back of one horse and some are
known to have zebra–like stripes. I have no trouble
picking out the stallions. Although no longer
young, they have a certain majesty dressed in their
shaggy, royal manes, forelocks, and tail, the length
of which sometimes reaches down to the sand. The
mares have shorter forelocks and manes. A few
months ago the horses were sleek and gleaming.
Now, in mid-September, I can see signs of winter
coats. Foals in winter have an unusually dense coat
of two or three inches thick which covers the
whole body, giving them a strange woolly bear
appearance. The little mare gives me another playful nudge in the back. Turning, I gently touch her
nose and stroke her flanks. She whickers softly.
Where did this beauty come from, I wonder. Who
brought her ancestors to this desolate island, and
why?

Historical accounts do not give a clear picture of the origin of the Sable Island horse. There are many stories and different theories. Some historians claim that horses along with cattle were introduced by the Portuguese fishermen around the time of Sir Humphrey Gilbert's expedition in the late 1500s. Then there are the tales of the Spanish adventurers; the holds of ships navigated by the Spaniards always carried horses. Perhaps when some of the ships were caught in the sand traps of Sable, the surviving horses swam ashore. Other theories suggest that the horses were left behind on the island by the Marquis de la Roche in 1598 during his brief colonization of Sable, or by Baron de Léry in 1539, when he sailed from France with men, cattle, and horses. De Léry did not colonize Sable Island but when winter threatened he decided to return to France leaving vague reports that he abandoned the animals on the island to lighten the ship on the journey home. Finally, there is the possibility that the horses were first placed on the island by the Reverend Le Mercier when he took possession of Sable in 1739.

Of the theories put forth, two of them are worth examining. One is the Le Mercier account, currently favoured by some historians; the other is the de Léry expedition which has been carefully examined by the Port Royal historian Lescarbot, a highly regarded and much quoted person in French Canada today. Unfortunately, he recorded the

Sable events almost a century after they occurred, which could make his reports questionable, and according to the Reverend George Patterson's excellent account of Sable, the diligent historian Charlevoix makes no mention of a Baron de Léry, even though his chronological table of early voyages to America was meticulously prepared. Champlain also said nothing of de Léry and he too was a most scrupulous historian who accompanied Lescarbot to Port Royal.

In 1885, J. C. Taché published a book, *Les Sablons et L'îsle Saint Barnabe*, which offered a pro-French theory of the origin of the horses on Sable. Whether he arrived at the opinion that Baron de Léry left the horses there simply to favour his own countrymen, or whether he knew something about de Léry that is yet to be revealed, makes little difference. His contributions are interesting and rich, and his suggestion of a special name and mythology for the little horses is delightful. The following is my own rough translation of some passages from Taché's book:

Since the reign of Francois the First, the legitimate king of their ancestor's country, generation after generation of horses have galloped along Sable Island with their long, abundant manes floating in the wind. They guard the cliffs, feed on grass and wild peas and have witnessed many of the hardships and unhappy scenes that happened there.

Names are given to the bands of wild horses in other

countries: the horse that runs wild in the steppes of Russia is called the "Tarpan": "Alzades" or "Mustang" is the name given to the horses of the pampas of South America. Why not give a distinctive name to the wild horses of Sable? In which case, no other name would be more appropriate than the one derived from the noble baron who placed them on the Island. Let us call them "Léris." They are bold, strong, handsome and proud. But they are of a good breed these little horses! Cousins of our own imcomparable Acadian horse, and like them, they originated from Brittany: the land of granite, of buckwheat, of heather—blessed with crosses, calvaries and churches—land of faith for the human soul, of poetry for the spirit.

The Sable horses (or *Léris* as Taché called them) are not descendants of the large Breton horses of the Leonnais, Taché claimed, but of the smaller horses from the Brittany mountains. According to a French legend, Taché explains, this is a horse from the same breed as the one that helped the young master of *Merlin Barz* (Merlin the Bard) win the race and the hand of Eleanor, daughter of Budik, King of Amorique. The tale includes a folk song which a Mr. de La Villemarque translated roughly like this: "The young man prepared his little horse, he shod it, bridled it, and put a saddle on its back. He put a gold ring about his neck and tied a bright ribbon on its tail. He mounted the little red horse and rode to the fair. As the young man arrived the crowd was in a festive mood as it cheered on the different riders putting their horses through practice jumps. Then the trumpets sounded and an announcement was made.

"'The rider whose horse can jump over the barrier at full gallop in one straight and perfect jump, will win the hand of the King's daughter.'

"When it came to the young man's turn he whispered into the horse's ear: 'Remember, proud and handsome beast, if you jump the barrier, I win the hand of the beautiful Eleanor and you will become famous. Fly through the air!' At these words the little horse whinnied and pawed the turf impatiently. The young man gave spur and the horse charged ahead with eyes flashing and nostrils flaring. It galloped at full speed, made the jump and floated over the barrier with ease. The crowd cheered the young rider and his brave horse."

According to Taché, no one during those days in Brittany invited a guest without also inviting his horse. This charming custom, taken to Canada by the early French settlers, resulted in a sweet song entitled "Madelaine," with these words translated from the French:

There is bread at our home
There is bread at our home
For your little horse, there are oats
  Faluré dondaine
For your little horse, there are oats
  Faluré dondé.

Here the translated Taché observations of his *Léris* end, a brief but poetic excerpt from his fine little book on Sable.

When the Reverend Andrew Le Mercier advertised Sable for sale in 1753, he had already invested fourteen years' interest in the island. "When I took possession of the Island, there were no four-footed creatures upon it but a few foxes, some red and some black (some of which remain to this day). Now there are I suppose about 90 sheep, about 30 or 40 cows, tame and wild, 40 hogs, between 20 or 30 horses including colts, stallions and breeding mares." It would be tempting to wrap the origin of the Sable horse in a mantle of mystery, but Le Mercier's claim makes it quite clear that he could very well have been the first person to introduce horses on the island. It is possible, too, that there were horses which died off prior to Le Mercier's possession. But this is conjecture, and it may just be impossible to trace the true origins of the little Sable horses, often referred to as "ponies."

It is a known fact, however, that "ponies" the horses are not, for the average Sable horse weighs from five hundred to seven hundred pounds and stands as high as fourteen hands (four feet, eight inches). Very little literature existed on the behavior of the Sable horse, today one of the last free roaming horse populations in the world, until Dr. Welsh's in-depth study of the grazing mammals in the early 1970s. For a zoologist like Dr. Welsh, the study afforded an "unparalleled opportunity to study a group of large grazing animals that have, as an isolated community, reverted to a wild state."

The role and position of each member of the herd, writes Dr. Welsh, "is clearly defined and any horse which attempts to alter these roles is usually driven from or abandoned by the herd." It is surprising to learn that it is the mare with the highest seniority and not the stallion who makes most of the herd decisions. Her control over all the animals is absolute; only the stallion can question her authority. Consequently, he plays a passive role and simply follows behind, happy to graze and allow the mare to move the herd in any direction she wishes. The stallion quickly asserts his dominance, however, when other horses approach or threaten the herd. With head held high and tail arched, the stallion trots out to meet the stranger. Will they become warriors? So much depends on the status of the visitor, usually a bachelor, and his ability to steal a herd. Bachelors begin their training early. The young stallions are joyfully serious in their rehearsal for future attempts at mare-stealing, and the waterhole is as good a spot as any to begin.

Hidden by tall grass, I watch for activity around a waterhole. I am situated this time far from the Main Station where the horses are reluctant to approach strangers. The Sable horse has an uncanny ability to divine fresh water accurately, and once located, the horse simply paws a hole into the sand for a depth of a few feet until water wells up. As the lead mare and the herd take turns drinking, the stallion marks his authority with droppings on a communal dung heap.

I nibble at dried fruit and nuts and, to pass the time, scan the dunes with binoculars for movement. My lenses pick out two bachelors: yearlings, one light brown, the other dark. My heart leaps with them as they race along the sand, shoulder to shoulder, manes flying in the wind. A pattern begins to emerge; what I am seeing is a playful but earnest game of heel-kicking with hind legs, and boxing with front legs. Mares demand protection and in order to keep his mares a stallion is constantly demonstrating his ability to protect the herd. Thus, the waterhole becomes the arena for daily interactions between the herds and roaming bachelors.

As the yearlings gallop out of sight, charged with life and exuberance, I swing the binoculars around just in time to see a family slowly approaching the drinking area. A few stragglers have chosen to flop down for an ecstatic roll in a field of daisies. Soon they all arrive to drink deeply of the fresh water. Before long another family enters the drinking area. I keep my eyes on the stallion to see what will develop from this chance meeting between two established herds.

The stallions leave their respective herds and trot towards each other to stand shoulder to shoulder. There are communal manure piles here and there.

After much whinnying, head tossing, and pushing, the horses indulge in mutual manure pile sniffing and defecating. Again, they push shoulders and toss manes. For a moment there is a tense feeling that something will happen, but there is not going to be any fighting. I am watching a common, everyday ritual, a highly stylized dance. In this fashion, the stallions are simply marking temporary territories between their two herds. This behavior pattern allows the stallions to trot back to their herds with great dignity to show the mares their ability to maintain protection. I marvel at this demonstration of animal integrity.

I move from a prone into a kneeling position. The horses are unaware of my presence. The first family to arrive now abandons the waterhole and moves away to allow the visiting herd to quench its thirst. At this moment, three horses canter onto the scene. They slow to a trot, then a walk, and take measure of the herd, especially the mares. Trouble is in the air! These three are marauding bachelors who have banded together to steal mares. Now, they are prepared to meet the lead stallion in territorial displays or to separate a mare from one of the herds. One brash bachelor trots forward to meet the herd stallion only to quickly turn tail with the stallion in pursuit. Perhaps the young bachelor in this, his first real confrontation, was intimidated by the authority of the stallion. Another bachelor takes up the challenge and rushes forward. But he is moving too rapidly. The herd stallion has him

figured—the bachelor is trying to slip in directly among the mares. The stallion charges the bachelor and there is an exchange of boxing, bites, and long whinnies. The young horse retreats and runs off.

As the stallion is being distracted, the third bachelor cunningly moves in closer to a mare lagging behind the herd. He waits for just the right moment. Only a few yards separate him from the mare and he has not yet been seen by the stallion. Suddenly, the bachelor nips the flanks of the mare; they whirl around kicking up a shower of sand, and then canter away over the dunes. The leader, furious at this hoodwinking, lets out a cry and gives chase. With murder in his eyes he quickly closes the gap between himself and the runaways; his powerful jaws are already snapping at the head of the younger horse. Their shoulders collide. Framed against a blue sky atop a sandy cliff, manes and tails flying, the battle begins. Rearing up, both animals flail the air with their hooves. Both come down, circle briefly, and charge again. They clash in a fury of snorts and snapping teeth, striking each other murderously. The mare looks on while the warriors fight for her. The younger stallion begins to weaken. Moving in swiftly, the leader turns and kicks out his powerful hind legs and delivers blows that stagger the marauder. The young horse, not yet a match for the experienced leader, suddenly breaks and gallops away. The leader rounds up his mare and returns to the herd. He stops, turns, takes a final look around, shakes his mane, and tosses his

head. He is beautiful: a magnificent example of a wild stallion in his full splendour!

Hiking through the central valley which is, in season, adorned with wild roses, asters, lilies, whortleberries, and trailing vines of cranberries, I can see a number of different herds. The typical Sable Island horse is distinguishable from other horses, because it is small and chunky in stature and usually very dark-coloured with a long black mane, very much like the small black mare I first encountered. The horses of Boston, imported to Sable by Le Mercier in 1738, were a mixture of early Dutch, Barbs, and the English Blood horse. It is probable that more of the same stock was introduced by Thomas Hancock in 1760 and according to Dr. Welsh, it is safe to assume "that these early horses were of mixed oriental and occidental stock." Other larger horses on Sable are descendants of the many introductions of new blood into the herd since the beginning of the Humane Establishment in 1801. In many of his letters, Superintendent Bouteillier mentioned imported stock; one stallion was named Samson, another was called Flying Frenchman, and a third was christened Telephone.

I recall that someone has made a special project of studying the imported breeds. Barbara Christie of Halifax, a researcher and horse lover, carefully culled the Sable records and journals for references to the periodic new blood imported to the island. The first record of mainland horses sent to Sable in 1855 mentions that two stallions, one of unknown name and breed, the other a bloodbay called Retriever, were thoroughbreds owned by Charles Hill Wallace of Halifax. Between 1841 and 1843, Retriever ran the mile and the mile-and-a-half heats in the annual races on the mainland and was retired to stud in 1845. He was sent to Sable Island in 1854, introduced to the herds, and returned to Halifax three years later on the schooner *Daring*.

In 1828 approximately three hundred horses roamed Sable, and in 1864 there were about four hundred, divided into six herds. When J. R. Bouteillier arrived on the island in 1884, the horses numbered well over four hundred. He gelded or removed all "entries from the Island's West End, except those on which the operation could not be performed in consequence of the breed running out."

The career of one of the introduced stallions during Bouteillier's time, well-known on the English and Maritime racing grounds, was short-lived. The dark bay, Jack of Trumps, was turned loose with fourteen native mares one sunny morning in July, 1885. Two months later Jack of Trumps was in the position of defending his new harem against some older stallions who had travelled fourteen miles looking for mares. They came from the east end where fifty horses had been rounded up and shipped off to the mainland. The old warriors now wanted mares from the newcomer's herd. A savage conflict was waged but like most imported stallions, Jack of Trumps was no match for the island horses. He was found with an enormous hole in his neck and Bouteillier was forced to shoot him. Shaken by this event, the superintendent exercised stringent control over introduced stallions for the rest of his tenure. That same month Telephone, a young colt, arrived on the S.S. *Newfield*. Bouteillier broke him in and passed many happy hours trotting him in a sulky along the south beach. In 1895 Bouteillier reported that Telephone, "about 11 years old, has been doing good service and is in fine condition and is yet at large."

The Flying Frenchman arrived on Sable in 1892. Originally named Tom Thumb, he was fourteen and a half hands high. Chestnut in colour, he was the son of a splendid pacer from the banks of the St. Lawrence River in Québec. He had spent many years racing and doing the mile in under three minutes. In 1895 this horse was "thin in flesh and lame but not diseased in any way." This fine stud held his own until 1898 when old age and lameness made him victim to some younger island stallions.

Other importations included Black Hawk, Columbus, a fine young Canadian pony named Sable Prince, and Pretoria. A Clydesdale-Thoroughbred cross, Pretoria kicked apart Bouteillier's splendid acquisition, a spanking new buckboard. The horse was allowed to stay, however, and produced fine quality stock.

Bayard II, a three-year-old Belgian bay draft stallion, was imported to Sable in 1903. Unhappy when taken in for winter quarters, he injured himself by trying to break out of the stable to return to his mares. Let loose, he collected his family and they all presented themselves at the Main Station to be taken care of by Bouteillier. Bayard II was still listed as being on Sable in 1908. At that time there were just over two hundred horses divided into five herds, each named after the locality to which it became attached. Some of the names of the localities came from wrecked ships; the herds at that time were known respectively as the *Eliza*, *Greenhead*, *Milo*, *York*, and *Smoky Hut*.

One of the stock horses on Sable in 1931 was Colonel, a large hunter. Starlight, a twelve-hundred-pound stallion, was sent to Sable by the Nova Scotia Agricultural College during the Second World War years.

In Barbara Christie's opinion the old blood is reasserting itself now that the horses are "entirely independent of man and are breeding successfully by a process of natural selection. If some of the governors of Sable Island of the past could now revisit their (often beloved) domain, they would see a much larger percentage of the original type of horse among the grazing gangs."

Some of the Sable Island horse herds have definite grazing patterns that they observe as regularly as clockwork. Others wander gypsy-fashion seeking rich pasture in the central valley. Dr. Welsh maintains that the most important regulating factor in the life of the Sable horse is water. Even a herd with erratic grazing patterns will go to a waterhole every day except in the most bitter weather. Other factors which alter the routine patterns of the herds are fierce winds and storms, winter, and marauding bachelors. Although the Sable horse is a hardy animal which adapts easily to conditions, a long, hard winter leaves only the healthy and strong standing. Sable Island is a marginal environment, so the problem for the island horse is one of quality of food and not quantity. About half of the island is covered with vegetation and of this more than two-thirds is considered "prime foraging ground." To survive in the winter depends on the amount of fat an animal is able to store up during the summer and fall months. Survival problems are compounded by other factors such as infection, out-of-phase foaling (colts born in midwinter), and poor teeth.

The other day, on a journey around the island, our group passed three horses, two adults and a colt. One of the adults was stretched out in the sun, the other two stood close by. It was an idyllic scene and appeared natural enough at first. On our return, we again passed the three horses who were in the same position as before, one stretched out, the other two standing. Curious, we investigated. The two horses reluctantly moved away as we approached to discover the prone horse was a mare who had recently bloated up and died.

"Poor teeth," said Dr. McLaren. He explained how, with poor teeth, the mare had difficulty chewing and subsequently starved to death. I looked over at the retreating stallion and the grown colt. They had stopped and were looking back and I was struck by their melancholy attitudes; they were grieving for the mare.

Poor teeth, not enough food, and long, hard winters are natural causes of death for the Sable horse. The winter of 1891 was a particularly fierce one. "Between 75 and 100 horses died last spring," wrote Bouteillier, "from exposure and want of food." Frequent and violent gales covered the

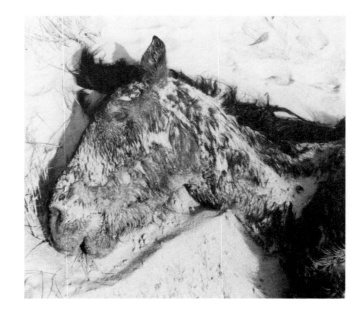

island grasses with sand and forced the sea water to spill into the ponds contaminating them with a heavy salt concentration. Because of the extreme shortage of food, the horses were consuming abnormal amounts of water resulting in severe debilitation. Superintendent Bouteillier designed what he called a "pony shelter" so the horses could be screened from the storms while they fed at hay ricks. But the superintendent discovered that any attempt to protect the animals by erecting shelters was met with suspicion by the stallions who simply demolished them by kicking them apart.

Almost seventy years later the same drama repeated itself when a series of violent storms ravaged Sable Island during the winter and spring of 1959. From Captain Williams' observations when he was superintendent of lights, it was the first time in thirty-four years that he had ever seen the island "turned into such a desert as it is at present." In spite of tons of hay dropped by the R.C.A.F. Search and Rescue Unit, almost 150 horses died during that cruel winter and spring; the animals would not eat food handled by human beings. Even though the weather had provided a terrible hardship on the horses and was partly responsible for the high death rate, the horses were simply going through a natural cycle, as do other wild animals.

The 1959 issue was an urgent one but became blown out of proportion through the media, mostly from the panic and ignorance of the condi-

tions of the Sable horse. After an investigation one official suggested a government ship be chartered to remove the animals, but cautiously pointed out that an attempt to remove two hundred horses by private enterprise in 1936 resulted in a high percentage of harm and injury to the animals. Another civil servant recommended a rather shocking solution. "Skilled riflemen from the Army," he wrote, "could be engaged to destroy as quickly and humanely as possible all but a few of the horses." This action would have brought on a huge outcry from animal lovers. Members of parliament from Nova Scotia suggested the Sable horse problem be approached "quite gingerly because people of Nova Scotia look upon the horses as an institution and would not wish to see them removed outright."

On October 1, 1959, the two hundred and fifty Sable horses were declared "surplus" by the Crown Assets Disposal Corporation in Ottawa. It is hard to believe that these fine animals, part of the heritage of Canada, had actually been declared surplus by the federal government, not once, but twice; the other incident was in 1948. It is just as distressing to learn that there were mercenary horse traders waiting for such opportunities and, indeed, they may have been applying pressure to their members of parliament to have the horses declared surplus.

Horse traders, ever since the American Revolution, have cast greedy eyes in the direction of Sable

Horses in corral.

Island. Governor Wentworth's 1800 report states that many of the horses were "wantonly shot by persons wintering on the Island;" the hides were taken to the mainland for sale. As early as 1803 the commissioners had requested a number of horses be caught and shipped to Halifax. This done, one horse went to Chief Commissioner Wallace, one to General Bowyer, and one to Governor Wentworth along with a small pony for his son. Later in the century, the exporting of Sable horses for private use and commercial sale became an important part of the Establishment duties on the island.

In 1936 a Mr. Huntley of Kentville, Nova Scotia, was authorized to remove one hundred horses to add to his stable; he paid $1.25 for each animal. That transaction fell through, but every time the horses were declared surplus, hundreds of letters arrived enquiring about purchasing the famous "ponies." Someone from Ste. Luce, Rimouski County, Québec, wanted to secure a carload of the horses. In 1949, a United Church missionary in Silver Water, Ontario, had heard of the "hardihood and gentleness of the Sable Island ponies" and wished to know what it would cost to bring a pair of them by way of rail. The Kentville horseman of 1936 would not let go of the matter. A voluminous correspondence on the subject continued right up to 1948 when the insistent demands of the horseman resulted in the horses being declared surplus and they were put up for sale; the Kentville horseman died in 1952 without removing them. The declaration of surplus was cancelled when it was learned that "livestock are most beneficial in encouraging vegetable growth."

By 1954 the number of horses rose to 280 and through all this the Sable horses enjoyed international press coverage as their fate hung in the balance. Despite threats of removal, only two horses left the island and that was in 1949 when the Kentville horseman gave them to a Sable radio operator and his wife. They tended the horses faithfully, and were anxious to take them to the mainland. The ponies were taken aboard the *Lady Laurier* for the trip.

"How utterly brutal!" was Isabel's reaction to Matthew Carney's description of the export of

Sable horses in the novel, *The Nymph and the Lamp*. "Ah, how can you be so callous! And why must they be sent away? They're perfectly happy here, aren't they?"

If the public had been aware of the terrible agonies that horses experienced during removal and transfer from Sable to the mainland, they would have raised an angry protest. Thomas Raddall's novel of Sable had not yet been published in the late forties. I heard a detailed and unforgettable account from the author himself.

Horse ready for transfer to surfboat.

"I was told," he recalled, "that in my book I had greatly exaggerated the horrors of removing the horses from Sable. But I kept a careful account in my diary, and photos of mine in the Dalhousie University Archives show the whole darn cruel business." Fifty or sixty horses were rounded up and driven into a corral that had been hidden in a ravine near the Main Station. A steamer was waiting a mile off Sable to take the horses aboard but the operation was often delayed because of dangerous surf. Sometimes the animals were corralled for two weeks without food. When it came time to move the horses, a Sable staffman slipped inside the corral and dropped a lasso over the head of one of the horses. The other end was fastened to a post near the corral gate. As soon as the horse felt the rope on its neck it jerked away and therefore tightened the rope. The horse would choke and sway on its feet. The staffman would leap forward, tie a rope to one of the forefeet, loosen the lasso, and lead the horse to the waiting surfboat.

The horse was then tripped with a rope and its legs lashed together. Six men rolled the animal over on a huge handbarrow and transferred it into the surfboat, which would take three horses piled one on top of the other, all with their legs lashed. The surfboat would be rowed or towed to the ship where the horses were hoisted upside down and lowered into the hold. Their lashings were cut and they were tied to stanchions, but the ship had no stalls and in rough weather the horses were badly shaken up "like dice in a cup."

On the mainland the animals were sold at auction for practically nothing. Often half the life would be beaten out of them just to tame them to the drudgery of pulling carts for poor whites and blacks from Preston (outside Halifax), who sold produce at the city markets. Raddall remembers seeing them in this condition and he used to come away feeling sick and angry. "I've never had any patience with these do-gooders who come along every fifteen years with the idea that Sable Island horses should be removed to the mainland where they'd be happier and all that nonsense. Like any other wild animal, the sick and the old die in the winters. I saw quite a number of dead horses in the spring I was there, and the result is the horse population stays stable. The island will support about three hundred horses. I have never hesitated to speak up whenever there is talk of removing the horses. The last proposal was made about twenty years ago and when the *New York Times* phoned me for an opinion about it, I told them it was a damned outrage."

The 1959 proposal to remove the horses was quashed. Animal lovers the world over, led by the Nova Scotia Society for the Prevention of Cruelty to Animals (S.P.C.A.), petitioned Prime Minister John Diefenbaker, asking for action to save the horses and allow them to remain on their island home. Diefenbaker's wise and instinctive feelings about wildlife on a remote island led to a cabinet decision on June 2, 1960. The prime minister, in a speech in the House of Commons, announced that the horses of Sable Island "and their progeny will not be removed but left unmolested to roam wild and free as has been their custom for centuries."

Today, the herd remains carefully protected and anyone visiting the island with the idea of feeding the animals or entertaining romantic thoughts of bareback riding along the beach, is in trouble. To molest, interfere with, feed, or otherwise have anything to do with the horses on Sable is an offence punishable by a fine of two hundred dollars, or two months in jail, or both. A new dimension has been added to Sable in that traces of gas and oil have been discovered beneath the sands. Guidelines, drawn up by governments and the oil companies, control the activity of men and their machinery on Sable in order to protect the terrain and vegetation which supports the horses.

The public, although often misinformed about the condition of the animals, has always displayed an intense interest in the Sable horse. Because of this, the S.P.C.A. with the cooperation of the provincial government, decided that two colts, Sandy and Sable, should be removed from the island and flown to the wildlife park in Shubenacadie, Nova Scotia. They were taken from different herds: Sandy, the female, was captured two miles east of the Main Station; Sable was taken from a herd that grazed three or four miles east of the west end of Lake Wallace. They were carefully placed aboard a Twin Otter aircraft, and with a veterinarian accom-

panying them, they arrived safely on the mainland; one was airlifted on June 19, 1973, the other the next day. The park, operated by the Provincial Department of Lands and Forests, is a well-maintained showplace of wild animals in as natural surroundings as is possible. Here, in their own paddock of five acres, Sandy and Sable have successfully adapted to their new and less hostile environment where they live on hay, vitamins, oats, and bran. Because of the much improved diet, they will grow larger than the island horses.

Sable was an island of sand, seals, birds, plants, and insects for many centuries until man imported horses and cattle. These latter animals have been harmful to the ecology of Sable, but the horses, although aliens in a natural and ecological sense, have become an essential part of the romantic image of the island.

In the very near future the question of the impact of the horses on the island's ecology will be raised. The opinion of almost every ecologist who has studied the situation is that "the horses are definitely responsible for much of the island's deterioration." The problem will probably be handled, not by removal, but by "fencing." Some of the most valuable parts of Sable need protection. Already there are a couple of experimental horse exclosures as part of a whole dune restoration scheme; probably the future will see permanent or periodic fencing off of parts of the island. "The consequence," in the opinion of Dr. McLaren,

"would be a new equilibrium between horses and environment that might be less damaging to Sable."

If the exclosures are not fully successful then it must be remembered that it was man who brought the horses onto Sable and man may, in the near future, remove some of them in order to protect the island. For Sable Island lovers this would perhaps be a painful thought since it is felt that the marram grass and the horses share an equal importance; they seem to be the very essence of Sable. Loss of either, or both, would gravely diminish the unique character of this fragment of ancient land.

Once more I visit the little family of horses near the Main Station. They are grazing high up on a dune overlooking the sea. From below, I call a greeting. Casually, heads are lifted. There is the dusky black mare! She ambles forward, chewing, and looks down on me for what seems an endless moment. I think of the long and rather peculiar relationship of interdependence between man and horse. The horse, a significant symbol in art and literature, is appealing because of its beauty, and its power. But its freedom is what appeals to many of us. The mare turns her head to scent the wind from the sea. Her long mane floats in the wind to flow in the direction of the waving grasses. She gives me one last look before she turns to join the other horses. As J. Taché wrote in his little book, "These wild horses are the poetry of the Island."

19 *Bestiary*

MOUNTED UPON HIS hardy poney, the solitary patrole starts upon his lonely way. He rides up the centre vallies, ever and anon mounting a grassey hill to look seaward; now he fords the shallow lake and ten minutes more he is holding hard to count the seals.

J. Gilpin on Sable, 1858

The old Ford tractor shudders into life under Dr. McLaren's persistent coaxing. Four of us position ourselves on the machine, Howard and Estelle up near the driver's seat, Al and myself at the rear. Then we rumble and roll over the great dessert on the south beach. We are off to patrol the east end of

Sable where large numbers of seal herds congregate. While in that area we will carry out a birdcount; birds of all descriptions dot the island in a profusion of colour and sound. Today, the ocean is grey-green. Yesterday when I had hiked along the south beach it was a startling veridian green that often comes with Indian summer.

It is easier to approach wildlife on wheels; the image of a man walking towards a wild creature is usually the danger signal for it to break and run. Yesterday, keeping this in mind, I waited until I spied seals near the shore and then, flat on the sand, I crawled slowly towards them. Carefully, I approached the small herd in this fashion, pulling myself by hand and pushing by digging toes into the sand so that I moved about a foot at a time, commando style. After fifteen minutes of this unnatural movement, I began to understand what a seal might feel like out of water. As I raised my head, I caught the glitter of waves and flash of gulls. Seals were lolling belly-up in the sand. Every now and then one would stretch its flippers, yawn, scratch its belly, and smack its lips, not unlike a human just before rising in the morning.

The heat of the sun was so comforting that I slipped off my shirt and lay soaking in the sun. Then inching forward, elbows chafing from the gritty sand, I advanced until the creatures were only forty feet away. I looked up to find myself staring into the dark liquid eyes of a small seal which had stopped scratching to gaze at me. Did I look anything like another seal, I wondered? Putting my head down, I moved forward again. When next I looked up, another seal was glaring at me suspiciously. The game was up. Soon I was too close and instinct gave them warning. Raising my head for the last time, I watched the seals scatter into the sea in that awkward, humping way they have. Soon they were splashing and frolicking in the water and turning to look at me, imps in the ocean. A remarkable sense of freedom pervaded my being. Affected by the sheer joy of their energy and the warmth of the autumn sun, I laughed like a crazy man, tore off the rest of my clothes, pulled off my boots, and ran naked into the waves to join the seals. Here these wonderful creatures, safe in their natural element, allowed me to get as close as fifteen feet. They kept swimming back and forth in a cocky fashion, just daring me to come further into the sea. But I had heard of dangerous currents and sharks. I waded back to shore, stretched out on the sand to dry off, and watched the bobbing heads in the water.

Though sporting in the rough sea, he loves the retirement of the tranquil lake, and quickly avails himself of any opening by the storms into its shallow bars. About the middle of May the new-born whelps are found sleeping on the sand, lumps of helpless fat in the smoothest velvet coats, with large black plaintive eyes. These little sea-babes do little upon land but snarl and flop from side to side, but the moment they reach the water they dive and directly re-appear, holding hard with their tiny flippers upon their mother's back, who goes off rejoicing in her load after swimming up and down in restless circles, whilst you tease her baby on the beach.

J. GILPIN

These are harbour or common seals which gather on the beaches, mostly on the south side well away from the other species, the grey seal, which predominates at the east tip of the island. The largest concentration of harbour seals in Eastern Canada is found on Sable. Elegant and sleek little mammals, they gather in groups of a half-dozen to sixty in number, averaging about thirty to a group. From early April to late July they chase each other in and out of the ocean, seeking mates.

J. Gilpin was the first to officially record observations of the seals on Sable. A natural history of Sable written by J. E. Erskine in 1952 listed several species of mammals including common porpoises and harbour seals. In the early sixties Dr. Arthur Mansfield, with Dr. H. Fisher and T. R. Welch, flew to Sable to investigate and estimate the harbour seal population. Recent studies show that in June of each year about four hundred seals are born. Of this number, eighty percent live through the first summer to join the stable population of fifteen hundred harbour seals that live on Sable for the entire year.

"In two or three months," wrote Gilpin, "the pups have attained to three or four feet and fifty or sixty pounds weight and snore the livelong day, and are overtaken and mercilessly clubbed for their skins and oil." Captain James Farquhar, who spent many years on Sable during and after Superintendent McKenna's tenure, won many tenders for sealing privileges on the island. Often, he and a crew would sail to Sable where, working from their boat or the beach, they would catch and kill as many seals as possible. Their haul for the season of 1895 was over a thousand skins and about nine hundred gallons of seal oil. "Around Sable," Farquhar wrote in a letter to Ottawa requesting further sealing privileges, "are found swarms of seals at present of no benefit to anyone and which feed upon and consume enormous quantities of cod and other valuable fish. A few years ago the State of Maine, realizing the great damage done to its cod fishing by the seals in the waters of that State offered a bounty to encourage the destruction of seals."

For many years the harbour seal was killed for bounty because of its supposed role in fish consumption, transmission of codworm, and damage to fishing gear. But new research, by Jean Boulva and Dr. McLaren, proves that the most common items eaten by harbour seals are herrings, flounder, and alewife, sometimes "swallowed whole, bitten in mouthfuls, or swallowed without head and tail." Small fish are swallowed beneath the water, but it has been discovered that seals bring a large fish to the surface where it is eaten piecemeal while held by the seal's foreflippers. They eat but one meal per day and have little impact on fish stocks. Today, the harbour seals are safe from the bounty hunters. Located far from fishing grounds, the island is a sanctuary for all mammals.

Sun-dried from my ocean plunge with the seals, I dressed and began my journey back to the A-frame. Before me the vast flat of sand on the south beach presented an endless brown-grey surface, rippled and shaped by the wind. Here and there I picked up patterned seashells, flung up on the beach during a storm, fragmented like broken china. About shellfish, Gilpin wrote that "I am not Conchologist enough to classify the various Shells and Shell Fish. The large Scallops, Beach Clam, and Razorshells are the most striking varieties. Lobsters and Crabs abound, and some parts of the lake are almost floored by large and pleasant flavoured clams."

There are other "treasures." Some coconuts, an opaque sand-blasted bottle, and "Devil's purse" (skate's egg cases), litter the shore. A rare find on Sable is the elegant argonaut shell, *Argonauta argo*. Delicately and beautifully sculptured, this light shell with its dark brown ridge is brought in from the eddies of the Gulf Stream.

As I strolled across this mini-desert, I passed three sand cliffs all in a row, separated slightly, and strangely isolated out on the sand flats. Further on I could see to the south how the sand meets the strip of deep blue sea. The horizon was another shade of blue and somehow the light sand and white clouds seemed to reflect a blush of pink. Looking east, I saw a perfect mirage. The three dunes I had passed appeared to be suspended above water, shimmering in mid-air. This wonderful illusion, which has the magic of a Magritte painting, is not an unusual one but for some reason it seemed all the more mysterious on Sable Island. Sometimes the effect on the viewer is a feeling that he is surrounded by water. For one historian who visited Sable in the 1850s, the sense of loneliness it created was "oppressive in the extreme for a moment or two."

We are now approaching the east spit of Sable; a tractor full of people lumbering and rolling towards hundreds upon hundreds of grey and harbour seals. Here, the island narrows down to just a finger of sand. Bearing down on them this distance away, the seals take on the illusory appearance of rounded rocks.

There they lie, old ocean flocks, resting their wave-tossed limbs; great ocean bulls, and cows, and calves. The rider marks them all. The wary old male turns his broad moustached nostrils to the tainted gale of man and horse sweeping down upon them, and the whole herd are simultaneously lumbering a retreat. And now he goes, plying his little short whip, charging the whole herd to cut off their retreat for the pleasure and fun of galloping in and over and amongst fifty great bodies, rolling and tumbling and tossing, and splashing the surf

in their awkward endeavours to escape. Let no man envy his fun, bred of well-fed man and high conditioned nag; many and many a bitter ride amply atones for it.

J. GILPIN

The approach by tractor is less disturbing, it seems, than a galloping horse. They are relatively tame, only a few begin to flop and slither towards the ocean. They are gradually becoming used to curious visitors, most of whom are biologists who recently have been keeping close tabs on the creatures. The island is the only spot in the world where so many mammals and birds leave a record of their movements which can be easily followed in the sand; for this reason Sable has become a working playground for biologists.

Dr. Henry James of Dalhousie University, Department of Psychology, established the A-frame as a field station to serve as a base for observing the social behavior of seals. Recordings were made of the spontaneous crossings of seals from sea-to-lake and lake-to-sea. Biologists then attempted to disorient some seals after capturing them and displacing them. This was done by releasing them at inland sites where seals have never been observed. Most displaced seals returned to the sea or directed themselves to reach the lake. No seals were lost during this experiment.

The field station for seal observations was at one time equipped with a rudimentary physiology laboratory which provided an opportunity to study the dive reflex of harbour seals. One summer a Smithsonian Institution biologist recorded the behavior of mother seals and their pups from their birth to several weeks of age. During her stay, the biologist was followed about by an amorous male seal that went so far as to make overtures to her.

We now greet the grey seal herds on the very east end of Sable. Dr. McLaren, Howard, and Estelle already have binoculars at the ready to catch a glimpse of the increasingly rare Roseate Tern. Dr. McLaren is using a tripod to steady his telescope. Al is moving close to the seals, camera whirring constantly. There are large colonies of grey seals at the east tip. Largest and rarest of all Canadian seals, these seals are easily distinguished from the harbour seals by their uniformly dark grey colour.

Gilpin wrote that "Sometimes in January but more often in February, a herd of several hundred large seals made their appearance upon the N. East bar, where they remain if undisturbed the whole summer, they and their little ones—for they usually whelp in early spring. They are called characteristically enough, by the patrolmen, ocean bulls. I saw them there in June of 1854, but had none of them in hand. By galloping down upon their line of retreat, I was enabled to close upon them as they shouldered or hummocked themselves into the sea."

Zoe Lucas, who began working on Sable Island with the Dalhousie seal research group in 1974, gave the following impressions of grey seals during breeding season:

Thousands of grey seals gather on the east end of Sable and move on to the beaches and dunes to mate and give birth to their white-coat pups. There were approximately 3,800 pups born this winter (1980). The males lie about on the sand, roll over slowly, and eye each other. Occasionally they utter challenges and warnings and issue a few reprimands to others who have come too close. The females nurse and guard their pups and then suffer the approaches of the large scrappy unhandsome but amorous males. When the winds carry sand, snow, and sleet almost horizontally across the east end landscape, the seals just close their crusted eyes and perhaps contemplate existance from inside the rolls of hair, skin, and blubber that encase them.

Most memorable about days spent in the seal colony are the sounds of the seals. The seals yodel, snarl, hiss, and bark, depending upon whether their ill-temper is directed towards another seal, seal-tagger, or photographer. The yodelling contributes to the primeval tone of the landscape.

According to the *Field Guide to European Mammals*, the grey seal's voice is a "loud, long-drawn-out, two or three syllabled, hah-eehou."

At the very end of the exposed east tip of Sable, breakers roll in from each side, meet in the middle, and slap together with tremendous force sending up great plumes of white surf. I go out as far as I dare, thinking of a short story by Eric Linklater. It is about a young, engaged woman who accidently meets a strange man wearing sealskin trousers. Somewhere among the Western Isles of Scotland, he has been able to change himself from human form to seal. During their brief meeting he kisses her, and, holding her in his arms, leaps off the high cliff into the green ocean far below. In the end, both of them return to the cliff as seals, happily swimming and singing in the sea near her fiancé, who eventually goes mad from his loss and loneliness. It is an unforgettable love story, and standing here at what seems the end of the world, I wonder if anyone through these centuries on Sable had such a mystical experience as invented in that story. Perhaps the grey seals here, through metamorphosis, became the singing sirens that beckoned ships, passengers, and sailors to disaster. In some of the legendary tales, a man or woman is enticed into the sea to drown and live happily ever "waterward," with a new-found love.

An hour later we are up on a dune top, four of us fanned out in a line, fifty feet apart, clapping hands and making "shooshing" noises as we advance through the thick grass. This strange behavior on our part is simply a successful method of flushing birds to the far end of the dune plateau to carry out a count. The ones that fly away are counted, and the ones that soar back over our heads are carefully noted.

Most of the birds nest close to the sand and are almost invisible while others can be seen flitting about in the low bushes. From an ornithologist's point of view, Sable Island is one of the most interesting places in the world. There are sea birds and land birds, marsh birds and coastal birds. Some seem to drop out of the sky to take up a lengthy residence. Others of a tropical variety are often flung by hurricane winds up on the beaches and meadows, exotic visitors from another world.

Our "shooshing" noise and hand clapping is

repeated; a cloud of birds rises out of the foliage in a rush of wings. There goes an ovenbird! A Louisiana waterthursh, a southern stray, flys by. A bank swallow shoots to the other end of the dune like an arrow. Several Ipswich sparrows change direction and fly back over our heads—one, two, three, four of them.

These white-breasted, pale brown-flecked sparrows are friendly and often perch on the dead yarrow stalk or sit on poles and fence posts around the houses. The visit of Dr. Jonathan Dwight, Jr., in 1894, confirmed that Sable Island was the only breeding place of this cousin of the savannah sparrow. The Ipswich sparrow, lately designated as a subspecies, *Passerculus sandwichensis princeps*, has been the object of considerable attention and affection for amateur and professional ornithologists. Dr. McLaren has been observing these little birds for many years and has co-authored a complete study of them. The bird counts, like the one today, have been carried out by Dr. McLaren ever since his first visit to Sable in 1967. His student, Howard Ross, has also been observing the Ipswich sparrow for a number of summers and completed his Ph.D. on this species.

"The Ipswich sparrow," writes Dr. McLaren, "can be cherished as a unique kind of bird, with many interesting and special qualities. It is a robust, adaptive bird, slightly larger than the savannah sparrow, with a reproductive vigour almost unmatched among small birds. Polygamy is com-

monplace in the Ipswich sparrow as it is with a number of North American birds." The pale hues of the bird clearly fit its environment. Its cryptic behavior in winter has been described by J. P. Hailiman in 1958: "Protectively coloured, a motionless bird is very difficult to find, and it was noticed that the birds never stop on the light areas of sandy

Ipswich sparrow.

ground, but run over them, stopping only on the darker areas. This appears to be a remarkable trait associated strongly with protective colouration, for one individual repeated the behavior almost a dozen times when pursued by the observer."

By late April the bird arrives on Sable from its southern habitat, coming in during or shortly after periods of westerly and relatively light winds. (Birds leaving the Cape Cod region are often harbingers of "good weather" for the Maritimes.) Observations of the Ipswich sparrow on Sable during spring, summer and fall, were made near the West Light, the same vicinity where Norman and Christel Bell lived for some years. Christel's recordings of bird activity were passed on to Dr. McLaren. The West Light area is composed of small dense clumps of shrubs. Bayberry, the most abundant shrub, provides a low but thick cover for the nesting sparrows. Strawberries and blueberries are important food for these birds.

In the early morning the males seek territories. The more experienced birds generally reclaim their old areas while newcomers gain unoccupied spaces. After finding a mate, the male announces his ownership by perching conspicuously and singing frequently. Their song, according to the study published by Drs. McLaren and Stobo, "was described by Dwight (1895) as a 'more polished and tuneful effort' and 'keyed a little lower,' compared with that of the savannah sparrow. Our impression is that songs of the Ipswich sparrows

are louder and lower pitched, perhaps related to the large average size of the singer, but we doubt that they differ in structure from some of the many variants given by savannah sparrows."

Ipswich, Massachusetts, is where the first described specimen of the sparrow was taken and where it often stays for the winter. During the cold months it is also known to take up residence in the states of New Jersey, New York, and Maryland, and in Halifax County, Nova Scotia. Some of the birds attempt to spend the winter on Sable and the loss is heavy. In their study, Drs. McLaren and Stobo have shown that the Ipswich sparrow suffers heavy mortality on its winter range on the United States east coast. The winter peak of abundance is at a latitude where there are numerous roadless and uninhabited islands off the coast of Virginia. "We hope," they write, "that the needs of the Ipswich sparrow can be considered in any future developments of these islands. Also, the long-term preservation of this bird will depend on repair and maintenance of its Sable habitat. Although the Ipswich sparrow is in no immediate danger of extinction, its longer-term survival is clearly in the hands of man."

Other breeding birds on the island include five species of duck, the most common being the black duck which nests around the ponds of Sable. On the long miles of beach I have seen the sandpiper running about and feeding. The soft, rather musical chuckle of the dark-backed semipalmated

Red-breasted mergansers, also known as "fish ducks."

plover can be heard along the beaches and salt marshes. This shorebird has the typical plover habit of running along the sand for several paces, then stopping abruptly and raising its head. The largest Canadian population of the roseate tern, white birds with a black cap and very pale gray back and wings, are found on Sable; there are colonies of about thirteen hundred pairs. Because the roseate tern is the least abundant east coast species,

Sable is important in maintaining the Nova Scotia population. Terns, thought to be the most vulnerable bird species on Sable, are suffering setbacks on the entire east coast.

Southwest of the Main Station are the nesting areas of the great black-backed gulls, herring gulls and terns. This is September; June and July are critical periods for disturbing their grounds. The approximate population is about fourteen hundred black-backed and three thousand herring gulls.

The sons of Superintendent Bouteillier regularly sent out lists of migrant birds to the Nova Scotia Museum at the turn of the century and some of these were published in the journal, *Ottawa Field-Naturalist*. These accounts have been added to in recent years, beginning with Erskine's ecological survey in 1952. Among the birds recorded on the island are the manx shearwater, the European storm petrel, the yellow-headed blackbird, the stilt sandpiper, and the cave swallow. Many birds found on Sable have not been observed anywhere else in Nova Scotia, Canada, or even North America.

Both breed in numbers, the Black Duck on the grassy tufts about the ponds, and the Shelldrake on the high sand cliffs or about old wrecks. Ring Neck, and Peeps were breeding in numbers, and towards the end of May the Terns or mackerel Gulls of several species arrived, and the bars were soon covered by their eggs, and presently their creeping young. Their eggs are collected by the bucketfull, and though small were well-flavoured. A little brown Sparrow also summered and wintered there. A few Hawks, a Robin or two, a wild Pidgeon Plover, and Shear-Waters are flung ashore in dozens after every gale.

J. GILPIN

Birds flushed and counted, we climb back on the tractor and head towards the weather station near the west end. I reflect on the many changes man has brought about on Sable through the introduction of animals foreign to her sands. The initial introduction of pigs was so successful that the animals broke out of pens to dig up the landscape and root like ghouls amongst the human corpses washed ashore from shipwrecks. Then there were the rabbits. Gilpin explains where they came from: "The Island owes the introduction of the common or Spanish rabbit, to the Honourable Michael Wallace. The rabbit finds the loose sands very fit for his long burrows, and rears his prolific brood and frisks among the high grass and affords many a fresh dinner when salt junk is plenty and fresh beef scarce, as well as exciting that love for sport natural to all; for I have known sailors just landing with their lives, and hardly dry, yet unable to resist running down a rabbit!"

Rabbits multiplied so quickly on Sable that they reached plague proportions. The situation took on tones of grim humour as cats were imported to get rid of the rabbits, foxes were brought in to kill the cats, and man had to resort to shotguns to eliminate the foxes. Superintendent Darby's journal of 1827 mentions sightings of the snowy owl which preyed on the rabbits. It visited the island often, sometimes bringing friends and, as Gilpin noted, it was curious to see this powerful bird "furred and feathered for a polar campaign" yet putting up with the hot August sun as it watched the rabbit burrows, a fondness for game "being too strong for his northern instinct." Eventually, rabbits vanished from the island.

We arrive at the Main Station where, on foot, I keep heading in a westerly direction. At the ponds near the West Light, there is a man clad in Indian summer colours: terra cotta cords, green shirt and brown jacket. His hair is light brown tinged with red. His whole persona seems to heighten the feeling and colour of autumn as he crouches to examine something among the greens and tawny browns of the grasses. Soft spoken, sure of himself, he tells me he is Barry Wright from the Nova Scotia Museum and he is on Sable to collect insect fauna. Already a dozen or more museum drawers have been filled with specimens of insects, labelled and under glass, and these will be sent to the National Museum in Ottawa and the Smithsonian Institution for viewing; this includes some new species that are found only on Sable. Barry invites me to join him on his "rounds" and I ask him about the first botanist on Sable.

"That would be John Macoun," Barry said. "He was working with the geological survey in Ottawa and he landed here in July of 1899. He studied the flora and made notes on terrain and fauna." Barry stops to pluck something from the grass and we continue on. "Later, in 1913, two botanists, Harold St. John and R. W. Glaser of Harvard University visited Sable for specimens of which duplicates were forwarded to Professor Macoun for permanent deposit in the Natural History Collection at Ottawa."

All visitors on Sable Island during Bouteillier's time made entries in a visitor's book. John Macoun's was a long one but one paragraph addressed to the superintendent's children is worth repeating: "To the young people I may, as a teacher, say go on as you are doing, observing and thinking and although shut out from the world and its vanities and follies you are not shut out from nature which, if taken aright, is the best teacher and the one that when accepted as a guide gives the purest happiness."

"Look at this," says Barry. We stop and he shows me a little creature. "This is a cutworm, in moth form and is closely related to one that occurs on mainland Nova Scotia but looks nothing like it. The markings on this moth are different and distinguish it immediately from mainland moths. You can see the brown bands going across the forewing, although in all other respects it is identical to the mainland ones."

Barry is working with invertebrate forms on Sable; animals without backbones like insects, spiders, worms, and snails. The information he gathers will be published by the Nova Scotia Museum and will cover sponges, worms, three different kinds of leeches, mollusks (snails, slugs and clams), pond plankton, isapods (cellar bugs, water bugs), amphipods (sand fleas), shrimps, insects (including fleas and lice, beetles, moths, butterflies, wasps, flies), centipedes, millipedes, and spiders. In all, the report will include more than seven hundred different kinds of insects and invertebrates, some of which can be found only on Sable. "What it will be," Barry explains as we continue walking, "is a basic reference for future change on Sable Island. I am listing what is there now and and in the future other people might come along and find that things have changed. They will be able to go back and say, well, such and such a thing used to be common on the island but it is not there anymore so that must be the result of some sort of change."

We sit down for a moment on a patch of marram grass while Barry opens a small package and takes out a specimen. "This is the white marked tussock moth and the tussocks refer to the pencils of hairs on the back of the caterpillar, which look like tussocks and they have four of them. The females are wingless and can't fly. Over the years on Sable this form of moth has developed quite distinct from the mainland form. The feeling is, these moths had been on the mainland prior to the Ice Age. With the ice moving south over the mainland, the moths moved out ahead of the ice on to the Grand Banks, the fishing banks, which were exposed. When the

ice retreated the moths didn't follow the ice back. They stayed and the only remaining part of the banks that remained was Sable Island. So that form of moth is still here." Barry slips the tussock moth gently back into its container as we get up and resume our walk. "A lot of moths on Sable are strays," he explains. "For instance, the red under-wing moth flies out from the mainland of Nova Scotia. It feeds on trees but there are no trees on Sable."

In 1901, as part of an experiment by the federal government, almost one hundred thousand trees were planted on the island. This was the enterpris-ing idea of Colonel Gordeau, deputy minister of Marine and Fisheries. It was his belief that because a large tract of land was redeemed by planting pines on the coast of Brittany in France, a similar scheme would benefit Sable. The conditions on Brittany, he wrote in his report, "are about the same on Sable Island." He was in error, for the coast of Brittany is mild in temperament compared to the damaging winds and storms on Sable.

Nevertheless, plans were approved for the plan-tation and seedlings. Twenty-five species of ever-greens and eighty species of trees and shrubs from northern France, were packed and shipped to Sable. After the planting, two huge ornate posts were sunk into the sand to officially mark the gate-way to the grand "Gordeau Park." The posts were still standing, almost covered by sand, nineteen years later when Tom Raddall arrived on Sable. It

became a customary prank to send newly-arrived wireless operators to view "Gordeau Park" in all its green splendour; the joke was that there were no trees to be seen, just the tops of the gate posts. The tree-growing experiment was not successful, for Sable was not kind to the seedlings. Incessant winds, drought, and frequent sand storms destroyed most of the trees that had been planted. The saplings had trouble surviving the salt spray and winter gales. Horses stripped the bark and used the little trees as scratching posts for their heads.

Nothing was ever heard again of Gourdeau on the subject of planting trees. The last word, how-ever, came from a scientist who in 1952 discovered one fifteen-inch shrub of buckthorn and a maple tree which has remained permanently stunted, spread very low to the ground—both remnants of the 1901 planting. Scotch heather, introduced on Sable in 1901, can still be found on the island. Rugosa rose bushes, planted by Bouteillier at the turn of the century, can be found still flourishing at the old Main Station site. *Rosa Virginiana* grows in the horse exclosures and other parts of the island.

The breeze brings up the scent of sweet grass from the grass and sedge meadows where moths flutter, luminous in the afternoon sun. Barry and I pass clusters of centaury, *Centaurium umbellatum*, nestled in wet dune hollows near the ponds. Suited only to sandy soil, it has fleshy leaves and a small rose-pink blossom that gives off a fragrance of fresh tea. Common in Europe, centaury is hardly

known in North America. J. S. Erskine, on his visits to Sable in 1952-53, suggests that the plant was "probably introduced in the ballast of wrecked ships." In Europe it is sometimes used to brew a tea said to be good for indigestion; on Sable it helps to bind the sand and is not eaten by the horses. Evening primroses can be found around the open dunes. The low flat areas near the brackish ponds that we pass are thick with cranberries, marsh arrow grass, and bog club moss. Here is where I now discover an exquisite miniature pink orchid.

It is late afternoon as we return to the Main Station. Barry describes a whale skeleton he found on Sable which is in the Nova Scotia Museum. Before he leaves he tells me of a large whale, still alive, that recently washed up on the north beach after a storm about a mile from the Main Station. I decide to investigate. The sun vanishes briefly under a gray cloud and I feel a slight chill. I have never been close to a living whale. I have seen their rotting hulks here on Sable and have watched them out at sea spouting their fountains. Now, as I come down an enormous sand culvert between two dune cliffs, I can see a dark form on the beach.

There Leviathan,
Hugest of living creatures, on the deep
Stretched like a promontory sleeps or swims,
And seems a moving land, and at his gills
Draws in, and at his breath spouts
out a sea.

MILTON, *Paradise Lost*

At least thirty feet in length, the pilot whale (actually a large dolphin which usually lives in warm, temperate seas) has been thrown by the force of the waves to remain lodged on its side in the sand, parallel to the shore. There appears to be no movement from the black mammal as seagulls strut back and forth on top of it, taking the measure of their find. As I draw closer the gulls scream and flap away. The whale seems to be alive as the bulbous forehead and triangular dorsal fin quiver; the huge body inflates, shudders, to suck in air. I look into the one exposed eye. With horror I see the socket is empty and red; the gulls have already begun their bloody work. Blood runs from a large split in the whale's stomach. This poor creature will swim no more and soon will enter its final sleep. So incredibly graceful in its liquid world beneath the ocean, this large being is now trapped to spill its life on the alien sands. In pain, spent from the terrible efforts to exhale air through its blow hole, the dark hulk shudders once again.

Kneeling beside the creature I try to cradle its nose in my arms. Lest it think my hands are tor-menting gulls, I stroke this huge dolphin as broadly as I can. What can be done? I decide to tell Dr. McLaren about the suffering to see if he will ask the officer-in-charge of the station to use a gun and end its misery. I leave this unhappy scene with great sadness.

Looking out to sea, I can make out what seems to be a giant ship advancing, coming over the horizon towards Sable. By narrowing my eyes the form takes the shape of an old-fashioned three-masted vessel from another century long ago. My romantic vision is self-induced. This steel four-legged monster comes not out of the past, but like a dark shadow the oil rig emerges from the present to adumbrate what is to come.

Thinking back to the suffering whale, I choose to hurry along the north beach and head east when I see the high wall of dunes standing out in relief in the soft light of the late afternoon sun. The west wind blows over the dunes bending the marram grass towards the ocean, then rushes out to the crested rollers at sea. Waves that began hundreds of miles away turn into breakers that rush towards the shore to cut into the dune walls. Everywhere, the unceasing ocean throws itself against the rocks, sands, and cliffs of the world; the sea challenges the land, the land tries to hold out. The continual force is relentless. For centuries this elemental drama has taken place on the island—the ocean versus Sable. Can this struggle go on forever?

THERE IS A prenatural shifting of scenes after every violent storm. Sandy hillocks fifty feet high, that have been landmarks for a generation, have tumbled into the sea; mountains of sand are piled today where yesterday the ground was level as a floor. Old wrecks, long buried, come forth to view. Scores of human skeletons are unearthed. Acres of land have disappeared beneath the sea, and old inlets are filled up, and hidden treasures revealed. Since 1820 five or six miles of the west of the Island have been submerged, and the ocean now rolls fathoms deep where the Superintendent's house formerly stood, and three miles out to sea. No secure anchorage in this world's haven has the heroic little community established here to rescue life and property.

Harper's Magazine, 1866

Sable can continue to exist only if the marram grass continues to grow in abundance. This is the most important plant on Sable and if it were killed most of the dunes would vanish into the air and the sea. Because of its enormously long fibrous roots, the marram grass plant can bury itself deep in the moist core of the sand where the roots intertwine to literally hold the sands together. Marram grass, in effect, is the anchor of Sable Island.

The tiny community that bunks at the A-frame each summer concentrates on repairing damage to the vegetated dune system. Scavengers, they comb Sable for debris: empty oil drums, corrugated tin sheets from an old government building, timber from a superintendent's decrepit house on the verge of collapse. This material is recycled for the construction of dykes at strategic points on the island.

Zoe Lucas is in charge of the restoration program on Sable that began in 1975 and she was appointed to carry on the work in 1976. An enchantingly vivacious young woman, small and

Zoe Lucas.

very pretty, Zoe combines quiet enthusiasm for her work with the cool detachment of the dedicated scientist. She was very animated when we chatted about her work on Sable.

"In 1976," she explained, "we began by building large debris dykes that would reduce salt-water washover into the fresh-water island ponds. By 1977 a great deal of sand had accumulated at the dyke and washover had been reduced. In 1979 we carried out a scheme of snowfencing and transplanting grasses in order to initiate the development of new dunes landward, on the older deteriorating south beach dune line."

Marram grass, as explained by Zoe in her own words, is also known as American beach grass and is the dominant vegetation on the dunes. It can capture and hold the sand, and given the right conditions, it will build dunes. It thrives in accumulating sand and begins to languish for lack of nutrients in areas where accumulation ceases. Where wind gets the better of it and sweeps the sand away, the marram is sparse and dull with exposed roots and rhizomes. But even then, small tips of green emerge from the battered and dry remains of previous growth. Marram seems to be a survivor. Bits and pieces of stems and rhizomes washed or blown into drift lines on the beach, or caught up amongst the flotsam and jetsam, will take root and grow into new plants, and then occasionally into new dunes. In many of the work sites where snowfences and dykes have been successful

Marram grass.

in preventing continued wind or water-caused erosion, transplanting is used to stabilize the area. Frequently these areas are too large to expect natural recolonization to occur soon enough. In other cases, the marram is used, rather than fences, to initiate the development of new dunes.

Exposed roots of marram grass.

"Such dunes," said Zoe, "become vegetated as they grow. Transplanting marram grass is a labour-intensive and sometimes tedious operation. The plants are collected from the well-vegetated dunes adjacent to the transplanting sites and are individually planted by hand into holes dug deep

into the damp sand. When the sun shines, it is warm for us, but the marram is in danger of drying out and must be carried and kept in buckets of water or wet cloths. Then too, the surface sand is dry and flows into the holes, in and around the delicate roots. But in the wet and foggy weather, when clouds and grey skies make the work less pleasant and the days long and cold for the crew, the cool wet sand welcomes the marram.

"Occasionally there is the fine sensation that tingles in the palms of the hands when the marram grass is placed down into the hole, and the fingers almost peel away from the moist stems and roots. The sand is pressed around the plant, the sand becoming familiar; the marram and the sand and the damp coolness settling down to a new cycle, a marriage of elements that might hold a dune or even build a dune if the marriage survives."

The horses, Zoe explains, are an extension of the contract between elements, as are the sparrows, terns, june beetles, cranberries, and so on. The horses wander about the dunes, grazing on marram mostly, but also nibbling the other vegetation such as fescue, rose, beach pea, and sandwort.

"It is startling to watch the horses die," she says. "Sometimes it is almost as startling to come upon a singular patch of tall verdant marram, lush and brilliant, at the base of the dune, or out on the sparsely vegetated undulating hills, and there in the middle of it discover a pile of white bones, empty skin and scattered curls of hair where a horse once was and then died, perhaps of winter, perhaps of age, or disease, or ill-timed pregnancy. But whatever the reason, died and finally returned to the sand and returned to the grasses. There might be a couple of horses grazing nearby, absorbing the energies of sunshine and organic matter as gathered up and reprocessed by the grasses."

The cycles seem to be manifest in almost every instance and every occasion, and though they can sometimes be somewhat shocking, they are not obtrusive.

"The sand slips down the sides of the dunes, the grasses thrive around the remains of a starved horse, and sometimes the flow is more of a jolt; the gulls depredate the nests of terns and ducks, and harbour seal pups are a sudden meal for a shark."

Zoe has been interviewed a number of times on film about her dune restoration work. No one else connected with the island—scientists, technicians, or others—seems able to evoke the spirit of Sable quite like her; listening to her I discover, as I did about Sable, a bewitching quality. There is no attempt to romanticize Sable for her perception of the island stems from her very personal relationships with its elements, and whatever feelings she has come from deep within her. It is as though she holds out her hands over the island grasses and sands, as over a flame; she can feel the strength of Sable, this strength sustains her and she gives this energy back to the island.

For Zoe, the future of Sable is fused with her own future. With increased familiarity with Sable she will learn to assess its needs, understand better the relationships between the grass, the dunes, the sand, the seals, horses, and all other creatures. This will take time but on her visits to the island she will be walking, listening, and absorbing the mysteries of continuous creation. I have the feeling that Zoe will someday help us comprehend these elemental relationships and reveal the hidden subtleties of Sable Island.

The dunes that surround the A-frame are in sight as I complete my long journey. The evening sun is ready to spill its colours into the ocean as I stop by the fence post close to the house. An Ipswich sparrow chirrups and flits away to vanish over the sand hills into the approaching dusk. The air is quite still now that the wind has fallen and the rumble of ocean breakers can be heard faintly on the south and north beaches. A ribbon of pale blue smoke undulates from the chimney to evaporate into the atmosphere; it is supper time. I stand for a while drinking in the pale shades of colour and think of the impressions I have experienced on Sable.

Those who have visited or worked on Sable, at one time or another, share very special feelings about the island. They speak of how, when they return to the mainland, Sable becomes more of a dream than a reality. They talk of how the lure of the island is so strong they long to return again and

Snow fencing.

again. They describe how jealous and protective they feel about it, for Sable's charm, like most unique islands, is that it appears to belong to each one who walks her shores.

As the sun slips downward, it begins to change shape flattening gently at its axis points. The upper half is a light orange, the lower half a shade darker; it resembles a perfect Chinese lantern. The sun, "that orbed continent, the fire that severs day from night," wrote Shakespeare, moves down to touch the horizon. Slowly, the orange ball sinks into the ocean. So strong was this illusion that I could actu-

ally see it drop as it slipped behind the ocean to throw out reflections that continued to hang in the canopy of sky over Sable. The dunes begin to dissolve into the soft evening dusk. I want to cry out the words of writer George Meredith: "Away with systems! Away with a corrupt world! Let us breathe the air of the Enchanted Island."

A sigh escapes me. Sable has a potent effect on its inhabitants. I am reluctant to move, but I must. Packing some things before supper I am suddenly gripped with a bittersweet melancholy. Tomorrow we leave the island.

Endpiece

Sable is left behind.

In the twentieth century an aircraft took me to the island and has taken me away again. A thousand years ago man reached Sable in a tiny cockleshell with the sail up. Since that time, many dreamers have dreamed of Sable and come to her shores.

Sable has summoned dreamers throughout the centuries: she drew Sir Humphrey Gilbert with his dream of fat cattle in pasture; a French king and his dream of empire; the ecclesiastical entrepreneur from New England who dreamed of a peaceable kingdom and had glimmerings of a lifesaving station. There have been self-seekers and scientists; good men, bad men, bureaucrats and politicians, all with their little dreams. Now, oilmen dream of oil.

I have the feeling, that for this dreamer, there will be no more visits.

Never shall I forget the compelling north beach on Sable, with her high sensuous dunes overlooking the ocean: the aromatic scent of sweetgrass in her meadows; the beautiful, low green cover lying like a fragile mantle over her body; the raging storm that shrieked through the dunes, shook the houses, and then hurled sand for miles out to sea. Her dramatic cloudscapes and her night skies hung with stars will pattern my memory forever.

The dusky black mare, my companion in the dunes, will be with me always; the elegant little seals scratching their white bellies; the vivacious birds, clouds of them, working with speedy industry, for their time is short.

Sable, a miniature world, is always shifting, always changing, giving and taking. Sable, with a ceaseless cycle of birth and death. Sable, with melancholy, serenity, beauty, and violence. Sable is a timeless world where we throw away the clock.

"Men are such stuff as dreams are made of..."

Sable is for dreamers.

Appendix A/Superintendents of the Humane Establishment

1801
to
1948

1801—1809	James Morris
1809—1830	Edward Hodgson
1830—1848	Joseph Darby
1848—1855	Matthew D. McKenna
1855—1873	Philip Dodd
1873—1884	D. McDonald
1884	J. H. Garroway (acting superintendent for seven months)
1884—1912	R. J. Bouteillier
1912—1919	Captain V. W. Blakeney
1919—1939	Jack Campbell
1939—1948	Don Johnson

Appendix B/Shipwrecks

THERE ARE MANY sources for this list: for material from 1583 to 1799 the writer referred to *Shipwrecks of the Western Hemisphere* by Robert F. Marx; "Shipwrecks and the Colonization of Sable Island," an article by Lyall Campbell; *Sable Island: Its History and Phenomena* by the Reverend George Patterson. Last names of the writers are used to indicate reference.

For material dating from 1802 to 1894, Appendix C of Patterson's book has been used. This list indicates the known wrecks since the founding of the Government Relief Establishment and it was drawn up by successive superintendents.

Shipwrecks that are listed from 1895 to 1921 were found in an article written by W. D. Taunton and published in the *Halifax Herald*, Saturday, July 23, 1921. The remaining shipwrecks are taken from a map, *Sable Island: Graveyard of the Atlantic*, originally drawn by Simon MacDonald, and revised and updated by Don Johnson (superintendent, 1939-48) in 1971. It is copyrighted by the Book Room Limited in Halifax.

Details of some of the shipwrecks have been woven into the main text of this book and are indicated with *See main text*. In the early Establishment years, up to 1848, details are scarce and loss of life not recorded. But from that year and up to 1912, near the end of Superintendent Bouteillier's tenure, details are expansive and in some cases, like the *Wm. Bennet* in December 1864, or the barque *Henry*, May 1892, a melancholy drama unfolds. Additional information on some of the shipwrecks from 1849 to 1862 was taken from the journal of Captain James Farquhar.

1583 to 1789

1583 English warship *Delight*, in the fleet of Admiral Sir Humphrey Gilbert. *See main text*. (Marx)

1714 French ship *Saint Jerome*, sailing from Québec to France, in autumn. Cargo of valuable furs and important passengers such as Charles D'Aloigny, the Marquis de La Groye, commandant of troops in France. In his early fifties, seriously ill for a year, D'Aloigny was returning home for a cure, or to die. The ship ran into a storm which drove her off course coming out of the Gulf of St. Lawrence. This was the first casualty on Sable which, since the Treaty of Utrecht in 1713, belonged to the English. The only survivors were two sailors who kept alive on Sable for a few months until rescued by an English vessel and taken to the mainland of Nova Scotia. (Campbell)

1716 In August, a fishing schooner from Gloucester, Mass.; no record of name; all six men vanished. (Campbell)

1725 Two merchant vessels on same day, both out of New England: ship *John and Mary* and the sloop *Eagle*; all crews saved. *See main text*. (Campbell)

1747 The corvette *Légère*, of the Duc d'Anville fleet, commanded by Charles Francois Guillimin. The crew lived with three Englishmen during the winter; nine months later they were put aboard a ship and taken to Boston. *See main text*. (Campbell)

1757   APRIL 22:   English merchantman, *Buchanen*, commanded by Captain Laurence, sailing from Gibralter to Maryland, was captured by a French privateer. Wrecked during passage to Louisbourg. (Marx)

1760 or 1761   A vessel with part of the British 43rd Regiment returning from the capture of Québec, Major Elliott in charge, stranded. Everyone saved except two sailors. *See main text*. (Patterson)

1766   Seven-hundred-ton ship sailing from Bristol to Boston. Fourteen of the twenty-eight crew members died. Survivors were picked up by a Cape Ann fishing vessel and taken to Louisbourg. Name of ship unknown. (Campbell)

1773   English merchantman *Sophia*, commanded by Captain Hastington, while sailing from Philadelphia to Québec. (Marx)

1777   The English ship *Aurora*. When the survivors got ashore they found seven negro women from a French ship that had been wrecked there sixteen years earlier. (Marx)

1779   A ship of unknown registry, *Fame Murphy*. (Marx)

1780   English merchantman *Jane*, commanded by Captain Wilson, sailing from London to Halifax. Crew saved. (Marx)

1781   English ship *Potowack*, commanded by Captain Mitchell, sailing from London to Québec, was captured by an American privateer and later wrecked. (Marx)

1786   Ship of unknown registry, *Telemachus*, commanded by Captain Sargeant, sailing from Georgia to Amsterdam, lost with most of her cargo. (Marx)

1792   Two ships of unknown registry. One not identified; the other was the *Rambler*, under Captain Kaquet, sailing from Philadelphia to Boston. (Marx)

1795   JANUARY 6:   The *Orb*, English merchantman commanded by Captain Brigs, sailing from Liverpool to Halifax. (Marx)

1797   NOVEMBER 9:   The brig *Princess Amelia*, commanded by Captain Wyatt, from London, on south side of island. All hands saved. *See main text*. (Patterson)

1799   Two-hundred-and-eight-ton government transport the *Francis*, sailing from England to Halifax with forty people and complete equipage of the Duke of Kent. Stranded and sank with all hands. *See main text*. (Patterson)

1802 to 1855

1802   Ship *Union*; ship *Packet*.

1803   Ship *Hannah and Eliza*; brig *Harriot*.

1804   Ship *Stark Odder*.

1805   Two schooners.

1806   Two schooners.

1807   Brig *Spring*; brig *John and Mary*.

1808   A schooner; an American fishing schooner.

1809   Brig *Prince Edward*, an American fishing schooner.

1810   One brig and one schooner.

1811   Schooner *Fortune*; brig *Hard Times*; brig *Orion*.

1812   H.B.M. frigate *Barbadoes*, with a sloop and a schooner under convoy.

1813   An American fishing schooner.

1814   An American fishing schooner; a schooner belonging to Halifax.

1815   Brig *Adamant*; wreck of ship *Demoscota* seen.

1819   A fishing schooner from France; schooner *Trafalgar*; schooner *Industry*; schooner *Juno*; a fishing vessel from Plymouth.

1820   Brig from Québec; schooner commanded by Captain Harvey.

1822 H.M.C.M. frigate *L'Africaine*.

1823 Brig *Hope*; brig *Marshal Wellington*; H.B.M. packet *Frolic*.

1824 Brig *James*.

1825 Brig *Nassan*; brig *Traveller*.

1826 Ship *Nassau*; ship *Elizabeth*; schooner *Brothers*.

1827 Ship *Agamemnon*; ship *Echo*; schooner *Four Sons*.

1828 Ship *Melrose*; ship *Franklin*; brig *Adelphi*.

1829 Brig *Hannah*; brig *Jamaica*; brig *Pegasus*; ship *Courser*.

1831 Schooner *Meridian*; brig *Mary Porter*; brig *Orpheus*.

1832 Ship *Tottenham*, (eventually got off again); brig *Floyd*; brig *Joanna*; brig *Ruby*.

1833 Schooner *Margaretta*.

1834 Brig *Tantivy*; brig *J. H. Albony*.

1835 Ship *Eagle* (of New York); schooner *Laban*; schooner *Ann*; brig *Abigail*.

1836 Brig *Lancaster*; brig *Sun*; galliot *Johanna*.

1837 Brig *Bob Logic*.

1838 Ship *Granville*.

1839 Ship *Maria*.

1840 Schooners *Barbara, Senator, Blooming Youth*; ships *Myrtle, Glasgow, Eliza, Australia*.

1841 Ships *Undaunted, Marmora, Mersey*; brigs *Triumph, Isabel*.

1842 Schooner *Louisa*.

1843 Ship *Eagle*.

1845 Ship *Eagle* of St. John's. (Patterson's notation: "There seems an *Eagle* too many here.")

1846 Brig *Afghanistan*; barque *Detroit*; schooner *Arno* (*see main text*); schooner *Lady Echo*; ship *Milo*.

1847 Ship *Levant*.

1848 Schooner *Fulton*; Spanish schooner *Bella Maria*.

1849 JULY 22:   Schooner *Brothers* of St. John, N.B., from Cumberland, N.S., bound for Liverpool, Great Britain, loaded with timber, deals, and treenails.
AUGUST 27:   Barque *Blonde* of Montreal, 676 tons, from Québec for Greenock, timber laden, run ashore.
DECEMBER 17:   Brig *Growler*, of and for St. John's, Nfld., from Baltimore, loaded with corn, flour, tobacco, pork, etc. Captain Farquhar notes that this vessel was a "typical Newfoundland sealing brig, sheathed for ice work and protected with iron round the bows." The figurehead was a little dog, carved out of wood and painted white.

1850 APRIL 2:   Schooner *Transit* of Prince Edward Island, from St.

John's for Boston, loaded with fish, wine, oil, raisins, and hides. "In some way or other," wrote Farquhar, "one of the Island crew managed to get at the wine, and took more than was good for him. When discovered he was perfectly helpless, and, a little later, when brought to the station, he became a raving maniac. His hands and feet had to be tied, otherwise he might have done serious damage. This was the first person I had ever seen drunk."
JULY 6:   Ship *Adonis*, of and from Portland, 538 tons, bound into the St. Lawrence River, in ballast.
AUGUST 3:   Brigantine *Hope*, of and from Baltimore, bound for St. John's, Nfld., 205 tons, loaded with flour, meal, and pork.
SEPTEMBER 4:   Barque *Margaret Walker* of Halifax, from St. John, N.B., 318 tons, for Liverpool, loaded with deals.

1851 FEBRUARY 11:   Brig *Science* of St. John's, Nfld., 143 tons, from Mantanzas for St. John's, with cargo of molasses.
APRIL 9:   Brig *Gustave I.*, 271 tons, of and for Antwerp from Havana, loaded with sugar, honey, tobacco, etc. The captain and crew were safely landed and a small portion of the cargo was saved. Captain Farquhar, a

young boy at the time, recalls his father receiving a box of fine Havana cigars from the captain. Farquhar picked up a partly smoked cigar his father had left and tried to finish it. Shortly after he was discovered by his mother, pale and sick from the effects of smoking. That was Farquhar's "first and last experience of tobacco."

AUGUST 26:   Schooner *Vampire* of Ragged Islands. Also the barque *Margaret Dewar* of Windsor, N.S., from Glasgow for New York, loaded with pig and scrap iron, wine, whiskey, etc.

SEPTEMBER 13:   Ship *Hargreave* of New York, from Newport, Great Britain, for New York, loaded with railroad iron. All hands made it to shore safely but the ship was broken up quickly. According to Farquhar, when the crew were getting their luggage into the boats, several rats scurried on board and hid themselves. "When the boats touched shore they jumped out at once, but they were caught and killed by a little rat terrier from our station. The officers told us that when the ship struck, the rats kicked up a terrible racket."

DECEMBER 4:   Schooner *Star of Hope* of New London drifted to the island.

1852   SEPTEMBER 14:   Schooner *Novara*, of and from Marblehead, on a fishing voyage.

NOVEMBER 21:   Brigantine *Ottoman*, of and from St. John's, Nfld., for Boston, with cargo of dry and pickled fish and oil.

DECEMBER 16:   Schooner *Marie Anne* of St. André, Québec, from Placentia Bay for Halifax, with cargo of codfish. One man lost.

DECEMBER 18:   *Ranger* of Pictou drifted ashore.

1853   JUNE 1:   Ship *Amazon* of Hull, 600 tons, from Shields with a cargo of gas coal for New York, stranded on the east wet bar, about three miles from the dry sand. Captain and crew safely landed on shore after dark. Next morning the superintendent and his men arrived and when they made their way to the wrecked ship in a surf boat, they discovered two Nova Scotia schooners busy stripping the sails and removing gear from the abandoned *Amazon*. They were ordered to proceed to the East Station and land all the gear they had taken from the *Amazon*. One schooner complied with the order. The other vessel refused to give up any of her loot. The superintendent reported this

matter to the commissioners and when the delinquent schooner reached home port it was seized by the wreck commmissioner.

JUNE 28:   Schooner *Guide* of London, 132 tons, from New York for Labrador, with cargo of flour, beef, pork, molasses, etc.

1854   MAY 5:   Brig *East Boston* of Pictou, from Catania, Sicily, with cargo of sulphur, sumac, rags, and oranges.

JUNE 29:   Schooner *Estrella* of Oporto, from Lisbon for Halifax, with a cargo of salt, corks, and corkwood.

OCTOBER 23:   Schooner *Maskonomet*, of and from Marblehead, from a fishing voyage on the banks.

NOVEMBER 26:   Ship *Arcadia* of Warren, Maine, 715 tons, from Antwerp for New York, with cargo of glass, lead, iron, silks, etc., 147 passengers. *See main text*.

1855   JANUARY 18:   Brig *Nisbis*, of and for St. John's, Nfld., 152 tons, from New York, with cargo of flour, cornmeal, corn, pork, sugar, etc. *See main text*.

APRIL 18:   Schooner *Albatross* of Kingston, Jamaica, from New York for St. John's, Nfld., with a cargo of beef, pork, flour, etc.

**1855
to
1873**

1855 DECEMBER 7: Schooner *Primrose*, commanded by Captain Myers, of Pope's Harbour, from St. John's, Nfld., for Halifax.

1856 JUNE 2: American ketch *Commerce*, under Captain Hincley, from Italy to New York. Discharged cargo and removed.

SEPTEMBER 23: American brigantine *Alma*, under Captain York, from New York, for St. John's, Nfld.

DECEMBER 7: Schooner *Eliza Ross*, under Captain Muggah, of and from Sydney, Cape Breton, drifted down south side of Sable dismasted, out of water, and decks swept. All hands saved in the lifeboat *Victoria*.

1858 MARCH: Brigantine *Maury*, commanded by Captain LeBlanc, of Lehave, from Harbour Grace for Boston.

OCTOBER 3: Brigantine *Lark*, commanded by Captain Pike, of and from St. John's, Nfld., for Prince Edward Island.

1860 SEPTEMBER 10: American brigantine *Argo*, commanded by Captain Auld, from Boston for Lingan, Cape Breton. Farquhar lists this as the brigantine *Arrow* as opposed to the *Argo* in Patterson's compilation. Apparently she was returning to Prince Edward Island in ballast when she was overtaken by a severe northerly gale. "On September 10th," Farquhar wrote, "she was

seen by the Sable Island lookout lying to under close reefed fore topsail and staysail. Immediately afterwards she was seen making sail in order to weather the North-west Bar." Superintendent Dodd and his men felt that it was not possible for her to do so and accordingly they drove as quickly as they could to the west bar with the lifeboat on the express wagon. When they arrived they found the vessel had already been driven onto the wet bar and quickly smothered in the heavy seas. The Sable crew were helpless to render assistance. "Only two things reached the Island," wrote Farquhar, "a capstan-bar and a bucket, with *Arrow* branded on them. Both of these had been washed off the brigantine's deck before she struck. Captain, crew and sixteen passengers were lost. No bodies came ashore."

1862 MAY 7: American barque *Zone*, under Captain Fullarton, from Shields, Great Britain, for Boston, struck on the south side of the northeast bar during the night, and broke up immediately. All thirteen hands were lost but one Russian Finlander, John Yanderson, who was washed ashore and saved by slipping his hand through a ring-bolt on one of the deck planks.

AUGUST 1: Barque *Jane Lovitt*, commanded by Captain Uttler,

of Yarmouth, from St. John, N.B., for Cork.

1863 JULY 22: Brig *Gordon*, under Captain Fitzgerald, of St. John, N.B., from St. Andrew's, N.B., for Wales.

AUGUST 4: Steamer *Georgia*, under Captain Gladell, from Liverpool, N.S.

1864 FEBRUARY: Schooner *Weathergage*, commanded by Captain McCuish, from Boston for Bacalieu, Nfld.

MARCH 8: American schooner *Langdon Gillmore*, under Captain Chase, from St. John's, Nfld., for New York. Captain and two men drowned. Four men got ashore in the ship's boat, the rest taken off in the lifeboat.

APRIL 12: Brigantine *Dash*, under Captain Coles, of and for St. John's, Nfld., from Cienfuegos.

DECEMBER 20: Brigantine *Wm. Bennet*, under Captain E. Bennet, of St. John, N.B., from Prince Edward Island for New York. Captain, crew and passengers, the captain's wife, sister-in-law and an infant three months old all saved by a line. But in the little graveyard of the island are two wooden headboards, one with the inscription, "Sacred to the memory of Henry J. Osborn, who died December 20th, 1864, while saving passengers and crew of the brig Wm. Bennet; aged 37 years"; and the other, not so legible, but of similar purport, regarding a second victim named Peter Day.

1865 Brigantine *Triumph*, commanded by Captain Wood, of and for St. John's, Nfld., from Figuera, Portugal.

1866 FEBRUARY 25: French packet, *Stella Maria*, under Captain Gauthier, from St. Pierre for Halifax, struck on the northwest bar; floated off during the night.

JUNE: Brigantine *Stranger*, under Captain Campbell, from New York for Pictou.

JULY: Steamship *Ephesus*, under Captain Collins, of Liverpool, Great Britain, from Norfolk, Virginia, for Liverpool.

AUGUST 16: Barque *Ada York*, under Captain York, of Portland, from New Orleans for Liverpool, Great Britain, loaded with cotton.

AUGUST 24: Barque *Bessie Campbell*, under Captain Lent of Plymouth, from Newport, Great Britain, for Portland,

Maine, struck the island, and found to be leaking, was run ashore, but afterwards got off.

1867 AUGUST: Ship *Rhea Sylvia*, commanded by Captain Roach, of Bristol, Great Britain, from St. Vincent, Cape de Verd Islands, for St. John, New Brunswick.

1868 JANUARY: Schooner *Malta*, commanded by Captain McDonald, of Annapolis, from St. John's, Nfld., for Boston.

JUNE 28: Schooner *S. H. Cameron*, commanded by Captain McDonald, of Southport, Maine, from Banquerall Bank, bound home with fish.

1870 FEBRUARY 24: Barque *E. Robbins*, commanded by Captain Hilton, loaded with peas. The first mate, Andrew Dunn, and one of the sailors, name unknown, washed off the wreck during the night; the rest of the crew were saved by a line.

MAY 2: Brig *Electo*, under Captain Finlayson, of Charlottetown, Prince Edward Island,

from Liverpool, Great Britain, for Halifax, with a cargo of salt and coal. Also the brig *Acton*.

1871 NOVEMBER: Brigantine *Black Duck*, under Captain Landry, of and from Québec for Bermuda.

1872 Schooner *Boys* of Gloucester, Mass.

1873 MARCH: Schooner *Stella Maria* of St. Pierre-Miquelon.

JUNE: Schooner *Laura R. Burnham* of Gloucester, Mass.

SEPTEMBER 15: Steamship *Wyoming* of the Guion Line, under Captain Morgan, from Liverpool to New York, touched on the northeast bar; got off after throwing overboard 20,000 pounds worth of cargo. Sent a boat's crew ashore for assistance, but sailed away leaving them on the island.

SEPTEMBER 25: Barque *Humbelton*, commanded by Captain Soreignson, of Sunderland, from London for New York.

NOVEMBER 9: Schooner *Zephyr* of St. Pierre came ashore with four dead bodies on board.

1874 MAY 20: Barque *Gladstone* under Captain Nelson, of Stavager, Norway, for New York.

JULY 6: Barque *Highlander*, under Captain Hutchinson, of Sunderland, for St. John, N.B.

JULY 20: Steamship *Tyrian*, from Glasgow for Halifax,

struck but got off, and proceeded on her voyage.

JULY 28: Barque *Nashwaak*, Captain LeBlanc, from St. John, N.B., for Ayr, Great Britain, timber laden.

1875 *Farto*, commanded by Captain

Jose Gomez de Sylva Lampais, of Lisbon, for Halifax, went to pieces instantly. The captain, cook, and steward lost; the rest, numbering eight, saved.

Ship *Ironsides*, under Captain Shedden, from Great Britain to New York.

1876 APRIL 15:   American ship *Neptune*, under Captain Spence, from Liverpool, Great Britain, for New York. One man drowned.

JUNE 29:   Barque *Norma*, under Captain Saunders, from St. John, N.B., for Great Britain.

OCTOBER 16:   American schooner *Reeves* struck on the northwest bar in a violent gale; all hands lost.

1878 AUGUST 22:   Barque *Emma*, under Captain Anderson, of Christiansand, Norway, from Great Britain to Philadelphia.

1879 MARCH 31:   Barque *Oriental*, under Captain Corning, of Québec, from Phildelphia for Queenstown, laden with corn.

APRIL: Schooner *Peasley*, abandoned, drifted on northwest bar.

JULY 12:   Steamship *State of Virginia*, under Captain Moodie,

from New York for Glasgow. The lifeboat succeeded in landing one load of passengers, but upset with a second load, and nine were drowned.

1880 JUNE 13:   Ship *Gondolier*, commanded by Captain Atkins, of Prince Edward Island, from Holland for New York. Three men drowned in the surf while attempting to land from the ship's boat.

NOVEMBER 22:   Schooner *Bride* of Bay Chaleur; the crew of three saved, exhausted and frostbitten.

OCTOBER 13:   *Schooner Lord Bury*, under Captain Power, of Cape Breton.

1882 MARCH 1:   Brigantine *Williams*, under Captain Warren, of Prince Edward Island, from Barrow, Great Britain, for Halifax. Had

been in the ice off Newfoundland. Provisions exhausted and all hands in a starving condition.

JULY 4:   Norwegian barque *Yorkshire*, under Captain Jacobson, from Barbados for Montréal. Two men lost.

AUGUST 12:   Norwegian barque *Balgoley*, under Captain Uglant, for New York, in ballast.

1883 AUGUST: Barque *Britannia*, under Captain Glaston, from West Indies for Montréal. Captain's wife and six children, with six of the crew, lost. Captain and three men taken off a raft.

1884 JULY: Steamship *Amsterdam*, commanded by Captain Luce, of Amsterdam, from Rotterdam for New York, with 267 persons on board, passengers and crew. Three drowned in the surf while attempting to land in the ship's boats.

1884 to 1947

1884 DECEMBER 19:   Brigantine *A.S.H.*, commanded by Captain LeMarchand, of St. Malo, France, from St. Pierre for Boston, with fish. The captain, mate, and steward succeeded in getting ashore. Mate managed with great difficulty to get to the West Light through a blinding snowstorm, but the captain and second mate perished before they could be found. The French

government presented William Merson with a silver medal and diploma of the first class, and the superintendent, a gold medal and diploma of the second class, for services rendered in connection with this wreck. *See main text.*

1885 MAY 26:   Schooner *Cora May*, of and from Provincetown, Mass., bound for the Grand Banks.

1886 SEPTEMBER 18:   Barque *Olinda*, under Captain Kendrick, of St. John's, Nfld., from Pernambuco for Sydney, Cape Breton, in ballast.

1889 Norwegian barque *Faerder*, under Captain Larsen, from Great Britain for Halifax, with coal.

1890 JULY 27:   Brigantine *Gerda*, under Captain K. F. Olsen, of

Drammen, Norway, from Barbados for Québec, with molasses and sugar.

1892 MAY 12:   Barque *Henry*, under Captain Jacobsen, of and from Tonsberg, Norway, in ballast. Six sailors left her in the long boat and boarded a fishing schooner, which landed them the next morning near the East Light. On that morning the wreck broke up, and the captain, mate, carpenter, cook, and two boys were drowned. The captain would not abandon the vessel while there remained a chance of getting her off. He stayed so long that rescue was impossible.

DECEMBER: Schooner *Bridget Ann*, under Captain White, from Margaree for Halifax. Also the American brigantine *Kaluna* of New York, under Captain J. H. Nelson, from St. John, N.B., for Buenos Aires, ran ashore, partially dismasted and waterlogged.

1893 APRIL 27:   *Inglewood*, commanded by Captain Tuuty, of St. John, N.B., 124 tons, from Halifax for Cow Bay, Cape Breton, in ballast, struck north side near centre of island, all saved.

AUGUST: Schooner *Valkyrie*, under Captain Hoar, from Cape Breton for Delaware. Wreckage picked up on island during September.

1894 JANUARY 12:   American schooner *Roby J. Edwards*, under Captain Bibber, of Gloucester, Mass., with frozen herring from Nfld., struck north side, lost with seven on board.

MAY 27:   S.S. *Laleham*, of Newcastle, under Captain Scrivner, via Halifax for Le Havre with cattle, struck north side in dense fog. With assistance from shore kedged off and proceeded on way.

JULY 30:   Barque *Nicosia*, under Captain Cole, of St. John, N.B., 1,047 tons, from Dublin for St. John, in ballast, struck south side at 5 P.M., dense fog, all hands saved.

SEPTEMBER 11:   S.S. *Nerito*, of and from Sunderland, for Hampton Roads, under Captain Skipper, struck south side of northeast bar at 6:30 A.M. in dense fog; all hands saved. Ship eventually floated, towed to Halifax, and repaired.

1895 NOVEMBER 27:   Steamer *Henri Reuth*, struck the northeast bar, pumped out water ballast, and floated off twelve hours later, arriving in Halifax next day with plates started.

1896 JULY 8:   Barque *Raffaele D.*, 629 tons, under Captain Caprile, of and from Genoa, Italy, in ballast, for Bathurst, N.B. Struck south

side four miles east of No. 1 Station at 3:30 P.M. Seven of the crew landed in a ship's boat, which swamped in, striking the beach, and leaving five men on the wreck, which was fast breaking up. Rocket apparatus went down from No. 1 Station to foot of lake, then up south side to wreck, arriving at 7:30 P.M. Made connection with the first rocket and hauled the captain and four men ashore in the breeches buoy at 8 P.M. All the spars had fallen at 7 P.M. This is the first instance of people being saved on the island from the firing of a rocket. *See main text.*

1897 APRIL 17:   Schooner *Charles H. Taylor*, 92 tons, of and from Gloucester, Mass., bound fishing. Struck south side, one mile east of No. 1 Station, 4 A.M. Eleven men left ship in dories and rowed around the bar, landing on the south side. Three more men got ashore in a dory direct from the vessel, while four other men were taken off with the whip and breeches buoy at 4 A.M. in a dense fog. Three of the crew went to Canso in a dory in thirty hours. *Newfield* took off the remaining men on May 12. Vessel owned by Davis Brothers.

APRIL 26:   Unknown barque, grounded near east end light, got off and proceeded.

NOVEMBER 11:   Unknown brigantine grounded on northwest bar, remained about one hour, got off without assistance.

DECEMBER 4:   Several pieces of *John McLeod*, wrecked off Halifax, came ashore.

1898   APRIL 17:   Four-masted iron barque *Crofton Hall*, of Liverpool, Great Britain, under Captain R. S. Thurber, from Dundee for New York, in ballast. Struck northeast bar, south side, three miles east of light. All thirty-three hands, including captain's wife and three children, safely landed, twelve by rocket apparatus. Owned by Charles G. Dunn & Co., Liverpool. (In Feb. 1902, three of the four spars were still standing.) *See main text*.

NOVEMBER 6:   Schooner *Mariner*, under Captain Henry Nelson, of Gloucester, Mass., with a full fare of fish, struck the northeast bar (wet) about twelve miles from the light. Weather moderate. Eighteen men rowed to the light in their dories. Schooner completely lost.

1899   FEBRUARY 12:   Steamer *Moravia*, 2,234 tons, of and from Hamburg for Portland and Boston with sugar and general cargo. Struck south side six miles from light, northeast bar. Vessel began breaking up after striking. Captain Jorgenson and twenty men left in the only ship's boat available and after much suffering landed at the East Light next morning, some frostbitten and the second mate dead. The island men landed fifteen men in two trips by the lifeboat *Relief*, on the 12th, and four on the morning of the 13th. Wreck completely broken up in a gale on the 14th. The German emperor presented gold watches to Superintendent Bouteillier, S. Small, coxswain, and A. R. Tobin, and twenty-five dollars each to George Bungay, Jos. Bowes, A. Lloy, W. Morash, and Gus Sodaburg. The deputy minister (Gordeau) came down in the autumn and made the presentations.

JULY 17:   American schooner *H. C. Worcester*, under Captain Crowell, struck on one of the bars during a dense fog and was totally lost. The crew all made the mainland in their dories. Vessel and crew were never seen by the island staff.

1901   APRIL: Two fishermen from the French fishing vessel *Aristide* drifted from Quero and landed at the West Light, six days out, much exhausted.

JUNE 2:   Brigantine *Stella Maris*, under Captain Beaudry, of Granville, France, from Turks Island with salt for St. Pierre, Miq., struck the northeast wet bar; total loss. Crew of ten landed in ship's boats and went to Canso in the *Dispatch*, July 2.

1903   OCTOBER 5:   French fish-tug schooner *Topaze*, of St. Pierre, Miq., came ashore bottom-up on the north side at No. 5 Station. She broke up at once and eight bodies, in an advanced stage of decomposition, came ashore and were buried. This schooner upset on the Grand Banks during the summer.

1904   FEBRUARY 14:   American schooner *Lizzie M. Stanwood*, of Gloucester, Mass., under Captain Oscar Lyons, from Newfoundland for Boston with frozen herring, drove ashore on the north side, near No. 2 Station, during a gale and snow storm. Crew of ten saved.

MAY 8:   Schooner *Olympia*, of Lunenburg, under Captain Westhaver, ran on the northeast wet bar at night in a fog. Crew saved themselves in their dories. Vessel a total loss.

1905   JANUARY 31:   Steamer *Skidby*, 2,421 tons, in ballast, of and from West Hartlepool, Great Britain, for Baltimore under Captain J. H. Pearson, struck north side of northwest bar, about 6 P.M., and remained there until 2 A.M. of February 1st, when it came off in a disabled condition, drifted down the north side, and grounded abreast of the schoolhouse, seven miles east of the Main Station. All twenty-six hands walked ashore at low tide. Officers and crew remained on the island until March 3rd and were then taken off by the government steamer *Lady Laurier*. *See main text.*

1906   AUGUST 14:   Schooner *Basil M. Geldert*, of Lunenburg, ninety-nine tons, under Captain Buffet, from St. Mary's, Nfld., with whalebone for Halifax, struck on the south side of the northeast bar at 8 P.M. Five men rowed in to the island and were landed by the lifeboat *Relief* the following morning. Owned by R. H. Cann, Louisburg.

1910   JUNE 18:   Norwegian steamer *Heimdal*, of Tonsberg, 1,875 tons, under Captain Gabrielson, from Santos, Brazil, twenty-six days, for Campbellton, N.B., struck on the south side opposite the *Eliza*, in a dense fog. Captain and crew remained on board for salvage. Efforts were made to float this craft, but she was finally lost.

1912   AUGUST 14:   British steamer *Eric*, of Cardiff, 1,788 tons, under Captain W. G. Corner, from Rosario for Québec, via Sydney, loaded with maize, struck on the south side at 11:35 A.M. in a dense fog, and moderate breeze from the southwest. Launched her lifeboat and Captain Corner came ashore and sent wireless messages for assistance. Steamers *Bridgewater*, *Cabot* and *Seal* came on the 17th and took some cargo out of her; more was jettisoned on the 18th. On the 19th, a southeast wind blew up, which made it too rough to get the crew off during the afternoon. That night the *Eric* broke abaft the engine room. On the morning of the 20th, all twenty-six hands went ashore and sailed to Halifax on the steamer *Aberdeen* on the 21st. The rescue was made in three trips of the lifeboat with J. A. Ritcey, coxswain. The ship and cargo became practically a total loss.

1915   Steamer *Silverwings*, loaded with munitions, U.S. port for France. Crew saved.
Auxiliary barque *Lota*, U.S. port for Europe. Crew saved.

1918   Tern schooner *M. P. Connolly*, Québec for Nfld. Crew saved.

1919   Greek steamer *Platea*, Genoa for Québec. Floated next year, uninjured; crew saved.

1921   Schooner *Esperanto*, from Gloucester, Mass. Crew saved.

1922   Schooner *Puritan*.
Schooner *Marshall Foch*.

1925   Schooner *Falmouth*.

1926   Steamer S.S. *Harold Casper*.
Schooner *Sadie Knickle*. *See main text.*
Schooner *Sylvia Mosher*. *See main text.*
Trawler *Labrador*.

1927   Trawler *Lemburg*.
Schooner *Mahala*. *See main text.*
Schooner *Joyce Smith*. *See main text.*
Schooner *Clayton Walters*. *See main text.*
Schooner *Ida A. Corkum*. *See main text.*
Schooner *Columbia*. *See main text.*

1930   Tern schooner *Geo. A. Wood*.

1942   Steamer *Independence Hall*. *See main text.*

1943   Steamer *Anna Mazaraki*.

1945   Trawler *Gale*.

1946   S.S. *Alfios*. *See main text.*

1947   S.S. *Manhasset*. *See main text.*

Appendix C/The Status of Sable

YOU CAN SEE it on the map of offshore gas and oil wells on the Scotian Shelf. There is the slender, delicate outline of Sable, a target area. Surrounding it are little circles which appear to be pierced holes; at first glance Sable looks like the centre of a dartboard dotted with gas and oil wells with exotic names such as *Iroquois*, *Abenaki*, and *Onondago*. Some wells have been christened to favour a ship, a flower, or a year, like the *Bluenose*, the *Primrose* and the *C-67*; altogether there are about thirty wells, most of them gas-producing, in the vicinity of Sable and on the island itself.

C-67, located about the middle of Sable and built in 1967, was the first hole to be drilled on the island. Boring to a depth of fifteen thousand feet, Mobil Oil set up the original program in the current phase of offshore drilling explorations on the Scotian Shelf. Two years later Shell Canada began an extensive drilling program in conjunction with several seasons of marine seismic research. To date, forty-seven wells have been drilled on the Scotian Shelf; land-based rigs are used for nine wells on Sable Island, and submersibles are used for the thirty-eight wells completed offshore. Ten miles to the west of the original 1967 test on Sable, the new 1971 Mobil Oil *E-48* well has produced a show of potentially commercial quantity with crude oil, natural gas, and condensate.

During the early seventies, oil rigs were conspicuous on the Halifax waterfront and the centre of much attention. By the mid-seventies, drilling operations slowed down around the world, rigs were pulled out of the harbour, and operations were suspended around Sable. Left behind at sea and under Sable were dozens of invisible well-heads marked with sonic transponders for easy location. Silent, capped under pressure and plugged, they are still waiting to be tapped.

Maritime consumers, impatient for their provinces to be energy self-reliant, express bewilderment at the potential natural gas supply out at sea, idle and not flowing into their houses. The provincial government of Nova Scotia, with oil and gas laws over thirty-eight years old, has been painfully slow in making decisions to determine the course of offshore gas

development, and a Liberal government in Ottawa has not been sympathetic to Nova Scotia's request for full control of offshore resources. In late 1979 and early 1980 a shortage of oil rigs caused further delays in offshore drilling for natural gas near Sable and Nova Scotia has recently taken steps towards assembling a consortium to build more rigs. Petro Canada has also responded with an interest in building rigs and associated drilling equipment on the east coast.

If the increase in production of oil rigs helps companies strike into a large enough gas source to make the whole offshore gas and oil operation commercially viable, then the Sable Island gas reserves will be tapped. That could result in the installment of a reversible gas line from Montreal, and the bringing of Alberta's gas to Nova Scotia until the Sable gas claims become realized enough to reverse the flow from the Maritimes to Montreal. After this, with the permission of the National Energy Board, gas could be sent from Sable by spur-line to the New England states (assuming that there are abundant resources for Canada first).

There are two ways of going about drawing gas from the reservoirs. One is to concentrate on only the largest wells, such as the *Venture*, and gather oil solely from offshore. The other method is to use Sable as a central gathering station for all the small wells.

The first alternative would use a separate man-made structure situated on a large well offshore. This structure would be a simple stripping mechanism on the well platform itself—a collection of separators which would take out the condensate. The gas would then flow under its own pressure to the mainland shore. But given a choice, this would be the least desirable method for the oil-seekers because a man-made platform out at sea would be capable of tapping only the few big fields where gas is at high pressure. To produce all the other smaller wells, a central reservoir on Sable would be required.

Using the second scheme of a central station or reservoir on Sable, the wells would be tapped by pipeline to the island where gas would go through separators. Here the condensate would be separated from the gas to go into the storage tanks; the gas would go through a dehydrating plant, usually a glycol plant, which removes the water from the gas. Left behind would be predominantly dry gas that would go to a compressor station to be compressed to the requisite pressure of 1,500 pounds per square inch. From there, it would run by one central line to the Canso area (the nearest point to Sable) and then across to Port Hawkesbury.

One of the greatest concerns associated with reservoirs on Sable would be the noise factor. The compressor noise in such an operation would be very loud and continuous for there is no silencer on the exhaust. Serious problems could develop should there be a gas leak, or should an oil-laden ship spill its cargo onto Sable's shores killing seals, birds, and fish.

It is difficult for many Sable lovers not to simply wish that all the oil companies would vanish from the island forever—an impossibility since oil-seekers were strongly encouraged to situate on Sable in 1959, the same year that the federal government declared the wild horses surplus and tried to remove them from the island. Federal, and especially provincial agencies were at that time more interested in having companies explore the gas and oil reserves on Sable, than in protecting it through formal status as a park or special reserve. Currently, Sable is considered only an official bird sanctuary.

For several thousand years, the shape and size of the island were changed only by natural forces but the more recent and rapid changes can be attributed to man. Sable residents, right up to the late 1940s, ploughed the fragile carpet of soil that hung precariously to the surface of sand with dreams of self-sufficiency. Increased activity in the late 1960s, and a concern for Sable's future, resulted in the formation of the Sable Island Environment Committee, set up to help monitor new groups that suddenly materialized. Made up of nominees from different government and private bodies, the committee still advises the Ministry of Transport on environmental concerns and terrain stabilization.

In 1976 a roads policy was drawn up by the Sable Island Environment Committee which included maps indicating specified vehicular traffic on the island. Today there is no restriction of travel on unvegetated beaches as long as the wildlife is not harassed in any way, but vegetated areas are out-of-bounds; even hikers are cautioned to tread softly, and certain existing roads are now closed to any motor traffic. An environmental guide booklet, given to each visitor on Sable, is designed to draw attention to the fragile elements of the island.

"How can I get to Sable?" is an understandable and recurring question. The answer: it is not easy these days and access is becoming even more difficult. The Ministry of Transport, which is charged under the Canada Shipping Act with the adminstration of the island and is responsible for the two navigation lights and the radio beacon, restricts admission to Sable to those who go there on official government business; those who land with permission from the District Marine Agent; and those persons wrecked on the island—a rather unhappy method of reaching Sable. At the present time, the only continuous residents on the island are a handful of Atmospheric Service personnel and one electronics technician.

It should be pointed out that whenever the oil-seekers have been present on the island, they have scrupulously followed government guidelines to avoid disturbing the environment. Also, they were the first to attempt a dune restoration program and today, Mobil Oil, along with a number of government agencies including the Department of Energy, Mines and Resources, still assists in funding a dune restoration program managed by Zoe Lucas.

A strange air of possessiveness hovers over Sable Island; its ownership is still in question. Nova Scotia has always considered Sable its property from the first day of the Humane Establishment in 1801; the federal government declares jurisdiction because of the construction of lighthouses in 1873 and its present maintenance of the Atmospheric Environmental Service Station. The interests of oil and gas company rights enter the picture to further compound the issue.

The island has its own right to exist; it must remain protected as a unique place, not only for further research, but also to make head-way on the important coastal dune restoration techniques now being implemented. "It is idle," writes Dr. McLaren, "to feel or assign guilt for past mistreatment of Sable Island, but we cannot remain indifferent to its future. It is as much a national treasure as the paintings of the Group of Seven or the restored fortress at Louisbourg."

Dr. McLaren believes the island would benefit most from declaration as a National Wildlife Area, for this would ensure that the environment and its living things would receive the full attention they deserve. "Altogether," he says, "restoration of the island to something more like its prehistoric condition seems a manageable ambition for the space age."

Selected Bibliography

BOWER, PETER, BRIAN DRISCOLL, GORDON DODDS, and BRUCE WILSON. "What Strange New Radiance: Sir Humphrey Gilbert and the New World." Public Archives of Canada, 1979.

CAMPBELL, LYALL. *Sable Island, Fatal and Fertile Crescent*. Windsor: Lancelot Press, 1974.

FARQUHAR, J. A. *Farquhar's Luck*. Halifax: Petheric Press, 1980.

GILPIN, J. BERNARD. *Sable Island: Its Past History, Present Appearance, Natural History*. Halifax: Wesleyan Conference Steam Press, 1858.

GROSVENOR, M. B. "Safe Landing on Sable, Isle of 500 Shipwrecks." *National Geographic Magazine*. 128 (September, 1965).

HALLECK, C. "The Secrets of Sable Island." *Harper's New Monthly Magazine*. 199 (December, 1866).

PATTERSON, REV. GEORGE D. D. *Sable Island: Its History and Phenomena*. Royal Society of Canada. 1st ser. 12 (1894).
—————. *Supplementary Notes on Sable Island*. Royal Society of Canada. 2nd ser. 3 (1897).

PERCY, H. R. *The Canadians, Joseph Howe*. Don Mills: Fitzhenry & Whiteside, 1976.

RADDALL, THOMAS. *The Nymph and the Lamp*. Toronto: McClelland & Stewart, 1950.
—————. *Halifax: Warden of the North*. Toronto: McClelland & Stewart, 1971.
—————. *In My Time: A Memoir*. Toronto: McClelland & Stewart, 1976.

STEPHENS, DAVID E. *Lighthouses of Nova Scotia*. Windsor: Lancelot Press, 1973.

TACHÉ, J. C. *Les Sablons et L'île Saint Barnabé*. Montréal: Nouvelles Soireés Canadiennes, 1885.

Acknowledgements

MANY PERSONS HAVE helped in the completion of this book and it is with great pleasure that I make these acknowledgements.

I am grateful to the Canada Council for their award of an Explorations Grant to assist in writing and preparing the book.

I am especially indebted to Dr. Melville Bell Grosvenor, Editor Emeritus, President Emeritus of National Geographic, for his generosity in allowing me to use material from his article, "Safe Landing on Sable," and for permission to use some of the splendid photographs.

I am forever grateful to Mabel Smythe for her consistent encouragement and the endless hours she spent in helping to shape the book.

Warm thanks to Thomas Raddall for his interest, suggestions, and for the time he took to read the complete script, and also for a pleasant and enlightening interview.

I am most grateful to Zoe Lucas for her valuable contributions, her special insights into Sable, and particularly for her superb photographs.

Thanks also to Dr. Ian McLaren who was constantly cheerful in supplying information, research material, photos; and thanks for arranging my second visit to Sable Island.

Cymru Khaelih, "The Keltic Wonder," has my enduring affection and admiration for her support and encouragement in this project.

Besides providing photographs, Mr. and Mrs. Don Johnson, through a delightful interview, helped to fill in the gaps of Sable's history for some of the 20th century.

Roger Crowther assisted in the dramatized portions of the CBC Radio documentary, "Island of Sand," 1968 (written and prepared in part by the author), some of which appears in this book.

Peter Donkin, who produced the documentary, suggested the idea which consequently lead to the later request from Doubleday for this book. I shall always be grateful to Peter for giving me my first opportunities in writing for radio and for casting me as an actor in some of these and other works.

Monique Gusset assisted with the Taché translations and provided encouragement, for which I thank her.

Special thanks to Lyall Campbell, whose Dalhousie University M.A. thesis, "History of Sable Island Before Confederation," was a most helpful springboard in creating the radio documentary, "Island of Sand," and a valuable research source for this book. Also, special thanks to Daniel Welsh, whose Dalhousie University Ph.D. thesis, "Population, Behavioural, and Grazing Ecology of the Horses of Sable Island, Nova Scotia," helped immensely in shaping the chapter on horses. I am indebted to both of these scholars.

My thanks to Tom Dexter of the Resource Management and Conservation Branch, Department of Mines and Technical Survey, for granting me an interview and providing needy information on the gas and oil reserves around Sable Island.

Thanks also to Mr. Robert S. Bouteillier of B.C., grandson of Superintendent Bouteillier, for making available, through Dr. McLaren, a taped interview of Trixie Bouteillier, the superintendent's daughter; this helped to define the family feeling at the turn of the century.

Ned Norwood was most generous in allowing me to use photographs of Sable from his private collection.

I am grateful to Al Chaddock for his fine slides of the island.

My thanks to Barbara Christie for her information on the imported horses to Sable Island.

My affectionate thanks to P. "Morag" MacDonald for so cleverly helping me to trim the script.

Others I would like to thank are: The personnel of the Public Archives of Nova Scotia, the Public Archives of Canada, the Halifax Regional Library, the Dalhousie University Archives, the N.S. Legislative Assembly Library, and the Nova Scotia Museum; Mrs. M. Josephine Caldwell Hamilton for the photo of Superintendent Bouteillier (her uncle) from her private collection; Louis Stephen of the N.S. Dept. of Culture and Recreation; Seymour Hamilton; Leslie, Jean, and Johnny Walker; Mars; Photo 67; Nancy Nichols; Barry Wright; Peacemeal Restaurant.

Finally I would like to pay tribute to my editors at Doubleday, Betty Corson, Rick Archbold, and Janet Turnbull. They have been most helpful and wonderful; thank you all.

Index of People and Ships on Sable Island

Sable Island

Shipwreck information from Lloyd's of London, Mariners Museum a Newport News, Virginia, The Maritime Museum, Halifax, Nova Scoti. Wreck positions approximate.
Design adapted from the National Geographic Magazine by Alf K. Ebsen

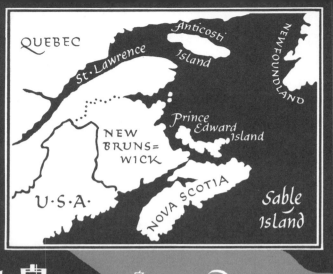

QUEBEC

St. Lawrence

Anticosti Island

NEWFOUNDLAND

NEW BRUNS=WICK

Prince Edward Island

U·S·A·

NOVA SCOTIA

Sable Island

a —

Afghanistan 1846
A·S·H· 1884
Fulton 1848
Spring 1807
Dolphin 1805
Black Duck 1871
Glasgow 1840
Novara 1852
Stranger 1866
State of Virginia 1879
Independence Hall 1942
Silver Wings 1915
Vampire 1851
Hard Times 1811

b —

Maskonomet 1854

Primrose 1855

Lark 1858
Arno 1846
Trafalgar 1816
Blonde 1849
no names (2)
Fortune 1811
Eliza 1840
East Boston 1854
Lady Echo 1816
Platea 1919
Lizzie M. Stanwood 1904
Industry 1816
Adamant 1810
Meridian 1831
Louisa 1842
Skidby 1905
no names (3)

1 —

1883
1888
1917

c —

1940
1947

West Light

e —

Lake Wallace

2

f —

N

Maury 1858
Weathergage 1864
Esperanto 1921
Maria 1839
Gustave I 1851
L'Africaine 1822
Jane Lovit 1862
Guide 1853
Gordon 1863
Adelpha 1828
Bridget Ann 1892
Lord Bury 1881
Harriot 1803
Charles H. Taylor 1897
Argo 1860
Lancaster 1835
M & Robbins 1870
no name
Olinda 1886
Raffaele D. 1896
Alma P. 1856
no name
Langdon Gilmore 1864
Myrtle 1840
Eric 1912
Nicosia 1894
Crowler 1849